THE ASE PRIMARY SCIENCE TEACHERS' HANDBOOK

SIMON & SCHUSTER
EDUCATION

First published in Great Britain in 1993 by
Simon and Schuster Education
Campus 400, Maylands Avenue
Hemel Hempstead, Herts HP2 7EZ

Printed in Great Britain by
Dotesios Ltd, Trowbridge, Wiltshire

A catalogue record of this book is
available from the British Library

ISBN 0 7501 0448 1

Contents

Introduction by Rosemary Sherrington

Introduction

The Primary Science Teachers' Handbook brings together a variety of viewpoints and perceptions which shed light on primary science and which open the debate to include more general aspects of primary education. One of the threads running through the Handbook is that of the subtle changes taking place in the professionalism of teachers. Now that science is becoming an established part of the primary curriculum, the skills of interpreting the curriculum, the development of understanding of how children learn, and the management strategies of the classroom are all coming under close scrutiny.

Children's experience of science depends on their teacher's ability to interpret the curriculum. In the opening chapter, Paul Black argues that the need to justify the place of science in schools and set out the aims of science education is especially important now that we are in 'National Curriculum country'. In order to make intelligent interpretations of the curriculum, we need to be aware of the social implications of scientific advance and have an understanding of its historical context.

Children's experience of learning depends to a large extent, on a teacher's view of how learning takes place. Wynne Harlen, in chapter 3, presents a view of learning as a change in ideas rather than taking ideas in from scratch. She demonstrates how understanding is created by development and change in these ideas.

David Oakley, in chapter 2, describes 'National Curriculum country' in some detail, with an account of the development of the National Curriculum and a critical look at some of its implications for schools.

The inclusion of Sc 1, Scientific Investigation, in the NC has introduced what, to many teachers, is a new approach to teaching and learning. In chapter 4, Rosemary Feasey defines scientific investigation as 'using and developing the concepts and procedures of science as a whole to find the solution to a problem, a question or to follow up an idea'. This would also suggest that solving problems contributes to developing investigative skills.

Science is now a part of the education of all children. However, not all children have equal access to science. Racism and sexism are, unfortunately, everyday realities in the lives of many children. Ways of interpreting the curriculum to allow and encourage access by all children, including those with special needs, are discussed by the authors of the three sections of chapter 5.

These serious issues should not detract from the fact that, for many teachers and children, science is a pleasure. The authors of chapter 6 bring science to life by providing 'snapshots' of activities in primary and secondary classrooms. Alison Bishop and Richard Simpson stress the importance of laying early foundations in science which harness children's natural curiosity. Terry Parkin and Jenny Versey describe a day in the life of a secondary science teacher.

It might be thought that primary and secondary education form a continuous and progressive whole. For the individual pupil, it may feel rather different. Inconsistency of experience is evident not only from phase to phase but from year to year and from subject to subject . In chapter 7, Brenda Keogh and Stuart Naylor suggest that what we plan for children should allow them to progress from a foundation of their own experience. This process of matching the pupils' ideas and the activities the teachers plan for them, is central to ensuring progression and continuity in learning.

The second section of the Handbook aims to put policy into practice, a task which Paul Black rightly describes as 'notoriously difficult'. Management of the classroom to create an effective and efficient learning environment is a crucial part of the task. Mike Schilling, in chapter 8, discusses some of the skills involved. He suggests that teaching and learning in science can require some radical re-thinking of classroom practice. Learning objectives in terms of knowledge, understanding and attitudes must be clearly defined, and the ways in which children learn clearly understood. In addition, he shows how various classroom strategies, such as grouping children in various ways, and the different roles a teacher can assume, significantly affect the opportunities open to children as learners.

In chapter 9, Anne Foden firmly grasps the nettle of assessment and offers ways of developing a system which is useful and manageable. The intuitive knowledge which teachers gain about children has a vital part to play, and the process of matching achievement to specific criteria will, she argues, help to build a more objective view of a child's progress.

In chapter 10, Kevin Hunn examines the teacher's role as the main resource in a classroom and ways in which the teacher may be resourceful. He offers practical advice based on a common-sense approach to the problems of equipment and safety.

Information Technology permeates the whole curriculum, but development of hardware and applications can be so swift that keeping up to date is a major problem. More to the point, argue Maddy Campbell and Dave Murray in chapter 11, is the need to know which software will support and facilitate learning in science. The chapter offers a current and critical overview of what is available for primary science and a tantalising glimpse into the future.

Science is a core subject in the National Curriculum, and as such, aids the learning of other subjects; it is, in turn, enriched by them. In chapter 12, Rosemary Sherrington addresses the question of integration. As it stands, the curriculum poses many management problems, and it would seem logical to continue to use a 'topic' approach to children's learning at primary level. Indeed, abandoning topic work may lead to an impoverishment in children's learning and enjoyment. However, the approach needs radical re-thinking. The author looks at the knowledge, methods of enquiry and positive attitudes to learning which science can engender, in order to clarify areas which are common to the whole curriculum and those which are particular to science. Plans for integrating the subjects in more rigorous ways could be developed from an increased understanding of these shared and discrete areas of the curriculum.

Learning necessarily involves children in communication of all sorts. In the following chapter on science and language, Rosemary Sherrington explores ways in which communication can enhance learning in science. She discusses how children talk, read and write in science and how teachers can improve children's opportunities for learning science through the use of various language skills. Providing science as a context will, in turn improve children's opportunities for language development.

The five cross-curricular themes of the National Curriculum can enrich and reinforce the learning of all children. Science has a major role to play in their development. Chapter 14 concentrates on three of them: Environmental Education, Health Education, and Economic and Industrial Understanding. Di Bentley looks first at ways of planning environmental themes so that knowledge and an understanding of the issues of the environment can be thoroughly taught. Then, in the second part of Chapter 14, she clarifies two main features of health education: children must gain knowledge about health concerns and be taught to make decisions about their own health. This has implications for schools, for they must provide an environment where, for example, informed decision-making can prosper.

David Sang looks at the meaning of Economic and Industrial Understanding and ways to extend its influence in teaching. EIU, he argues, can benefit science learning by providing relevant contexts which show the importance of science to industry.

Organising a science curriculum in a school is, clearly, a complex task. Derek Bell , in his chapter on the science co-ordinator, describes the complexities of the role. It is one that involves skilful management and one that is not yet fully realised in schools. Anthony Cudworth and Deirdre Medlar provide illuminating and positive examples of the role in action.

In the final chapter, Anne Watkinson brings together the worlds of home and school. She documents the benefits of developing home-school relationships in terms of improved parental attitudes to education in general and science in particular.

Rosemary Sherrington
October 1992

Acknowledgements

I would like to thank the following people who have made contributions to the Handbook:

Tessa Carrick with whom the outlines of both Handbooks were originated;

Richard Hull editor of the companion Secondary Handbook;

members of the ASE committees for Primary Science and Primary Science Review;

David Bevan, now ASE Hon. Treasurer;

John Nicholson for his help and advice;

Magaret Dibdin who produced the cartoons.

Very special thanks go to the authors of the Handbook who contributed so willingly and with such commendable promptness.

Section 1: Science Education

The Purposes of Science Education

Paul Black

1

Why Discuss Purposes?
An introduction

It is not inevitable that science be given the high priority that it now enjoys in the school curriculum, or even that it be a subject at all. A case could be made out, for example, that medicine, or politics should be essential components. Thus one priority in a discussion of purposes is to justify the place of science in schools. Why, for example, should science be required in both primary and secondary stages, rather than, as for languages, at secondary only? And does it have to be a separate subject, when other aspects of education are deemed worthy only of cross-disciplinary or extra-curricular attention, notably personal and social education and environmental education?

The orientation and practice of science education have to be consistent with the justifications given for its place in the curriculum. So a second function of any discussion of purposes is to set out the aims which science education should deliver and in the light of which it should be evaluated.

There could be a cynical response to the inevitably general and idealistic tone of this chapter. We are living in National Curriculum country (D.E.S. 1991) and whilst a trip to an imaginary island could provide entertainment and relaxation, it might also generate frustration on return. One justification here is that there is a wide range of classroom interpretations of the curriculum and it is in the classroom that each teacher's personal hopes strongly influence their children's experience.

A second justification is that the motivations behind a formal curriculum document need to be understood by anyone who has to put it into practice. Many of the issues discussed in this chapter receive no explicit mention in the national curriculum order, yet teachers' views about these issues must influence their practice. This point leads onto a more general justification – curriculum thinking is a product of its time and is open to change. We all need to be prepared to contribute to change in the future, and not just to be victims of its tides (A.S.E. 1992)

This last issue is taken up in the next section of this chapter, which surveys the historical context, and in section 3, in which the factors that might influence change are reviewed. Following these preparatory discussions, section 4 discusses the main aims of science education for all whilst section 5 discusses the needs of future specialists. These lead to an outline, in section 6, of a proposal for the main elements of science learning which could

1

implement the purposes. Section 7 then takes up the problem of the place of science in the whole school curriculum. Section 8 concludes with discussion of some implications.

Little has been said here of the concept of "scientific literacy" (Champagne and Lovitts 1989, Atkin and Helms 1992). It could be said that the phrase stands for no more than the science needed by all. However, the use of the metaphor of "literacy" might be a way of giving a particular emphasis, giving priority to narrowly instrumental needs. In short, the phrase either adds nothing to the arguments here, or is used to introduce, by implication, a bias of priorities. Therefore, it does not seem to be helpful.

How Did We Get Here?
The historical context

The nineteenth century beginnings of science education in schools have been described in David Layton's book "*Science for the People*" (Layton 1973). Conflict arose between two groups holding opposed views about the purposes of the new development. One proposed a science that would focus on everyday practices and artefacts. The second wanted to focus on academic science so that school science would help to recruit future scientists. The second view prevailed then and has done so ever since, although that original tension continues to bedevil school science to this day.

Whilst such influence dominated in the first part of this century, there also emerged educational reformers, notably Armstrong, who had a vision of a change which would give pupils a more authentic engagement with the practice of scientific enquiry (Jenkins 1979). However, the style of science teaching remained largely formal, based on teaching of definitions and derivations, and on experiments which illustrated foregone conclusions, with some discussions of applications added at the end.

This tradition was transformed in the 1950's and 1960's by a worldwide movement for reform, driven by and originating from two main foci. One was in the United States, where fears of technological inferiority sparked off by a Russian lead in space flight served to generate support for curriculum reform. The other was in Britain; here, it was the dissatisfaction of science teachers themselves which led them to press for reform. However, the outcome, in the Nuffield Foundation's science teaching project, was supported and influenced strongly by university scientists.

The assumption in the USA movements was that better school curricula would lead to better prepared students for science and engineering. In consequence, the courses were "top-down" in their construction, showing originality in devising quite new routes to the understanding of fundamental concepts. The agenda of these was chosen to represent current science in an authentic way, an aspect in which existing courses notably failed. This new strength was also a weakness, for the courses were ambitiously abstract and paid little attention to everyday consequences. A later physics project, *Project Physics*, differed from the others in giving more emphasis to the history of the development of ideas and to showing how they developed within the societies – and technologies – of their times. Subsequent evaluations showed that on the whole these courses, and the many international applications and imitations which they fostered, did not achieve their aims (Tamir et al 1979).

The Nuffield courses were more successful in holding those originally committed. The first courses were designed for the most able and were thereby biased to academic science, again giving priority to clearer emphasis on modern concepts rather than to any broader perspectives on science. They were characterised, however by more emphasis on changes in teaching method. A second generation of Nuffield courses struggled with a different problem, the provision of courses firstly for those placed in streams or schools designed for the less able, later for the mixed ability groups of the secondary comprehensive school.

The implementation of comprehensive schooling led to new challenges, as it became increasingly clear that quite new arrangements for science teaching would be needed. Growing dissatisfaction, with courses that were too specialised, and with the need for pupils to opt out of one or more of the separate science subjects, culminated in the 1980's in a move for broad and balanced science, supported by the A.S.E., the D.E.S. and, notably, by the Secondary Science Curriculum Review. (A.S.E. 1981, S.S.C.R. 1987)

These changes were motivated by a desire to realise the purpose of making science education accessible and meaningful to all pupils. However, this needed more than a change in the arrangement of courses. Three further aspects were given a powerful impetus in the 1980's. One emerged from research studies reporting both that pupils' enthusiasm for science declined from a high point of enthusiasm at age 11 to a low level by the end of schooling, and that only a small minority attained any satisfactory grasp of even the most elementary concepts by age 16 (Driver et al 1985, Osborne and Freyberg 1985).

The second trend started from the new emphasis given to the processes and skills of science, particularly through the work of the A.P.U. science monitoring (Black 1990). This led to more complex views of the essential links between the learning of concepts and of skills. These developments also led to a new empha-

3

sis on pupils' own science investigations, culminating in the emergence of Attainment Target One of the national curriculum.

The third trend started with the growing concern with environmental issues and with the moral responsibilities of scientists, which led some to promote the study in school science, of its technological and social implications (Lewis 1980, Solomon, 1983, Holman 1986, Hunt 1988). Others argued for a more human approach which would discuss scientists as persons developing their contributions in particular historical contexts. A third group criticised science teaching for failing to give explicit attention to the methods of science, and yet presenting, by implication, quite false views about them (Hodson 1985, Lucas 1990). These strands have converged in arguments that a broader, more humanistic, definition of school science is now needed (Matthews 1990, 1992).

The position is no less stable in the area of primary science (Black 1985). The early predominance of the "nature table" approach was first replaced by attempts to set up a broader agenda of interesting topics for basic knowledge. This was further replaced by an emphasis on process skills, with reduction or even exclusion of specific topic knowledge. This has been replaced again, notably in the national curriculum, by a model which emphasises investigative skills, together with a mixture of basic topics ("know that" statements) and elementary concepts ("understand that").

The sum of these trends has been a definition of the science curriculum for the present decade which is different in several fundamental respects even from that of the early 1980's. Indeed, there have been fundamental changes in every one of the last few decades.

Stop The World We Want To Get Off!
The future for change

It might be comforting to imagine that future decades will be marked by greater stability. However, it seems unlikely that the forces which have driven the changes of past decades will disappear. The first of these is the influence of changes in science and technology themselves. Areas such as genetic engineering, the AIDS epidemic and the burgeoning environmental crises, let alone others that are yet to emerge, must surely affect priorities in science education.

The second drive for change will come from changes within education itself. In the last ten years, research in education has become notably more relevant to pedagogy than at any previous time and this process is hardly likely to stop. At the same time, developments in information technology have yet to achieve anything like the impact which is currently foreseeable. For example, when vast resources, in knowledge bases and training systems, are available to anyone at the touch of a button, what then will be the point of much of the work that now takes up time in classrooms ?

The third drive will come from changes in society, leading to changes in expectations for schools. The national curriculum itself is not an accident arising from the 1987 general election, but rather the culmination of longer term political and social trends. There is no sign that public and political interest in education has since declined, and no evidence at all that the definition of a national curriculum will be followed by suspension of debate about curriculum purposes or practices.

Finally, there is the less evident but most potent catalyst, changes in pupils themselves. Radical changes in influences outside the school, notably in family life and in the media may well be producing profound changes in the needs of the pupils. A recent authoritative review of the condition of children in the USA (Hamburg 1992) talks of a generation in crisis, because of the disastrous stresses for those growing up in poverty in inner cities, and the neglect of parenting in all classes. As society starts to suffer the consequences of such changes, it may look to schools to provide a redeeming framework for many children – a task which far transcends their traditional role.

Given all this, it is up to teachers and school to develop to the full their understanding of, and so their commitment to, their purposes for education. They might thereby be better able to hold on to their own interpretations of change, so that they can filter or distil the pressures in the interests of their pupils, rather than be disoriented and de-skilled by them. They might also be better prepared to influence public debate about re-definitions of their purposes and priorities.

However, the influence of teachers is bound to be limited. Others professionally involved in science education, whether as academic researchers, as inspectors, as trainers or as administrators will all exert pressure. The growing emphasis on the need to expand the numbers in tertiary education will give that sector more influence. More uncertain will be the strength of public, notably political pressure. Business, industry, and environmentalists may play enhanced roles, whilst it seems that political control over the curriculum, far from leading to stability, is leading to more questioning of school practices and to weakness in the face of the temptations to exert one's powers to "improve" as soon as difficulties are publicised.

Thus, the determination of purposes and priorities for the science curriculum has to take place in an essentially political struggle between competing traditions, perspectives and interests. In this respect, it does not differ from other significant social issues. However, the point deserves emphasis here, both because current trends and proposals have to be examined in this light, and because formulation of policies and practices in the future have to be made in this context. However, whilst schools are not in full control of specification, they have very strong control over implementation, so that their own priorities, and their views of the priorities of others, are of outstanding importance.

Science for All?

The starting point must be to consider the purposes of a curriculum which might be the only experience of serious learning about science that pupils have in their lives. Given the large and growing relevance of science in the private, social and political spheres, the optimum planning of this experience must be of the utmost importance.

None of the main purposes can be achieved unless certain subsidiary purposes are met. The first of these is accessibility. Pupils must understand and feel confidence with the science they are studying. This purpose may present very difficult dilemmas, for it is clear that in experience to date, it has not been achieved.

Likewise, the main purposes cannot be achieved unless pupils can see the relevance of what they are trying to learn and can find stimulus and enjoyment in it. Very few pupils can persevere with work which, being difficult and apparently irrelevant, brings little immediate reward.

To turn to the main purposes, the first is that pupils should be given a basis for understanding and for coping with their lives. Science has a lot to say about problems in people's personal lives, notably in health, including nutrition, drug abuse, the AIDS epidemic and in broader issues, such as those concerned with sexuality. Here, as for most applications of science in personal and social life, impersonal knowledge and understanding has to develop in conjunction with appreciation of issues of moral and social value. This purpose embraces the need to look after oneself, and to help protect oneself and others from the flow of incomplete and misleading information which seems to be an inevitable feature of a democratic society.

The need to become capable of taking part in positive initiatives to improve life for all follows naturally. Indeed, the social dimension expands this agenda to such an extent that a further purpose, that of understanding the applications and effects of science in society, is worth formulating. The considerations here also need to be related to issues of value and morality, and also raise the question of whether such issues should be be tackled only, or even mainly, in the science classroom. Almost any of the main examples, for instance pollution or global warming, could well be tackled from a variety of non-science perspectives. This point is taken up further below.

The two aspects of the purpose discussed so far involve learning *from* science, using its results as a starting point, rather than *about* science, studying how those results are achieved. Learning about science constitutes the second main purpose. It involves learning about the concepts and the methods which are combined in scientific enquiry. Pursuit of this purpose in isolation can give too much emphasis to purely instrumental reasons for learning science One function of schools however is to be the guardians and transmitters of a society' culture. Science is one of mankind's greatest achievements, and without some knowledge of its history, some appreciation of the personal genius of famous scientists in determining the course of science, and some insight into the particular way in which science searches for truth, a pupil will have little insight into what science, seen as a human activity, is really like. For example, a pupil struggling with the ideas that air fills the space around her, and that it has weight and that it even exerts a very large pressure, might understand her own confusions and the nature of science better if she was told about how some of the greatest intellects grappled with the same difficulties in previous centuries. Historical examples can also make clear that imagination and creativity are essential to the development of science, and that it proceeds through obstacles of misunderstanding, and controversy, rather than by the smooth deductions and experimental "proofs".

Such purposes should be so pursued that the experience of science that school learning gives will be authentic. This need affects the style of the work undertaken, the range of issues covered and the image of science that is conveyed.

Science education cannot be planned as an isolated experience, contributing only to its own particular purposes. Thus a third main purpose is that it must contribute to the general personal and intellectual development of the pupils. Such a contribution tends to be considered automatically in primary education, but to fall away at secondary level where the practice of subjects working in isolation is too prevalent.

There are many possibilities here. One is that a pupil should gain experience, in science, of the logic of explanation using assumptions, models, evidence and argument to reach conclusions. Such experience can build up pupils' confidence in their power to construct explanations. A different emphasis appears in the possibility of pursuing practical investigations. These can contribute to building up practical capability, since such investigations call for powers of initiative, of making decisions, of overcoming obstacles. They can also provide outstanding opportunities for learning to work in small groups. For both of these aspects, it is essential that emphasis be given to helping pupils to reflect on what they have done so that they become more aware of the way in which science works (White and Gunstone 1989). Here the pursuit of the goal of authentic understanding of the nature of scientific enquiry contributes powerfully to pupils' general development. Such contribution can be enhanced if pupils can relate the way in which they work in science to the ways in which they work in other disciplines.

This agenda cannot be complete without attention to the fact that a common curriculum should provide pupils with a basis for making choices, together with positive motivation to consider seriously a further commitment to science. This, the fourth main purpose, is discussed in the next section.

Your Country Needs You!
Providing future specialists

Given this spectrum of purposes set out above, it can be asked whether a curriculum which gave its main priority to the selection and preparation of future scientists ought to be very different. The needs of understanding science, with its implications for developing powers of explanation and of practical capability, are of direct significance for future specialists. It can hardly be argued that a broader view of science as a human activity is not needed by those in whose hands the future development of science will lie. Indeed, it can be argued that the neglect of this aspect at all levels of study, particularly in specialised tertiary education, has been an intellectual weakness and a practical impoverishment of the scientific community. The need for the experience of science to be authentic would seem to be a top priority in providing pupils with a basis for choice. It might be argued that a far narrower range of subjects, studied in greater depth, and giving less attention to the broad range of everyday applications, might be appropriate. This raises the prospect that future specialists would be less well served than their peers in using science to cope with their personal and social needs.

However, it is also necessary to consider the need to attract pupils to specialise in science as well as the need to prepare them if they are attracted. The number attracted has always been too small and, for science and engineering, has always included far too few girls. This means that the images and experiences of science presented to school pupils have to be changed. Studies of the links between adolescent personality development and choice of science (Head 1986) indicate that the closed and algorithmic view of science that courses usually present, tends to repel those extrovert pupils, particularly boys, who wish to challenge authority and question values. For girls, the impersonal view of science presented by a narrow concentration on "basics" is a severe obstacle. Thus, emphasis on a narrow preparation can limit recruitment. It might have the further disadvantage that those who are attracted are being misled, because the reality of professional practice will be quite different from their experience of "preparation".

The conclusion from these arguments is that future specialists cannot do without any of the work that all pupils require. However their needs argue for the provision of more in-depth work in at least a sample of areas of science so that any pupils who wish can explore their commitment and test out their ability to take science further. This particular part of the argument has no relevance for primary science. However, insofar as primary science generates enthusiasm, an appreciation of science as the work of people, and a growth in capability and in understanding it is laying essential foundations for all of the purposes discussed as well as providing the first inspiration for future scientists.

Evidence that students in tertiary education suffer from the same misconceptions about science fundamentals as their secondary peers, and that transfer of learning to new contexts is notoriously difficult to achieve, cast doubt on the notion that school study can at present provide a "firm grounding". A counter-argument, that a spiral curriculum in which a broader range of aims is addressed at each stage may be more effective, is at least plausible. Thus, for example, an interplay between principles, applications, and "hands-on" investigation should characterise both sides of the secondary – tertiary interface, just as it should at the primary – secondary interface, for which it would be absurd to propose that primary pupils should learn only concepts, leaving project investigations to build on this "preparation" at secondary level.

The arguments may be different if the aim is to provide pupils with preparation that is more directly vocational. Arguments about the needs of different vocational groups are often in mutual conflict, so that it emerges that the range of needs can only be met by distilling out what they have in common. Thus the argument reduces to one about basic knowledge and skills. The metaphor of "basic skills" has many attractions. There are dangers here also. The implied assumption, that these skills are the same across different contexts, needs careful examination; this assumption may be evident in the case of reading instrument scales but it is very doubtful if (say) problem-solving is assumed to be the same skill in many different occupations. It is also notorious that pupils are usually unwilling or unable to apply a skill, learnt in one context, to a problem in a quite different context.

Finally, it should be noted that some parts of higher education are also calling into question the view that specialist education should proceed by the learning of required components at early stages and should only tackle the "synthesis-in-application" of these at advanced stages. There is, for example, a move in engineering schools in the USA to emphasis the integrative and holistic activity of tackling real problems right from the start of freshman courses (Bordogna 1989), whilst science degree courses in this country now incorporate substantial components of project work where thirty years ago they would have assumed that such work had to wait until the postgraduate stage.

A Model for Purposes
Essential Components of a Learning Programme

A brief discussion is offered here about components essential to any learning programme designed to achieve these purposes, partly because this will help to bring out some of the implications of the aims presented.

A first essential is that students should come to understand science and to understand how science is made by being engaged in doing it. This involves three main aspects. One is that they have to learn about its main concepts, seen as abstract yet powerful agents for predicting and controlling natural phenomena. This in itself is a formidable requirement. The difficulties pupils of all ages have in grasping and accepting many science concepts have been well documented. it seems clear that to overcome this problem requires that more classroom time be spent on any one idea, so the range of concepts to be covered will have to be reduced (Scott et al 1992).

The second aspect is that pupils should be able to use the main skills which go to make up the scientific method. Such skills as observation, measurement, making generalisations, inventing hypotheses, devising fair tests, designing experiments, analysing data and interpreting results should all be included. A full exploration of many of these has been made in the work of the science teams of the A.P.U. (Black 1990, Strang 1990, Strang et al 1991)

However, neither the concepts nor the skills can be properly understood in isolation from one another. It is not possible, for example, to propose hypotheses except in the light of some preconceived model of the system under consideration. Conversely, understanding of the ways in which concepts have developed can only be conveyed through activity which uses these skills. This leads to the third aspect – which is that pupils should have personal experience of working with the interaction of concepts and skills in planning, designing, carrying out and interpreting their own experiments. Only through such activity can pupils develop an authentic understanding of what is involved in doing science. It is important that at least some of these should involve the application, and subsequent modification, of scientific ideas to test explanations. Science involves far more than systematic comparison of materials or products, and whilst consumer tests may have some value in teaching some skills, some published materials so emphasise this approach that they give a misleading image of science.

It is not implied that every new idea must be developed through students' own personal investigations. However, their own personal experience of investigating some ideas and phenomena should help pupils in understanding the way in which others have come to new ideas through scientific investigation.

Whilst it should be clear that the careful pursuit of these three aspects in an interconnected way must be the main vehicle for achieving some of the main purposes, other activities will be needed to complete the agenda. Students should come to know about science as a human activity, by studying how its achievements have emerged in particular historical contexts and have depended on beliefs, technology, social systems and above all the human personalities of those involved. Reflection on their own investigations should help pupils to develop understanding of the ways in which evidence, experimentation, hypotheses, models and mathematics are combined in the development of science.

The above requirements demand that more time be spent on some science topics, because there is evidence that unless this is done we shall continue to leave pupils with serious misunderstandings, not only about particular scientific ideas, but also about what the whole activity of science is about. However, this need conflicts with the purposes of giving pupils a basis to cope with everyday needs, for this requires that they know about the many results of scientific work which are important to them in their lives. It seems neither possible nor necessary that all of this large number could be studied in the depth suggested in the tripartite interaction of concepts, skills and processes discussed above. Whilst a few must be studied in this way, others could be studied more superficially, with emphasis on those features which must be known about in order to lead a healthy and responsible adult life.

The need to know about the many applications of science, and about the ways in which, through its contribution to technology, science has had a profound effect on our society, is indisputable. However, it is difficult to specify what level of understanding of a scientific idea is needed to be able to make use of it in daily life (Layton 1991): electricians know far less about circuit theory than physicists, but they are better at fixing a new ring main. At a more general level, the extent to which science has been the driving force of modern technology is often exaggerated, there being many technological changes in which the contrivance technology of craftsmen and entrepreneurs has been the main driving force (Gardner 1992). Finally, since technological change is a complex human activity in which many areas of thought and action play a part, it may be misleading to present it to pupils in the restricted context of the science classroom

(Black and Harrison 1985). This point will be taken further in the next section.

All of this discussion has treated science as a single entity. The conceptual basis of science has a structure in which the separate components of biology, chemistry, physics and earth sciences are identifiable, albeit overlapping, components. Furthermore, these different areas of science differ significantly both in philosophy and in their styles of work – so, for example, biologists overlap with social scientists in the way that physicists do not, and biologists have to do experiments with many of the variables uncontrolled, the design of which would be unthinkable for a physicist (Black 1986).

Opinions differ about the implications of these features. Several varieties of combined, or co-ordinated, or integrated science are used. Almost all agree that to teach three or four sciences separately and without close co-ordination is unacceptable and that up to age 16 all the main areas should be encountered by all. It is also the case that in almost all courses, whatever their ideology, there is a mixture of separate discipline topics and topics which clearly cross the boundaries. These features contribute to an overall purpose of understanding the nature of science, which has within itself elements both of unity and of diversity.

Across the Curriculum?

If a broad definition of technology is adopted, then it has a place of its own in the curriculum which does not derive from science. In this view, one problem about implementing technology in the curriculum is to ensure that in their learning and involvement in technology, pupils summon up and bring into use contributions from many school subjects, of which science is one. Science teachers should try to make their contribution to technology, both to serve other parts of the curriculum, and give their own pupils a mature appreciation of the role of science in technology.

There is a broader set of possibilities to which similar considerations apply. Science is an arena in which the purposes of other important parts of the curriculum can be realised, e.g. uses of descriptive and imaginative language, or application of mathematical modelling, or development of moral education in relation to the choices presented by science. Conversely, it can be enriched by work in other subjects. Examples are overlaps between earth sciences and geography, and overlaps with history; the latter would be important if the scope of science study were to be broadened to make it more human (Watts 1991).

Such opportunities are taken up in primary schools, although it needs careful planning if topic work is to bring out the interconnections. There are more serious difficulties at secondary level. Where school subject departments work as separate empires, the pupils are left to make the inter-relationships which their teachers have failed to make for them; most cannot do so and keep their learning of subjects in separate compartments. This grave weakness can be overcome if schools give priority to planning the curriculum as a whole. This requires that overarching themes be formulated and agreed, from which the roles of separate subjects can be assigned and the possibilities of inter-subject work explored. Sadly, the national curriculum, with its almost exclusive concentration on separate subjects and avoidance of general curriculum principles or aims, gives too little encouragement to such important work.

Making it Happen

The realisation of purposes in classroom work is notoriously difficult. Of course, where discussion of them is treated as academic indulgence without any vision of accepting the struggles needed to make any important changes, there can be little point in discussing purposes at all.

If the possibility that they are to make a serious difference is accepted, then one approach would be to carry out an audit of present activities to judge which are being served and where gaps occur. This would then lead to difficult decisions as to whether the purposes can be more fully met by a set of small adjustments, or whether quite radical changes are needed, at least in part.

A helpful part of any such planning is to derive from the broad aims some secondary aims which necessarily follow from them, for such aims, being closer to practice, can help cross the bridge between high-minded purposes and day-to-day work. Some of the discussion in Sections 6 and 7 can be read as contributions to such a strategy.

Within such a strategy, the issues of progression, implying the matching of the purposes to the development of pupils with age, would also need consideration. This has not been attempted here, apart from a few references to the differences between primary and secondary stages. It is not proposed that any of these purposes should be uniquely reserved for one phase only – they all apply at most ages, albeit in different ways.

Realisation of new purposes can imply more than shuffling of lesson plans so that new topics are introduced or the old ones realigned. For example, if moral issues are to be taken up, discussions which cannot lead to the right answer have to be managed; if pupils are to learn from taking responsibility for their own experiments, the role of their teacher will be quite different from the role needed to guide routine practical exercises (Black et al 1992). Such role changes are the most difficult obstacles in the path of any large shift in the purposes of a curriculum.

Finally, success might also require that pupils be aware of the underlying plan and perhaps build up their own portfolio of ideas about science and about the point of studying it (Claxton 1990). Central to any debate about purposes is the need to achieve reconciliation between what is needed by all, what is wanted by all and what is feasible for all. What is wanted by all is an oft neglected aspect.

What is feasible for all is the great uncertainty. Wherever new purposes, or a radically different balance between purposes, are explored, implementation changes the view, not only of what is feasible, but of what is really desirable (Roberts 1988). Commitment to a new vision of purposes is a moral adventure – a voyage in which the purposes themselves are explored as well as the uncharted tracks that lead to them.

References

References are given in the sections above where they are relevant to particular points and a list of these is given below. However, for more general discussions of purpose, a few of those listed are particularly valuable – these are identified by asterisks.

Atkin, J.M. and Helms, J. Private Communication Stanford University, California. 1992

*A.S.E. *Education Through Science: Policy Statement.* A.S.E. Hatfield. 1981.

*A.S.E. *Change in Our Future; a Challenge for Science Education.* A.S.E. Hatfield. 1992.

Black P. and Harrison G. *In Place of Confusion* Nuffield/ Chelsea Curriculum Trust London 1985.

Black P.J. APU *Science: the Past and the Future.* School Science Review. Vol.72 (258) pps. 13–28. September 1990.

Black P.J., Fairbrother R., Jones A., Simon S. and Watson R. *Open Work in Science: a Review of Practice.* King' Research Paper. C.E.S. King's College London 1992. *see also* Black P.J.Fairbrother R., Jones A., Simon S. and Watson R. *Development of Open Work in School Science.* A book to be published by the A.S.E.

Black P.J. *Integrated or Co-ordinated Science?* (Presidential Address given to Association for Science Education at University of York on 4th January l986). The School Science Review, Vol.67, No.24l., pps.669–68l, June l986.

Black P.J. Why hasn't it worked? Chapter in: *Approaching Primary Science* (ed. B. Hodgson & E.Scanlon), pps.61–64, Harper & Row, London, 1985.

Bordogna J. *Entering the 90's: A National Vision for Engineering Education. Engineers' Education* 79 (7) November 1989.

Champagne A and Lovitts B. Scientific literacy : a concept in search of a definition. In Champagne, A., Lovitts,B., and Calinger, B. (Eds.) *This Year in School Science 1989: Scientific Literacy.* Papers from the 1989 AAAS forum for school science. AAAS Washington DC, USA 1989.

Claxton G. Science Lessens? *Studies in Science Education* 18. pps.165–171. 1990.

D.E.S. *Science in the National Curriculum* 1991. H.M.S.O. 1991

Driver R., Guesne E and Tiberghien A. (eds.) *Children's Ideas in Science.* Open University Press. Milton Keynes U.K. 1985.

*Fensham, P.J. (ed.) *Development and Dilemmas in Science Education.* Falmer. Lewes UK. 1988.

*Fensham P.J. Science and Technology. pps. 789-829 in *Handbook of Research on Curriculum.* Macmillan. New York. 1992.

Gardner P.L. The Application of Science to Technology. To be published in *Research in Science Education* – papers from the 1992 ASERA conference at Waikato University New Zealand.

Hamburg D.A. *Today's Children: Creating a Future for a Generation at Risk.* Times books – Random House, New York 1992.

Head J., *The Personal Response to Science.* Cambridge University Press. 1986

Hodson D. Philosophy of Science, Science and Science Education. *Studies in Science Education 12.* pps.25–57. 1985.

Holman J. *Science and Technology in Society. General Guide for Teachers.* Association for Science Education. Hatfield Herts.U.K. 1986

Hunt A. SATIS Approach to STS. *International Journal of Science Education.* 10. pps.409–420. 1988.

Jenkins E. *From Armstrong to Nuffield.* Murray London 1979

Layton D. *Science for the People.* George Allen and Unwin London U.K. 1973

Layton D. Science Education and Praxis: the Relationship of School Science to Practical Action. *Studies in Science Education 19.* pps.43– 78. 1991.

Lewis J. *Science in Society: Readers and Teachers Guide.* Heinemann. London. 1980.

Lucas A.M. Processes of Science and Processes of Learning. *Studies in Science Education. 18.* pps.172–177. 1990.

Matthews M.R. History, Philosophy and Science Teaching: a Rapprochement. *Studies in Science Education 18.* pps.25–51. 1990.

Matthews M.R. History, Philosophy and Science Teaching: The Present Rapprochement. *Science and Education 1.* pps. 1–47, 1992.

Osborne R. and Freyberg P. *Learning in Science: the Implications of Children's Science.* Heinemann Auckland N.Z. 1985.

*Rutherford F.J. and Ahlgren A. *Science for All Americans.* Oxford University Press. Oxford 1989.

Roberts D.A. What Counts as Science Education? pps.27–54 in Fensham, P.J. (ed.) *Development and Dilemmas in Science Education.* Falmer. Lewes UK. 1988.

Scott, P.H., Asoko, H.M. and Driver,R. (1992) Teaching for conceptual change: a review of strategies. in Duit, R. et al.(eds.) *Research in Physics Learning: Theoretical Issues and Empirical Studies.* Kiel: IPN – Institute for Science Education.

*S.S.C.R. *Better Science: Making It Happen.* A.S.E./ Heinemann. London. 1987.

Solomon J. *SISCON in Schools – Readers and Teachers Guide.* Blackwell. Oxford 1983.

Strang J. Measurement in School Science. *Assessment Matters No.2* Schools Examinations and Assessment Council. London 1990.

Strang J., Daniels S., and Bell J. Planning and Carrying Out Investigations. *Assessment Matters No.6* Schools Examinations and Assessment Council. London 1991.

Tamir P et al. *Curriculum Implementation and its Relationship to Curriculum Development in Science.* Israel Science Teaching Centre. Jerusalem 1979.

Watts M. (ed.) *Science in the National Curriculum.* Cassell London 1991.

White R. and Gunstone R., Meta-learning and Conceptual Change. *International Journal of Science Education.* 11 (5) pp.577–586. 1989.

Paul Black is Professor of Science Education, King's College, London.

A National Curriculum for Science

David Oakley

2

Why a National Curriculum?
The background
The political imperative

The National Curriculum (NC) was introduced as a result of the reforming philosophy of a Conservative government which culminated in the Education Reform Act of 1988. ERA contained a mass of legislation (nearly 1 cm thick) which gave the Secretaries of State for England and Wales (SoS) unprecedented powers over the education system in this country. As well as the legislation for the National Curriculum, it included that for Local Management of Schools (LMS), open enrolment, the establishment of the National Curriculum Council (NCC), the Curriculum Council for Wales (CCW) and the Schools Examinations and Assessment Council (SEAC). Many objected at the time to the setting up of separate organisations for curriculum and assessment, and indeed the government white paper of August 1992 proposes to combine them again in the School Curriculum and Assessment Authority (SCAA).

In 1989 the Secretary of State (Kenneth Baker) summed up the aims of the National Curriculum (in a speech at the North of England Conference) as:

1 giving a clear incentive for all schools to catch up with the best and the best will be challenged to do even better;
2 providing parents with clear and accurate information;
3 ensuring continuity and progression from one year to another, from one school to another;
4 helping teachers concentrate on the task of getting the best possible results from each individual child.

All state schools in England and Wales are required by law to provide a balanced and broadly based curriculum which will prepare young people for the opportunities, responsibilities and experiences of adult life and promote the spiritual, moral, cultural, mental and physical development, of pupils at the school and of society. Fears about the prescriptive nature of a National Curriculum were deflected by statements that it is a "framework not a straightjacket" and is a "minimum entitlement". How the "Programmes of Study" were to be taught and learned was not specified, though government concern about teaching methods resulted, in 1992, in the setting up of a three-man commission (Alexander, Rose and Woodhead) to consider primary practice, and in the setting of new guidelines for a reduced role for course-work at GCSE. Both steps encouraged debate about how pupils should best be taught, and challenged aspects of current practice.

A view of the curriculum

The curriculum model presented was subject-dominated, with ten subjects plus Religious Education to be accommodated. Cross-curricular themes, dimensions and skills were added later, part-way through the process of introduction of the subjects. Science was deemed to be of fundamental importance and was elevated to the "core" curriculum alongside English and Maths. The recognition of science as an essential part of the curriculum represented a major success for those influencing national policy on education. The seminal HMI document "*Science 5–16: A statement of policy*" (DES 1985) the ASE and the Secondary Science Curriculum Review, all played a part in preparing the ground for the core curriculum status for science, as did the Education Support (ESG) Grants to help LEAs' to strengthen the primary science curriculum.

The making of the curriculum

Once the government had embarked on this course of action, someone had to advise on, and write, the curriculum. The first group set up to pave the way was the Task Group on Assessment and Testing (TGAT). Chaired by Professor Paul Black of Kings College, London University, this was influential, in particular, in suggesting the ideas of attainment targets (AT), the ten levels of attainment profile components, (groups of attainment targets for reporting purposes) and standard assessment tasks, for national testing of achievement. Many of their original ideas have evolved; some have fallen by the wayside. With TGAT to give guidance, working groups were set up by the Secretaries of State to produce recommendations on what the curriculum should be. The science working group was chaired by Professor Jeff Thompson of Bath University: academics and practitioners were represented, and HMI and NCC officials attended the meetings. The remit of the group also included Technology 5–11. The timescale was short. They met at regular intervals over a twelve month period. Their early thoughts were summarised in an interim report in December 1987. The thinking of the group produced, from five "themes", a number of attainment targets, 22 in all in their final report, reflecting not only subject content areas but also skills. The attainment targets (ATs) were packaged into profile components as a way of grouping them for reporting purposes. Consultation conducted by the NCC resulted in recommendations to the Secretaries of State and in March 1989 Draft Orders were framed, followed, after brief consultation, by Final Orders, which itemised 17 Attainment Targets grouped into two profile components. Only 14 ATs were thought to be appropriate for pupils from 5–11. 4 ATs were proposed for Primary Technology. Fig's 1 and 2 summarise the sequence of events and the "evolution" of National Curriculum Science. One notable feature in fig 1 is the changing balance between knowledge and understanding and skills.

	Attainment Targets	Profile Components	Weighting of PCs %				Examples
Interim report December 1987	5 "themes" define the scope of science • living things and their interaction with the environment • materials and their characteristics • energy and matter • forces and their effects • the earth and space						
Final report & proposals of SoS August 1988	1 – 16	knowledge and understanding	KS1 35	2 35	3 40	4 40	No
	17 & 18	exploration and investigation	50	50	30	25	
	19 & 20	communication	15	15	15	15	
	21 & 22	science in action	–	–	15	20	
NCC consultation & recommendations Dec 1988 and draft orders January 1989	1	exploration of science	50	45	35	30	No
	2 – 17	knowledge and understanding of science	50	55	65	70	
Statutory orders March 1989	1	exploration of science	50	45	35	30	No
	2 – 17	knowledge and understanding of science	50	55	65	70	
Proposals of SoS May 1991	1	exploration of science	50	45	35	30	
	2 – 5	knowledge and understanding of science	50	55	65	70	
NCC consultation & recommendations September 1991	1	no profile components	weighting of ATs 50	50	25	25	Yes
	2 – 4		50	50	75	75	
Draft orders October 1991	1	no profile components	weighting of ATs 50	50	25	25	No
	2		}	}	25	25	
	3		}50	}50	25	25	
	4		}	}	25	25	
Statutory orders 1991	1	scientific investigation	50	50	25	25	Yes
	2	life & living processes					
	3	materials & their properties	50	50	75	75	
	4	physical processes					

Figure 1 The Evolution of the National Curriculum for Science

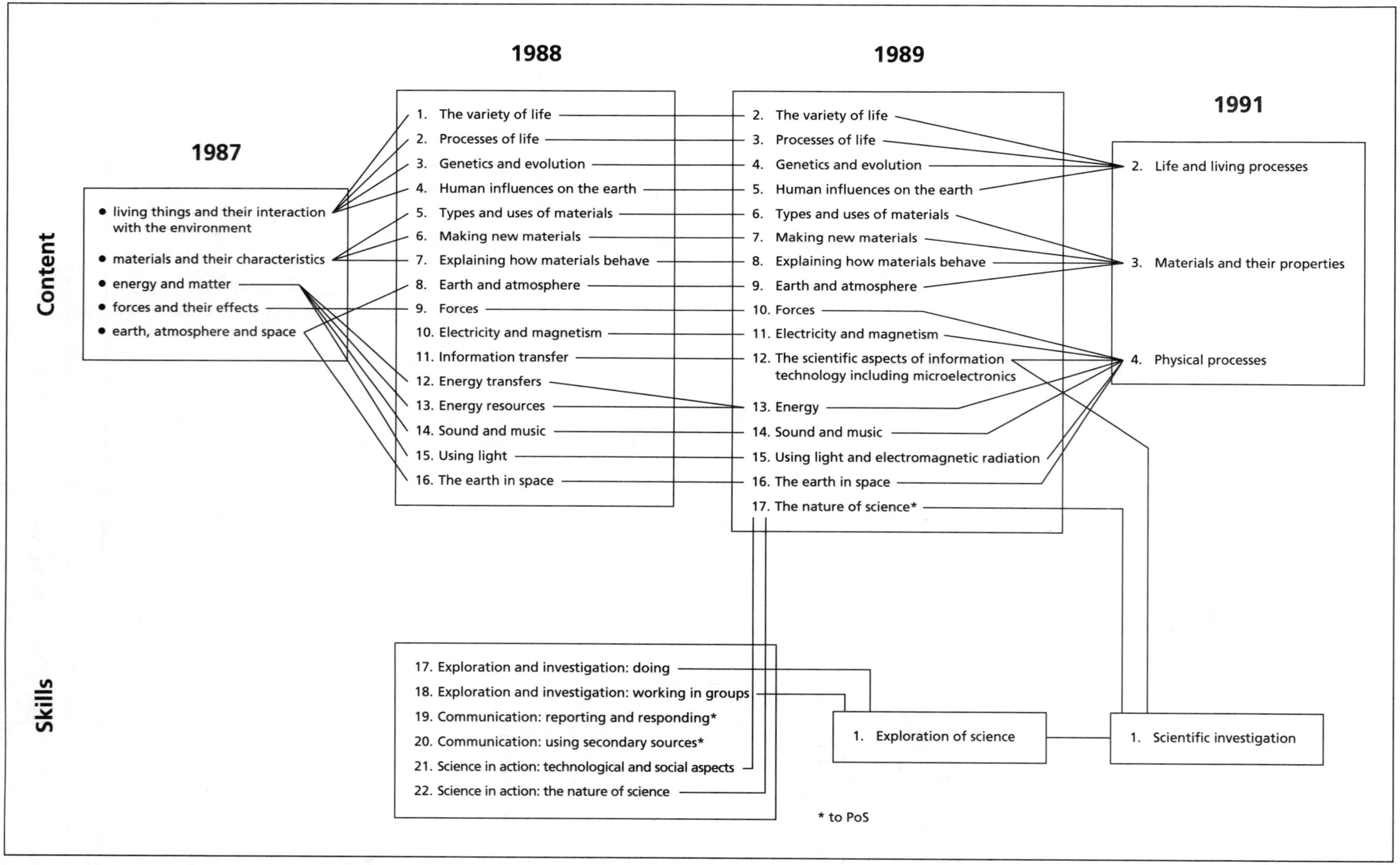

Figure 2 *National Curriculum Science: Content and Skills Attainment Targets 1987–1991*

Implementing the National Curriculum

Schools were required to start to implement NC Science, from August 1989 for five year olds and twelve year olds, and from August 1990 for eight year olds. A massive in-service training exercise was mounted by LEA's to prepare teachers for delivery of the new curriculum. Fortunately, many primary advisory teachers were in post, funded by Education Support Grants and the Secondary Science Curriculum Review had stimulated the appointment of secondary advisory teachers. Advisory teachers were recruited from amongst good classroom practitioners to lead in-service training, to prepare support materials for teachers and co-ordinators, to work alongside teachers in the classroom and act as consultants and advisers. Many were seconded to the role and returned to the classroom; others became education lecturers or advisers/inspectors. With the demise of ESG's, the rise of LMS and the devolution of finance to schools, the number of advisory teachers has declined, but their support was crucial at the time.

The issues

In primary schools, the immediate task of teachers was to come to terms with National Curriculum in Maths, English and Science and incorporate them into the curriculum. The emphasis on subjects initially caused problems, as a result of the apparent conflict with the integrated nature of the topic work characteristic of primary practice. Guidance focused on detailed planning for coverage of the Programmes of Study (PoS) and attainment targets over a year and a phase. Overemphasis on Attainment Targets tended to spoil the coherence of some of the topic work by narrowing its focus, and it took a while for teachers to realise that ATs are not "taught" but attained. This also proved to be true for secondary schools. Even though the NC was to be phased in gradually, primary schools soon realised the value of implementation in all year groups, to allow more coherent planning, particularly as the NC provided more of a framework for continuity and progression, and offered more specific guidance on what pupils at a particular age should be capable of, than existed before. It was no longer sufficient for individual teachers to plan in isolation from their colleagues and disregard what had gone before and what came after. This has perhaps been one of the greatest benefits of the National Curriculum.

Key Stage 1

At KS1, teachers were able to provide a much better and more consistent and complete coverage of science. For many, the problems of lack of funding and the speed of curriculum development were more than balanced out by the sharpening of their own practice, although detailed planning to some extent reduced the spontaneity, flexibility and serendipity of the early years.

Key Stage 2   KS2 presented the additional problem of the lack of background subject knowledge of primary teachers. Initially, topic work became very science-orientated as teachers put a lot of effort into ensuring that this new (for many) area of the curriculum was delivered properly. This was probably an inevitable consequence of the statutory "threat", as well as of the novelty of some of the skills and knowledge to be covered. The pendulum swung in the direction of the humanities in a similar way with the introduction of NC Geography and History. The integrated nature of topic work has been more difficult to maintain at KS2: many schools have opted for a more subject-orientated approach in the upper years of KS2. The Alexander Report, (Alexander Rose and Woodhead 1992) questioned whether it is realistic to assume that the generalist class teacher, aided by the curriculum co-ordinator, can effectively deliver nine subjects plus Religious Education. The tendency towards specialisation in the upper years of KS2 was predicted as a likely outcome for both teaching and learning. Some support for the science background knowledge of science co-ordinators and classroom teachers was provided, as a result of grant-aid from the DES for "20-day courses". These courses are, in the main, delivered in conjunction with higher education. An Open University distance learning course is also available. The DES courses began in 1989-90 and end in 1993; they are likely to reach only a third of schools. The NCC also embarked, in 1992, on the publication of distance learning materials specifically aimed at enhancing subject expertise in particular aspects of science. Primary school teachers in general feel the need for support with physical science topics such as forces, electricity and magnetism.

Key Stage 3   Science at KS3 had less impact. Science teachers assumed or asserted that they were "doing most of it already", as integrated courses were the norm at this stage. The arrival of the NC gave added impetus to the movement towards balanced science. It was in the areas new to school science, such as earth sciences, astronomy and the history of science, that most activity was stimulated, but in a search for resource materials rather than in any drastic revision of methodology or the structure of the curriculum. Publishers rushed to show how NC compatible their schemes were and produced materials to fill the gaps. Modifications to practice took a little longer in secondary schools than primary schools. Coming to terms with the new emphasis on IT in science was an awareness-raising and in-service training issue, sometimes sidestepped as a problem of under-resourcing – though this is a contributory factor. The recognition of the importance of a comprehensive scheme of work was a salvation for many science departments. Using PoS to define areas of content and enable achievement of attainment targets (which can then be specified in the scheme of work), and supporting this by suggestions for pupil activities, appropriate teaching/learning strategies, assessment and IT opportunities and homework, together help the planning and delivery of NC science. Changes in the management structure of science departments towards supporting and reflecting the organisation of the NC rather than the subject disciplines are also increasingly common, with incentive allowances being identified for responsibility for a key stage, assessment and recording, or organisation of a specific course.

Key Stage 4 KS4 National Curriculum GCSE courses, consistent with NC criteria, started in 1992 for examination in 1994. Double award (formerly model A) and single award (formerly model B) courses are available. Between 1989 and 1992 schools were required to meet the "reasonable time requirement": that is all pupils had to study science, the majority a double subject equivalent, with a single subject equivalent for the "minority" of pupils who might need

> *".... to spend more time on other subjects, for example to develop a special talent in music or foreign languages"* (DES 1989).

The continuance of separate science subjects was legislated for by the Secretary of State. These must be taken as a "suite" of subjects, physics, chemistry and biology: existing syllabuses are to be examined in 1994 with new subject criteria for subsequent years. The survival of separate subjects was felt by some, perhaps many, to subvert the broad and balanced science philosophy of the NC. Many still feel there is a danger that it could become a "second-class" option for girls or that it will be used for the less able. The reduction from double science is achieved by leaving Sc1 intact and excluding strands from the PoS for Sc2-4. The single science option (model 'B') has always been a controversial compromise.

The Structure of the National Curriculum for Science
The elements that make it up
The framework

The National Curriculum is a statutory framework which encompasses what is to be taught and what it is intended will be learnt by pupils or, more specifically, what pupil achievements are to be assessed. It should be remembered that the whole curriculum comprises cross-curricular elements and Religious Education as well as the NC. The "what is to be taught" are the programmes of study (PoS), continuous commentaries explaining what pupils should "do". Programmes of Study are defined as:

> *...the matters, skills and processes which must be taught to pupils during each key stage in order for them to meet the objectives set out in the attainment targets.*

A PoS is, then, more akin to a syllabus than a scheme of work.

The Attainment Targets (ATs) are the learning outcomes and are defined as:

...the objectives for each foundation subject, setting out the knowledge, skills and understanding that pupils of different abilities and maturities are expected to develop within each subject area. They are further defined at ten levels of attainment by means of appropriate statements of attainment.

The NC for science is currently set out in a document called *Science in the National Curriculum* (DES and Welsh Office 1991) which supersedes the 1988 version. The pages of parliamentary jargon bracketing the document reflect its legal status. The statutory requirement to teach the NC only applies to state schools in England and Wales but there is widespread adoption of it the independent sector. Northern Ireland has it's own NC which, as far as science is concerned, closely resembles that of England and Wales. Scotland has a different approach to the curriculum – it has NO National Curriculum!

Programmes of Study   The Programmes of Study need further interpretation and extension before a teaching programme can be devised which structures and sequences the scheme of work for science in a school. It is possible to group together the guidance in the programmes of study under various headings.

(i)   Those that have a practical emphasis – for example, pupils should ....

     .... be encouraged to develop skills ....

     .... collect and find ....

     .... explore the properties of ....

     .... explore the effect of .... .

     ... observe ....

     .... classify ....

     .... have the opportunities to experience ....

     .... investigate practically ....

     .... make predictions ....

     .... have experience of ....

which enable a teacher to identify suitable activities as part of the scheme of work.

(ii)   Those that deal more with ideas and concepts e.g. pupils should ....

     .... be encouraged to develop .... understanding ....

     .... learn that ....

     .... be introduced to the idea that ....

     .... be introduced to the concept that ....

     .... appreciate the relationship between ....

     .... explore the nature of .... consider ideas about ....

These will figure as part of the knowledge to be acquired as part of a scheme of work.

(iii) Those where relevant links with everyday life and the impact of science on society are detectable themes. pupils should ....

    .... consider everyday uses of ....

    .... develop an awareness of ....

    .... relate their experiences to ....

It is useful to use such statements to identify cross-curricular themes in the scheme of work.

(iv) Some imply guidance on teaching method. pupils should ....

    .... be given opportunities to discuss ....

    .... to investigate ....

but these are rare, and in general teachers can put flesh on the bones of the Programmes of Study in their own teaching and learning styles.

The emphasis in the NCC definition of the PoS is on teaching rather than learning, but both DES and NCC have always stressed that the National Curriculum has never prescribed methodology; it states, the "what" but not the "how". This leaves teachers with some freedom to interpret the programmes of study as they would a syllabus. The PoS can be used to initiate planning, or as a check on the scope and coverage of a topic or scheme already planned.

Fig 3 attempts to summarise how the demands of the NC may be incorporated into the planning process for schemes of work, for a piece of science with a fairly small amount of cross-subject linking and integration.

Each PoS is aimed at a Key Stage. Key stages are a way of packaging the years of compulsory schooling. Each Key Stage ends with national testing at ages, 7, 11, 14 and 16. Key Stage One (KS1) thus covers two years, Key Stage Two (KS2) four years, Key Stage Three (KS3) three years and Key Stage Four (KS4) two years. Programmes of Study are preceded by general statements which set the scene for each key stage and stress the importance of the development of communication skills and other key areas:

    – *the importance of science in everyday life at KS1 and KS2,*

    – *the application of science and the nature of scientific ideas at KS3,*

    – *the application of economic, social and technological implications of science and the nature of scientific ideas at KS4.*

Many of these fundamental themes featured in their own right as attainment targets in earlier versions of NC science. It is interesting to follow through some of the evolutionary pathways in Figures 1 and 2.

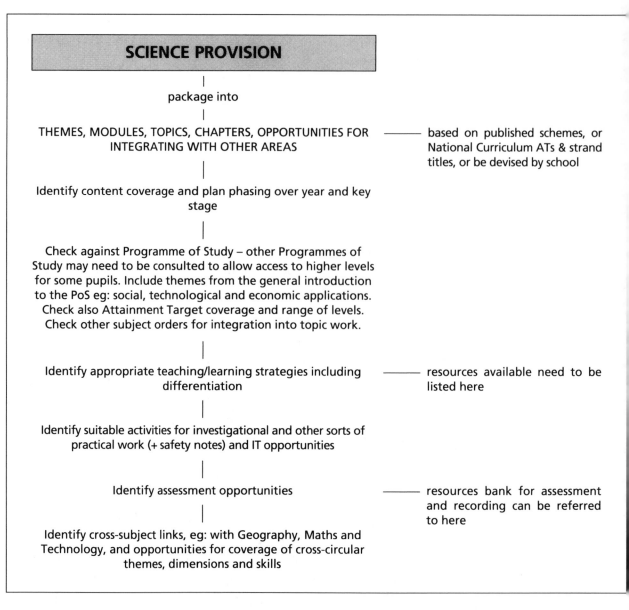

SCIENCE PROVISION

|
package into
|

THEMES, MODULES, TOPICS, CHAPTERS, OPPORTUNITIES FOR ——— based on published schemes, or
INTEGRATING WITH OTHER AREAS   National Curriculum ATs & strand
| titles, or be devised by school

Identify content coverage and plan phasing over year and key stage
|

Check against Programme of Study – other Programmes of Study may need to be consulted to allow access to higher levels for some pupils. Include themes from the general introduction to the PoS eg: social, technological and economic applications. Check also Attainment Target coverage and range of levels. Check other subject orders for integration into topic work.
|

Identify appropriate teaching/learning strategies including ——— resources available need to be
differentiation   listed here
|

Identify suitable activities for investigational and other sorts of practical work (+ safety notes) and IT opportunities
|

Identify assessment opportunities ——— resources bank for assessment
| and recording can be referred
| to here

Identify cross-subject links, eg: with Geography, Maths and Technology, and opportunities for coverage of cross-circular themes, dimensions and skills

Figure 3 Planning a Scheme of Work for National Curriculum Science

Attainment targets   Attainment targets are, in effect, learning objectives. They specify what it is expected pupils will have achieved as a result of having been taught the Programmes of Study. The interpretation of attainment targets and statements of attainment as assessment criteria has superseded the intention of the original authors of the NC science. They regarded them as general indicators of the performance to be expected by pupils at particular levels of achievement. Guidance by means of non-statutory examples helps teachers to visualise the sort of activities that pupils could experience, to enable them to achieve a particular level, in a particular Attainment Target. The inclusion of examples was a result of the consultation exercise on the revision of the original science national curriculum. There was some reluctance, on the part of the DES and NCC, to include, them because of the danger that the examples could become a dogmatic and prescriptive syllabus rather than guidance. Teachers however welcomed them, as ways of interpreting the statements of attainment and providing ideas for classroom activities. The pupil is put very much at the centre of these activities and the teacher is not mentioned ....

Pupils could ....

- use information .... from an extended family ... to show that a feature may be inherited ....
- identify processes .... such as feeding, growing ....
- explain how .... the heart acts as a pump in the body
- describe .... a local example of human impact on the environment
- compare .... a candle and a car engine
- identify variables .... which affect the rate at which water cools ....
- sort .... and group materials according to their shape, colour or hardness
- take measurements .... of the biological and physical factors involved at different sites ....
- select techniques .... such as decanting, filtration, dissolving and evaporation
- use knowledge of .... heating, evaporation, condensation .... to explain the water cycle
- deduce .... the products of heating elements ....
- design and make .... a circuit ....
- use diagrams to show .... the direction of forces on objects ....
- calculate .... the mean speed of vehicles from measurements ....
- predict .... the effect of the Sun's mass on the paths of a comet ....
- apply knowledge .... of energy transfers and of course ....
- investigate!

One weakness of the examples is that they are the same for each level irrespective of the context of that level in a particular key stage. Pupils may be at level 3 attainment in KS1, KS2, KS3 or KS4: a single example cannot be adequately relevant to all these age-groups. This reinforces the categorical (and arbitrary) nature of the ten-level scale but teachers are free to use their professional judgement to provide comparable alternatives. The word "comparable" however hides an inherent problem in the whole structure: the underlying assumption that what pupils can do in one context they can do in another. Once statements of attainment are used as assessment criteria this becomes a crucial issue: one that has not been fully addressed.

The science attainment targets

There are four attainment targets for science, *Sc 1 Scientific investigation, Sc 2 Life and living processes, Sc 3 Materials and their properties* and *Sc 4 Physical processes.* Sc1 (or AT1 in references to the first version of National Curriculum Science) is about practical skills, which are to be acquired in the context of the areas of knowledge and understanding specified in the programmes of study for Sc 2, 3, 4.

Sc1

Specific to Sc1 are those skills concerned with the process of scientific investigation, sometimes described as procedural understanding. They come together in the context of a whole investigation, fig 4.

Other kinds of practical work are part of teaching and learning about science but are not Sc1 because they illustrate concepts or processes in a prescribed way or involve practical skills and observational exercises outside the context of an investigation. The different kinds of practical work are summarised in fig 5.

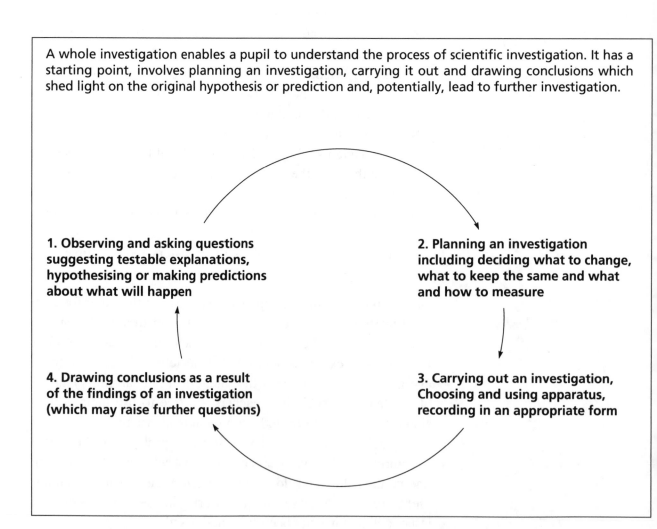

A whole investigation enables a pupil to understand the process of scientific investigation. It has a starting point, involves planning an investigation, carrying it out and drawing conclusions which shed light on the original hypothesis or prediction and, potentially, lead to further investigation.

1. Observing and asking questions suggesting testable explanations, hypothesising or making predictions about what will happen

2. Planning an investigation including deciding what to change, what to keep the same and what and how to measure

4. Drawing conclusions as a result of the findings of an investigation (which may raise further questions)

3. Carrying out an investigation, Choosing and using apparatus, recording in an appropriate form

Figure 4 Whole Investigations

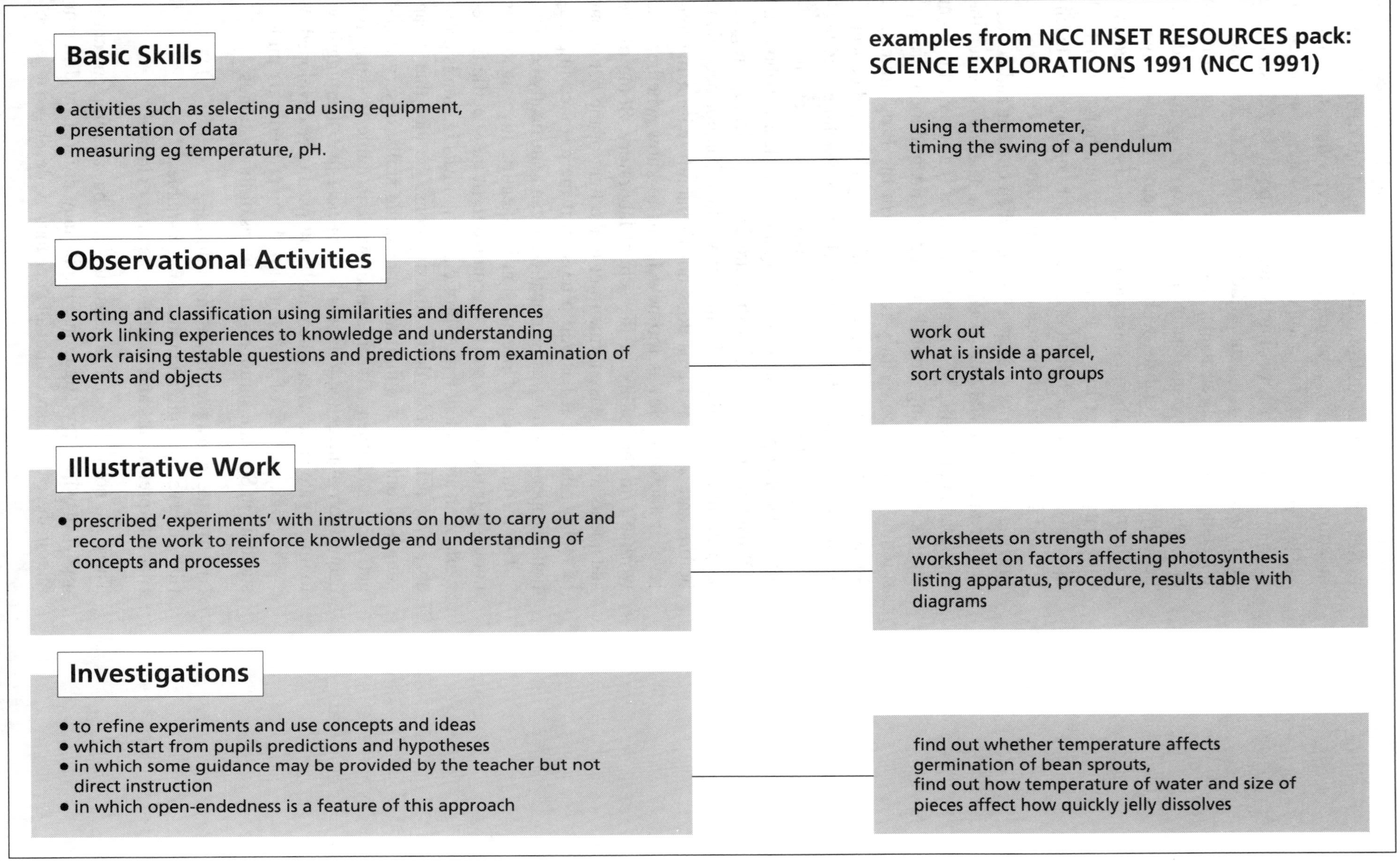
Basic Skills
• activities such as selecting and using equipment,
• presentation of data
• measuring eg temperature, pH.
examples from NCC INSET RESOURCES pack: SCIENCE EXPLORATIONS 1991 (NCC 1991)
using a thermometer, timing the swing of a pendulum
Observational Activities
• sorting and classification using similarities and differences
• work linking experiences to knowledge and understanding
• work raising testable questions and predictions from examination of events and objects
work out what is inside a parcel, sort crystals into groups
Illustrative Work
• prescribed 'experiments' with instructions on how to carry out and record the work to reinforce knowledge and understanding of concepts and processes
worksheets on strength of shapes
worksheet on factors affecting photosynthesis listing apparatus, procedure, results table with diagrams
Investigations
• to refine experiments and use concepts and ideas
• which start from pupils predictions and hypotheses
• in which some guidance may be provided by the teacher but not direct instruction
• in which open-endedness is a feature of this approach
find out whether temperature affects germination of bean sprouts,
find out how temperature of water and size of pieces affect how quickly jelly dissolves

Figure 5 The different kinds of practical work in science

The NC has, in a way, attempted to tease out the essence of what makes science different from other subjects. It has defined science in terms of a body of knowledge and concepts that is peculiar to science and, perhaps more importantly, the way in which science works. The view that it is intellectually impossible to disentangle the two threads and that an artificial division of the two ways of understanding has been made, is probably true, but the structure and nature of science process is more likely to be appreciated, particularly by non-specialists, with the arrangement that we have.

Giving investigation prominence in the ATs has ensured that this critical aspect has to be tackled by teachers from KS1 upwards. Sc1 has been, and is still, a major challenge for teachers and it is taking them some time to come to terms with it. Investigation for investigation's sake, when content and context are, or appear, trivial, has been criticised. The NC stresses the importance of setting Sc1 in the context of the other attainment targets and drawing upon knowledge and understanding of science, a point constantly reinforced in the Programmes of Study. Sc1 helps pupils to refine and clarify ideas and concepts. An investigation may be used as a vehicle for teaching a particular concept or for reinforcing it by exploring its practical manifestations after pupils have been taught or have learned about it.

What the attainment target structure does is to identify progression in investigational skills in a way which has not been done before and which perhaps does not fit happily within the ten-level framework. Sc1 is too new for us to know whether it is workable in the reality of the school laboratory. Some of the statements are not easy to interpret in the light of the behaviour of real pupils, and it has yet to be seen if the resource implications of open ended investigational work can realistically be met.

The identification of progression in scientific investigation is not easy, particularly when it is required to fit the specific framework of an attainment target. Proficiency in investigation is probably only achieved by doing investigations: the idea that it can somehow only be acquired after practising skills, observational activities and illustrative practical work is liable to delay the acquisition of investigational skills. It is clear that "learning how to investigate" is an area where materials need to be developed.

The components of investigational (or procedural) understanding in Sc 1 are summarised in terms of three strands:

(i)   ask questions, predict and hypothesise;
(ii) observe, measure and manipulate variables;
(iii) interpret results and evaluate scientific evidence.

These are not to be seen as separate skills but as complementary aspect of whole investigations. Pupils may progress at different rates in these three aspects but all three must be developed together.

"Stranding" Sc1 in this way has produced a more accessible approach to investigations which has many similarities with the "Planning, Implementing and Concluding" version of science process adopted by the Graded Assessment in Science Project (ULEAC 1992). For recording progress and to help diagnose where pupils need help to improve, teachers may assess one, two or three strands from a single investigation. When a level has to be reported at the end of a key stage, teachers will be able to aggregate the three strand levels using their professional judgement rather than a formula. If a pupil scores level 1 for strand (i), 2 for strand (ii) and 3 for strand (iii), the teacher may choose an overall level 2 as an average, level 3 using the "best" level or level 1 the "trailing edge" level! At the time of writing it is not clear how the teacher assessment of Sc1 will be moderated by any quality audit process. Fig 6 attempts to summarize Sc 1 by picking out the main features at each level of the attainment target.

Sc 2, 3, 4 The Attainment Targets Sc 2, 3 and 4 hark back to the first attempts of the science working group in 1987 to categorise science content. That, in turn, had been based on *"Science 5–16: A Statement of Policy"* (DES 1985 and Welsh Office). Sc2 packages the biological and ecological aspect of science. The physical sciences are split between Sc3 and Sc4, Sc3 being mainly chemical with earth science and Sc4 being physics with astronomy. The individual strands reflect their pedigree through the various stages of the science NC. Many strands were once attainment targets in their own right: fig 2 attempts to trace the ebb and flow.

The Revision of National Curriculum Science
The rationale

The reduction in the number of attainment targets and the abandonment of profile components was the result of a ministerial decision, announced in January 1991, that the curriculum needed simplifying, to make assessment more manageable. The revision was carried out by HMI in consultation with NCC. They used the opportunity to improve progression and continuity in the attainment targets, using research into children's learning in science which had taken place since the original version. This creativity was strictly outside their brief, as a major review was not intended, merely "re-brigading" – to use the jargon of the time!

The proposals for revision were initially met with more resistance than the revisers expected. Teachers had taken considerable trouble to come to terms with the original targets. They felt that the hard work that they had put in had been wasted and that the rules had been changed yet again.

	Strand	(i)	(ii)	(iii)
Plan and carry out investigations drawing on an increasing understanding of science				
Level		**Hypothesising & Predicting**	**Carrying Out**	**Interpretation & Evaluation**
Level 1		Observational		
Level 2		Predictions & observations		Compared
Level 3		Predictions	.. Tested	.. Fairly?
Level 4		Predictions based on prior knowledge	Fair test with selection of equipment and measurement	Draw conclusions
Level 5		Hypothesis Construction	Range of variables chosen to test hypothesis	Conclusions evaluated
Level 6		Predict and investigate the relationships between continuous variables		Explain relationship and results theoretically
Level 7		Predict relative effect of two or more independent variables	Compare effects	Draw conclusions on relative effects and limitations of evidence
Level 8		Make quantitative predictions based on theory and decide what to investigate	Select instruments to suitable accuracy	Evaluate effectiveness of strategies in determining relative effects of individual factors
Level 9		Use a theory to make quantitative predictions. Collect valid data	Systematically using a range of techniques to judge relative effect of factors	Analyse in terms of complex functions, calculations, graphs, etc.
Level 10		Hypotheses based on laws, theories and models	Collect data to enable	Evaluation of a law, theory or model as an explanation etc. observed behaviour

1. Identification and control of variables begins at level 4 as part of 'fair testing'
2. Evaluation begins as part of the 'fair testing' process

Figure 6 Summary of Sc 1: Scientific Investigation

The changes In the event, the number of statements of attainment was reduced from 409 to 176. Some statements changed levels and in general there is now a greater consistency in their scope, though some are still much broader than others. Some of the "pruned" Statements of Attainment (SoA) appear in the Programmes of Study but are still liable to be tested. Reference to fig 2 illustrates the expansion and contraction of the National Curriculum over the years. One cannot help reflecting that in some ways the wheel – if it has not been reinvented – has come full circle. At least the evolution of NC Science suggests a combination of natural and artificial selection with the final version looking more manageable.

Fig 7 shows the origins of the strands, and is the sort of analysis done when converting schemes of work from the 1989 to the 1991 orders.

Assessment influences The 1989 orders, though demanding, gave much more detailed guidance than the current version on what was to be assessed. Primary teachers, in particular, find some of the new SoA too generalised and still rely on the 1989 orders for interpretation and amplification. The streamlining process has resulted in a reduction in emphasis on social implications, the history of science, multicultural aspects, health education and communication. At least that is what transference from SoA to PoS may

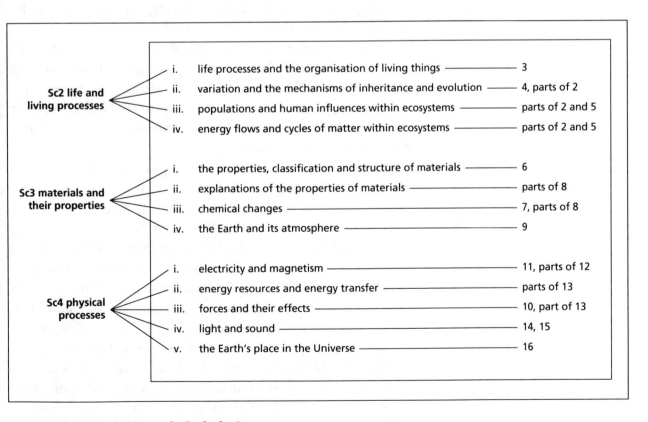

Sc2 life and living processes
i.   life processes and the organisation of living things ——————— 3
ii. variation and the mechanisms of inheritance and evolution ——— 4, parts of 2
iii. populations and human influences within ecosystems ————— parts of 2 and 5
iv. energy flows and cycles of matter within ecosystems ————— parts of 2 and 5

Sc3 materials and their properties
i.   the properties, classification and structure of materials ————— 6
ii. explanations of the properties of materials ————————— parts of 8
iii. chemical changes ———————————————————— 7, parts of 8
iv. the Earth and its atmosphere ——————————————— 9

Sc4 physical processes
i.   electricity and magnetism ————————————————— 11, parts of 12
ii. energy resources and energy transfer ——————————— parts of 13
iii. forces and their effects —————————————————— 10, part of 13
iv. light and sound —————————————————————— 14, 15
v.   the Earth's place in the Universe ————————————— 16

Figure 7 Origin of Strands Sc 2, 3, 4

cause, even though PoS are statutory. Aspects not assessed may well be de-valued in a curriculum that started life as a basic entitlement but has become all-embracing.

The issue of how trends in national assessment will affect teaching is a real one. The prospect of paper and pencil tests at all key stages, rather than the extended assessment tasks originally proposed by TGAT is bound to make teachers less willing to stray far from the documentation. The balance between national tests and teacher assessment has also undergone various modifications. Originally it was suggested that some kind of combination of the two, or moderation of one by the other, would result in a final level for the subject being determined. In practice, the reality is of short national tests for assessment of knowledge and understanding (conceptual understanding) and teacher assessment for Sc1 (procedural understanding). There is evidence from KS1 assessment that, in the absence of a standard task for Sc1 in 1992, teachers have devoted less time to it, and that performance by pupils in Sc1, as measured by teacher assessment, has gone down. There is a danger that a vital vehicle for learning in a fundamental aspect of science could become neglected.

The nature of the KS3 assessment – 3 × 1 hour pencil and paper tests for Sc2, 3, 4 and teacher assessment for Sc1 – may influence practice in this key stage. The testing of three years work at the end of Year 9 and four years work at the end of KS 2 certainly calls for some kind of strategy to cope with it! The most acceptable answer seems to be that a revisiting of attainment targets and strands is planned for, with revision in the context of current, related, learning. A regime of revision tests punctuating the KS3 or KS4 course at regular intervals is a depressing prospect. Pupils' written work will be kept for reference and their organisational and study skills will need more practice and thought than in the past.

At KS 4 assessment of Sc1 will replace current schemes of assessment of practical skills. The requirement for assessment of investigational skills in the context of a whole investigation will require some re-alignment of existing practical assessment. Departments will differ in their capacity to integrate Sc1 into the normal run of work. In practice, continuous assessment of practical skills in many schools has turned into a series of 'set-piece' practical exams: the difficulty of assessing an individual's contribution to group work has tended to reinforce this strategy.

The complexity of provision at 14+ extends beyond the issue of which GCSE course to choose, though even that is difficult enough. Potentially, the introduction of vocational courses can increase the repertoire of a science department. The un-certificated levels of GCSE are also generating courses. How the key stage will evolve in the light of the Secretaries of States wish for "more flexibility" remains to be seen. Once again, decisions taken nationally to change the rules have to be sorted out in detail afterwards by teachers.

Conclusion

Both primary and secondary teachers have shown remarkable resilience and stamina in the way in which they have tackled the nine versions (yes nine – count them on fig 1) of the NC Science that they have had to consider or implement since 1987. As a period of some stability is expected for science before the next review, it seems likely that schools will have an opportunity to refine existing practice and even consolidate in the light of experience. Whether there will be time for reflection is doubtful. The quality of the guidance offered by the National Curriculum is high. It was always intended to reflect good practice; what has been missing has been the time to plan for change. Changes have been forced on schools as a result of policy and logic beyond the control of teachers. The National Curriculum has been described as "a cure for which there is no known disease" by Professor John Tomlinson (quoted in Times Educational Supplement 1992). The measure of its success will be whether the quality of education after its implementation is better than before it. The reaction in science is probably "we were getting there quite nicely on our own thank you!". How OATs (Old Attainment Targets) became NATs (New Attainment Targets) after briefly being PRATs (Proposed Revised Attainment Targets) is now history, but you may still hear more experienced (older) colleagues musing about GOATs (Good Old Attainment Targets!).

References

Alexander R, Rose J, Woodhead C. (1992) *Curriculum organisation and classroom practice in primary schools: a discussion paper*, DES.

Department of Education and Science and the Welsh Office (1985) *Science 5–16: A Statement of Policy*, HMSO.

Department of Education and Science (1989) Circular No.6/89 The Education Reform Act 1988: National Curriculum: *Mathematics and Science Orders under section 4*, HMSO.

Department of Education and Science and the Welsh Office (1991) *Science in the National Curriculum* (1991) HMSO.

ULEAC (1992) *GCSE Science Syllabus: Graded Assessments in Science Project(GASP)*, ULEAC

INSET Resources pack : *Science Explorations* (1991), NCC.

David Oakley is General Inspector (with responsibility for Science) for Dudley LEA. He taught science for over 20 years in comprehensive schools, a tertiary college and adult education, before becoming a Science Advisory Teacher. He was Chair of the Science Advisers and Inspectors Group of the ASE 1991–92.

Children's Learning in Science

Wynne Harlen

3

Introduction

Everyone has a view of learning and how it takes place. For many of us, teachers included, our view of learning was formed by what we did in school. Less often do we think of it in terms of the learning we do everyday, in grappling with a problem and finding a more useful approach than before, or in making our ideas more useful by extending them through understanding a new experience. However, everyday learning events involve the same mental activity as more formal learning; reflecting on them can help us to envisage what is happening when children learn in school.

A teacher's view of how learning takes place is very important, since it determines what experiences and materials s/he provides, what role s/he takes in the learning and what role the pupils are expected to take, what is assessed and how success is evaluated. For example, a teacher convinced that learning takes place by rote will provide facts and procedures to be memorised in digestible packages, the mastery of each being tested before the next is presented. A quite different approach will follow from the view of learning which is presented here.

The model discussed in this chapter is derived from evidence of observing children and adults making sense of new experiences. It also fits what scientists do in trying to explain new observations, leading to the suggestion that learning science and doing science are much the same. After presenting the model the subsequent sections discuss the main elements involved in learning science: ideas, process skills and attitudes.

A View of How Children Learn Science

When faced with something new we search around, often unconsciously, in our minds and use previous experience in trying to understand it. Suppose someone shows you a shell of a type, size and colour that you have never seen before. Although you could not identify it as the shell of a particular creature, it is likely that you would be able say that it had come from a living thing and was not man-made and perhaps even whether the creature was likely to have lived on land or in water. You would be linking previous experience to the observation of the texture, shape and density of the object. You may well have thought at first that it was made of china or plastic but by tapping and fingering the object these ideas were dismissed, on the basis of knowledge from previous experience of the properties of these materials.

Figure 1

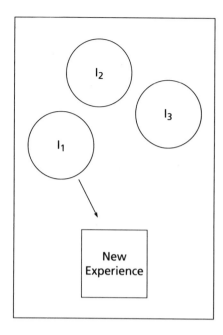

Figure 2

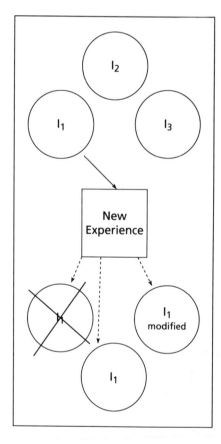

Children go through the same processes in trying to make sense of new objects or events, but because of their more limited experience they may not have an idea available to them which really fits and they use what seems most reasonable to them. For example, faced with the evidence that varnished cubes of wood stick to each other when wet, several groups of eleven year olds concluded that the blocks became magnetic when wet (Harlen, 1985, p20). The resemblance of a block sticking to the underside of another, without anything to hold them together, to a magnet picking up another magnet or a piece of iron was clearly very strong. An equally good alternative explanation was not available to them and so they held onto their view of magnetism, modifying it to accommodate the observation that the blocks only stuck together when wet by concluding that 'they're magnetic when they're wet.'

These examples illustrate several points which are found in learning in general and which are represented in the model. Figure 1 is an attempt to show diagrammatically a number of existing ideas (I) which are already in the mind to be called upon to help understand the new experience. It may be that perceived similarities between a previous experience and the new one results in one or more of these ideas being linked in an attempt at understanding. Other processes also may create links – for example, similar words used in description may suggest connections. It is not always logical reasoning and careful observation which lead to ideas being linked, but creativity and imagination have a part. Indeed, in the case of the scientist faced with an unexpected phenomenon, it is the ability to try ideas from outside the immediately obvious that provides the start of a 'break through'.

But once an existing idea has been linked, its usefulness in *really* explaining the new experience has to be tested (Figure 2). The testing has to be done scientifically if the result is to be of value in making sense of experience. In essence, this means that more evidence has to be sought to find out whether it is consistent with predictions based on a linked idea or on possible alternative ideas. The 'testing' can be as simple as tapping the shell to see if it makes the kind of sound which would be expected if it were made of plastic. Here the idea that the object is made of plastic is a hypothesis which leads to a prediction and the tapping is the means of testing this prediction.

There are three main possibilities of what may result from the testing:

(i)   the linked idea is confirmed, in which case it becomes strengthened by successfully explaining a new phenomenon or having its range extended;
(ii) the linked idea is not confirmed and so an alternative is tried (if there is one);
(iii) the linked idea will fit the evidence if it is slightly modified.

Both i and iii result in a change in ideas which enables the new experience to be understood in terms of previous experience. Ideas have been extended or changed so that what was not previously understood can now be understood because it fits into ideas that make sense. In other words, learning has taken place.

This model, then, represents learning as a *change* in ideas, rather than the taking in of ideas from scratch. In practice, ideas which are not related to previous experience and thinking are of very little use to us. They do not arise from past experience and so are not called forth when past experience is used to explain new experience. Such ideas have to be committed to memory by rote and are usually usable only in contexts close to those in which they were learned. *Understanding*, which by definition is more widely applicable, is created by development and change in ideas.

.... jumping to the wrong conclusion.

But will ideas necessarily become more scientific during the process of change embodied in the model? It was assumed in the argument above that the testing of ideas was rigorous and systematic, in the way associated with scientific investigation. When this is so, then ideas which do not fit the evidence will be rejected and those which do will be accepted and strengthened. But it may not be the case that the testing has this quality. The skills of young children – and those of some adults – have not developed to the appropriate degree. Children may ignore contradictory evidence in interpreting findings and hold on to their initial ideas even when these do not fit the evidence.

Thus the extent to which ideas become more scientific (by fitting more phenomena) depends on the way in which the linking and testing are carried out, that is, on the use of the process skills.

> *The development of understanding in science is thus dependent on the ability to carry out process skills in a scientific manner.*

This is the reason for attention to development of these skills in science education; because of their role in the development of scientific concepts and not just because they are valuable skills in their own right.

Children's Ideas

That some of children's ideas are different from those of adults has been known for a long time; it is nothing new. Before the second quarter of this century these ideas would have been dismissed as childish and silly; their expression perhaps tolerated as quaint in the home but certainly not in school. The significance of these ideas in the context of learning became recognised mainly through the work of Piaget. His publications from the early 1920s influenced many educators, such a Susan and Nathan Isaacs, who developed child-centred teaching approaches which acknowledged and valued children's ideas.

The spread of child-centred teaching approaches in primary science can be followed through the Nuffield Junior Science and Science 5/13 projects, both strongly reflecting Piaget's work, through to its reconstruction in the valuing of children's ideas by the Working Group which developed the National Curriculum in Science. The Working Group's recognition of the importance of children's ideas, expressed in its Final Report, was repeated in almost identical words in the Non-Statutory Guidance produced by the NCC:

> *In their early experiences of the world, pupils develop ideas which enable them to make sense of the things that happen around them. They bring these informal ideas into the classroom and the aim of science education is to give pupils more explanatory power so that their ideas can become useful concepts. Viewed from this perspective, it is important that we should take a pupil's initial ideas seriously so as to ensure that any change or development of these ideas...become 'owned' by the pupil. (NCC 1989, A7 paragraph 6.2)*

So the tenets of constructivist learning clearly now have widespread support, although it is necessary to look more closely at what taking 'a pupil's initial ideas seriously' means. The extent to which pupils' ideas are used, rather than merely revealed and noted, makes all the difference to whether or not the children have the intended 'ownership' as their ideas are modified.

Research work began on the scientific ideas of secondary pupils in the 1970s in New Zealand and then spread to Europe and North

America (see, for example, the reader edited by Driver, Guesne and Tiberghien, 1985). The main work to date at the primary level has been carried out by the *Science Processes and Concepts Exploration* (SPACE), a joint project based at Liverpool University and King's College, London. Its research phase, which revealed the nature and extent of different ideas held by children across the whole range of concepts relevant at the primary level, was funded by the Nuffield Foundation. The methods for revealing children's ideas were designed to ensure that children had the chance of experience in the topic before their ideas were sought. Teachers were asked to introduce into their classrooms materials and exploratory activities relating to the topics that the researchers wanted to discuss with the children. For example, when children's ideas about sound were to be discussed, the materials provided were a range of musical instruments, home-made and conventional, and other articles which could be used to make non-musical sounds. When interest was in ideas about growth, the materials were growing plants, seeds which were germinating, stick insects and even an incubator with hen's eggs hatching.

The following examples represent some of the most common of children's ideas but they cannot represent the full variety. For that, the full research reports need to be consulted (SPACE, 1990–92). The research involved children from the age of 5 to 11 and many ideas were found across a wide age range, although a trend with age was often discernible.

Ideas about growth inside eggs

In a class where hens' eggs were being incubated, children were asked to draw what they thought was inside an egg whilst it was incubating. The most popular idea was that there was a miniature but mainly complete animal inside the egg, feeding on what was there (Figure 3).

Figure 3 (SPACE Report: Growth, 1990, p31)

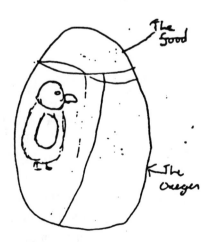

An alternative was that the complete animal was inside simply waiting to hatch.

Figure 4 from SPACE Report:
Growth, 1990, p10

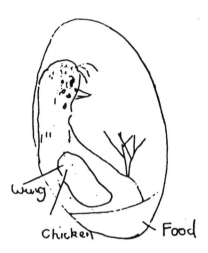

There was also the view that the body parts were complete but needed to come together. The more scientific view that transformation was going on, was evident in some children's ideas and it was also clear that they used knowledge derived from experience – of reproduction of pets and observations of human babies – in trying to understand what was going on inside the eggs.

Ideas about growth in plants

Infant children generally mentioned one external factor in response to the question 'what do you think plants need to help them grow?' For example, Figure 5 suggests that a position by a window is necessary which may or may not mean recognition of the need for light.

Figure 5 SPACE Research,
unpublished

Other young children mentioned soil or water or sun, but rarely all three. Characteristically the younger children made no attempt to explain why these conditions were needed or by what mechanism they worked. Junior children, however, made efforts to give explanations, as in Figure 6.

Figure 6 from SPACE Research, unpublished

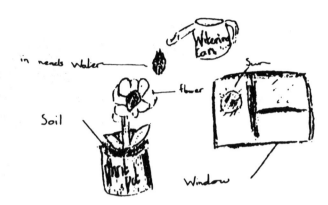

Ideas about how sounds are made and heard

The example in Figure 7 suggests no mechanism for sound being produced by a drum or for it being heard; it is as if being 'very loud' and 'listening hard' are properties which require no explanation.

Figure 7 (SPACE Report: Sound, 1990, p36)

The simplest mechanism suggested is that the impact of hitting produces 'sound'. In contrast, Figure 8 explains the sound in terms of vibration. But notice that the vibration comes out of the drum through 'the hole'. A very common understanding of children was that sound travelled through air, or at least through holes in solid objects and not through the solid itself.

The notion of 'vibration' was associated with sound in ambiguous ways, sometimes sound being the same as vibration and sometimes having some cause and effect relationship to it.

The findings of the SPACE research have immediate relevance to teaching. In some cases these are only hinted at in the

*Figure 8 SPACE Research,
unpublished*

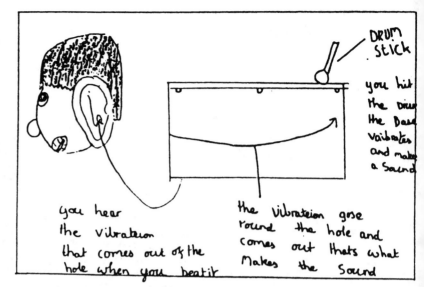

examples given above, but they have a considerable basis of evidence in the full research findings. The general features revealed were that the children's ideas:

(i)   emerged from a process of reasoning about experience, rather than from childish fantasy or imagination;

(ii)   would not, however, stand up to rigorous testing against evidence that was often available for the children to use had they wished to do so;

(iii) sometimes required additional evidence to be made available if they were to be tested in practice;

(iv)   were influenced by other information than that which came from evidence of actual events, these other sources including the media, conventions of speech and of ways of representing things, influential adults and peers;

(v)   were often expressed in terms of words which seemed scientific, yet had, for the children, a meaning which was ill-defined, difficult to pin down and not apparently consistent with the scientific meaning.

These features of children's ideas are important in suggesting ways of 'taking their ideas seriously': for example, by practical activities which test predictions based on the ideas or which extend experience, or by discussion of words, thus helping children to clarify the meaning the words have for them.

The Process Skills

Process skills are described in various ways, all of which suffer from the problem of trying to draw boundaries between things which are not separable from each other. This will soon be apparent here, for when we describe an example of 'observing' there is some 'hypothesising' going on as well and even some degree of 'investigating'. Almost any scientific activity begins with 'observation' and so it is an integral part of other process skills. In the light of these points it is reasonable to ask, how useful is it to attempt to separate aspects of scientific activity? It may be best to regard it as a whole. However, the whole is so complex that, whilst admitting that they are not separable in practice, it is useful to describe certain aspects of scientific activity and to name them. In this way we can at least hope to arrive at a common and clear notion of the parts which are inter-woven in the investigation of the world around and the develop-ment of understanding.

There are overlapping sets of process skills involved in linking and testing ideas. Those involved in linking existing ideas to try to understand new experience: observing, hypothe-sising, predicting and communicating; those involved in testing ideas: predicting, planning and carrying out investigations, observing, interpreting findings, drawing conclusions from them and communicating. Putting these together provides the list of skills that will be considered here. The description of each is mainly in terms of a list of actions which anyone involved in using the process skill may be carrying out.

Observing

For an image of observing in action let us return to the example of someone given in their hand an object which resembles a shell; it might be a shell of a kind they have never seen before – or it might not be a natural object. They rub their fingers over it, hold it to the light to see the detail (or use a hand lens if there is one), they smell it, even put it to their ear (as people do with shells); they might tap it and listen to the sound. They may men-tally, or actually, be comparing it with something known to be a shell, seeking points of similarity and difference. All these things add up to careful observation in this particular situation.

In another example, imagine a person watching a 'cartesian diver', made from a dropper floating in water inside a large plastic bottle. When the bottle is standing, firmly capped, the dropper floats at the surface upright, with water about half way up the tube. When the sides of the bottle are squeezed the dropper slowly sinks to the bottom. More than this can be noticed, however, by looking carefully and noting the order in which events take place. The level of the water inside the dropper's tube rises when the bottle is squeezed and this happens before the droppers starts to sink; indeed it could be the reason for the sinking (which would be a hypothesis based on the observation). At this point, however, we keep the focus on the observation. In this situation the careful observation of detail and of the order of events are important aspects of what we mean by 'observation in action'.

Figure 9 Cartesian diver

From thinking about these and other examples we can identify the kind of actions which indicate 'observation in action' as including the following:

- making use of several senses
- noticing relevant details of the object and its surroundings
- identifying similarities and differences
- discerning the order in which events take place
- using aids to the senses for study of details (eg hand lens).

Hypothesising   In the cartesian diver example a hypothesis was mentioned in the context of attempting to explain why the dropper sank. A hypothesis is a statement put forward to attempt to explain some happening or feature. When hypothesising, the suggested explanation need not be correct, but it should be reasonable in terms of the evidence available and possible in terms of scientific concepts or principles. There always is some knowledge brought to bear on the evidence in making a hypothesis. In the case of the dropper, the suggestion that it sank because of the extra water inside it was based not only on the observation of the water level in the tube but also the knowledge that adding more mass to a floating object can make it sink.

Often there is more than one possible explanation of an event. This underlines the point that hypotheses are plausible but not necessarily correct. Take for example the observation that one of two puddles of water left after a rain storm dries up more slowly than the other. The reason could be that there was more in one than the other to begin with, that one is on more water-permeable ground than the other, that only one is in the sun, that there is greater air movement over one than the other. Several more might well be thought up. In each case there is knowledge brought to bear – about the conditions which favour evaporation, about the differences in properties of materials with regard to water permeability, and so on. If the suggestion were that the water ran uphill out of one of them or that it dried up more quickly 'because it wanted to', these would not be scientific hypotheses because they conflict either with the evidence or with the scientific knowledge.

Even though one may not oneself be able to think of alternative explanations it is important to recognise the possibility of alternatives. In turn this brings the realisation that any hypothesis has to be regarded as provisional since there may always be another which is more consistent with the evidence.

So the indicators of hypothesising include:

- suggesting an explanation which is consistent with the evidence
- suggesting an explanation which is consistent with some scientific principle or concept
- applying previous knowledge in attempting an explanation

- realising that there can be more than one possible explanation of an event or phenomenon
- realising the tentative nature of any explanation.

Predicting   A prediction is a statement about what may happen in the future, or what will be found that has not so far been found, that is based on some hypothesis or previous knowledge. For example, if you know how far a car will go on 5 litres of petrol and how far it will go on 10 litres, it is possible to predict how far it will go, say, on 12 litres. In another case, if your hypothesis about why a table lamp is not working is that the fuse has blown, then you predict that changing the fuse will make it work again.

A prediction is quite different from a guess, which cannot be justified in terms of a hypothesis or evidence. Given no information about how far the car goes on a certain amount of petrol the suggestion of how far it would go on 12 litres would be a guess, not a prediction (except that evidence of other cars may be used, in which case the prediction would be based on that evidence). However even when there is a rational basis for a prediction there is always the possibility that it will not be supported by evidence of what actually happens. This may be because a relationship assumed to hold does not do so indefinitely. For example, an elastic band may stretch 10cm under a force of 5 Newton, 20cm under a force of 10 Newton but break under 15 Newton! Caution is thus needed in making a prediction which depends on applying a relationship beyond the range of available evidence (extrapolating). Interpolating (predicting within the range of evidence), such as predicting how far the elastic band will stretch with a force of 8 Newton is much safer.

There is often confusion of the meaning of a hypothesis and a prediction, partly because the hypothesis on which a prediction is based may be implicit, not explicit. So, a statement such as 'I will be able to see myself better in that spoon than this one because it is shinier' is a prediction. The related hypothesis is that shininess makes surfaces reflect better.

The behaviours which indicate that predicting is in action thus include:

- making use of evidence from past or present experience in stating what may happen
- explicitly using pattern in evidence to extrapolate or interpolate
- justifying a statement about what will happen or be found in terms of present evidence or past experience
- showing caution in making assumptions about a pattern applying beyond the range of evidence
- distinguishing a prediction from a guess.

Investigating   The whole range of process skills could be regarded as being part of 'investigating' and some people do in fact regard it as such and therefore omit it from a list of constituent skills. However, a slightly more restricted meaning can be given, covering what happens from the point where a question for investigation has been raised, or a prediction made on the basis of a hypothesis which has to be tested, to the point where evidence is gathered and needs to be interpreted. Even this more restricted meaning, which is taken here, involves bringing together several kinds of thinking and action concerned with planning and carrying out investigations. Sometimes it is helpful to separate planning from the practice of carrying out an investigation. But often the two occur together, particularly in the case of children, and parts of the investigation are worked out along the way rather than being all thought through before taking action.

As an example of what investigation involves, take the possible reasons for one puddle of water drying up more than the other. The first hypothesis which someone might decide to test is that it could be caused by different movement of air over the water movement. But there are a number of things which can vary (variables) and to find out whether air movement can make a difference, it it necessary to set up a test where this is the only thing which is different. It would be much easier to ensure that 'all other things are equal' by making 'puddles' in equal containers indoors. One variable, the amount of movement in the air, has to be different in the two cases. This is the *independent variable*, the one which is being changed by choice. An investigation set up in this way is described as 'fair' in the sense that there is (or should be) no other variable than the one we choose to change which will affect the result, so any difference observed can be said to have been caused by the independent variable.

What may change as a result of the change in the independent variable, in this case the amount of water left, is dependent on what is done and so is called the *dependent variable*. The change in this variable has to be compared or measured to obtain the result and this has to be done in a suitable way. Thus first planning ways of doing this, using measuring instruments if necessary, and then using the equipment effectively in carrying out the plan, are all parts of the process of investigating. If the result shows that there is no difference resulting from varying the air movement, then another investigation may be carried out with another variable, say the exposure to sun, as the independent variable. In that investigation the air movement would be kept the same and not varied.

Indicators of this skill in action would include all these actions involved in setting up and carrying out an investigation:

- deciding which variable is to be changed (independent) and which are to be kept the same (controlled)
- carrying out the manipulation of the variable so that the investigation is 'fair'
- identifying which variable is to be measured or compared (dependent variable)
- making measurements or comparisons of the dependent variable using appropriate instruments
- working with an appropriate degree of precision.

Interpreting findings and drawing conclusions

Interpreting involves putting results together so that patterns or relationships between them can be seen. The results of water evaporation investigation might be in terms of the amounts of water present in two containers at various times. To interpret these would mean relating what happened in the different conditions in a statement such as 'the water went down more quickly when the air was moving than when it was still'. The further step of drawing a general conclusion, such as 'water evaporates more quickly in moving air than in still air' requires some caution, since it suggests not only that this relationship was found in one particular investigation but that there is reason to suppose that it would hold in other cases.

Where several pieces of information have been collected (as in seeing how far an elastic band stretches under various forces), interpretation involves looking for patterns in them. These patterns might be regular – as in the case of the elastic band, as long as it is not stretched too much – or merely trends, such as in the tendency for taller people to have larger hands and feet than shorter people. In the regular-pattern case all the information will fit the pattern without exception, but in the latter there is an overall association although there may be exceptions to it in some cases.

If there are only two sets of data, as in the comparison of the rate of evaporation of the two puddles, the interpretation would only be in terms of what happens with and without movement of air. Only if there were at least three different conditions (eg still air, slowly moving air, fast moving air) would it be possible to draw a conclusion about the effect of wind speed on the rate of drying.

It is often tempting to jump to the conclusion that a pattern exists on the basis of only some of the data, ignoring other information which conflicts. Thus checking a pattern or trend against all available information is important. Even then the possibility that more data, were it to be collected, might conflict with the pattern has to be kept in mind. 'On the basis of our results .....' would be a fitting start to a statement of a pattern or conclusion.

Thus indicators of this skill in use are:

- putting various pieces of information together to make some statement of their combined meaning
- finding patterns or trends in observations or results of investigations
- identifying an association between one variable and another
- making sure that a pattern or association is checked against all the data
- showing caution in making assumptions about the general applicability of a conclusion.

Communicating

Talking, writing, drawing or representing things in other ways are not only means of letting others know of our ideas but also help us to sort out what we think and understand. Thus communication is important in learning and takes various forms according to the subject being learned. In science, talking and listening are particularly valuable for making ideas explicit and for helping the understanding of scientific vocabulary. Children often use words which they pick up without necessarily realising the meaning which attaches to the words. Encouraging children to talk about what they mean by these words and to listen to what others say can help to reveal differences which can be the source of misunderstanding. Discussion also helps where children may have ideas but no words to express them.

Communication in science involves using various conventions of representation which help in organising information and conveying it efficiently. Graphs, charts, tables, symbols, etc serve this purpose and have to be chosen to suit the particular kind of information. Communication is, of course, two-way, and involves the ability to take information from written sources, to use information presented in graphical or tabular form, thus expanding the evidence which can be used in testing ideas.

Thus indicators of scientific communication skills include:

- talking, listening or writing to sort out ideas and clarify meaning
- making notes of observations in the course of an investigation
- using graphs, charts and tables to convey information
- choosing an appropriate means of communication so that it is understandable to others
- using secondary sources of information

Scientific Attitudes

A distinction is to be made between two kinds of attitude: those *towards science as an enterprise* and those *towards objects and events in the environment* which are studied in the course of scientific activities. To form an attitude towards science it is necessary to have an idea of what 'science' is. There are many myths about science and about scientists which persist in popular belief and in caricatures which are perpetuated in the media and in some literature. Young children do not have enough experience of scientific activity and its consequences to form their own opinions and attitudes towards science. If they seem to hold such attitudes it is a result of accepting adult prejudices and parroting views which are not their own.

At the primary level the concern is to give children experience of scientific activity as a basis for a thorough understanding, which will only come much later, of what science is and is not and of the responsibility we all share for applying it humanely. Therefore attention is given here only to those attitudes which we might call the attitudes *of* science, those which support scientific activity.

Many attitudes fall into this category and would also fall into the category of supporting learning in several subject areas. Perseverance is one of these; it is certainly needed in practising science but it is equally relevant to learning a foreign language or writing a poem. The generalised nature of attitudes is such that no clear line can be drawn between 'scientific' and other attitudes, but the ones chosen for discussion here are particularly relevant to developing ideas through exploration of the world around. They are: curiosity, respect for evidence, willingness to change ideas and critical reflection.

Curiosity

Although this could be considered in the 'general' category, its importance for young children's learning is such that it deserves inclusion here. Curiosity leads a child forward into new experiences and so is essential for learning from exploration of things around. It follows that for children to benefit from opportunities provided for first hand investigation, their curiosity should be encouraged.

The curiosity of young children is inevitably immature. It is spontaneous and impulsive, easily stimulated by new things but just as easily distracted by something else. A child who has reached a more mature level shows greater powers of concentration and will be less impulsive. The number of questions asked is likely to decline but the ones which are asked will be more perceptive and relevant. There will be more thought behind them in the attempt to equate new experience with previous knowledge. Mature curiosity shows in wanting to 'come to terms' with each new experience and reach an understanding of it. Thus curiosity becomes an active component in learning with understanding.

It is useful to sum up in terms of some general indicators of children showing curiosity:

- noticing and being attracted to new things
- showing interest through careful observation of details
- asking questions of all kinds including those which seek explanations
- spontaneously using information sources to find out about new or unusual things.

Respect for evidence   Many new ideas have been born as a leap of the imagination, but they have a short life unless they can be shown to fit evidence and help make sense of what is already known to happen. Children's keen desire for things to 'be fair' provides a basis for respecting evidence. They will readily challenge each other to 'show me' and not be prepared to accept something as true unless they see evidence for themselves. Of course, it is impossible for evidence to be obtained for every statement and it is equally immature to accept nothing as it is to accept everything. The sign of mature respect for evidence is willingness to place ones own ideas under test in relation to evidence, in the understanding that any ideas which are worthwhile stand up to such testing. As a corollary the understanding develops that no ideas are worthwhile unless the evidence is there to support them.

Actions which, if a general pattern of behaviour, indicate respect for evidence include:

- reporting what actually happens even if this is in conflict with expectations
- querying and checking parts of the evidence which do not fit into the pattern of other findings
- querying a conclusion or interpretation for which there is insufficient evidence
- treating ideas or conclusions as provisional and as being open to challenge by further evidence.

Willingness to change ideas   This attitude is sometimes described as *flexibility* but it is not to be mistaken for adopting whatever is the current way of thinking and having no ideas of one's own. At all times ideas are changing with new experience. For example, recently identified holes in the ozone layer have extended many people's understanding of ecology and indeed introduced a new concept of ecocide. However, for young children the rate of experience of new phenomena and events is particularly high and there need to be frequent adjustments in their ideas.

Unless there is a willingness to change ideas then there would be devastating confusion as new experiences conflict with existing ideas. The importance of legitimising these changes, making them open and acceptable and considered as normal, cannot be over-emphasised. It is helpful to discuss with children how their ideas have changed, and to give some examples of how other people's ideas, including those of scientists, have changed. With maturity, and bolstered by greater experience, ideas need to change less often but it is important to retain the possibility of change and the tentative nature of any ideas. This can be facilitated by expressing conclusions in terms of the evidence available. 'So far we have found that all the pieces of wood float', lays a better basis for accommodating evidence that some wood (eg lignum vitae and ebony) does not float.

In summary, indications of children's willingness to change ideas include:

- being prepared to change an existing idea when there is convincing evidence against it
- considering alternative ideas to their own
- spontaneously seeking alternative ideas rather than accepting the first one which fits the evidence
- realising that it is necessary to change or give up existing ideas when different ones make better sense of the evidence.

Critical reflection This increases the potential learning from experiences and class activities. It manifests itself in deliberate review of the way in which activities have been carried out, what ideas have emerged and how these could be improved. It is the beginning of reflecting on one's learning, but only the beginning, for this is a mature activity, requiring a degree of abstract thinking not available to young children. But as everything has a beginning at an earlier level than that at which it shows in its full form, we should begin to encourage critical review as a normal part of work. This requires teacher guidance at first; making time to talk through activities, to compare different approaches and to make suggestions of how thing might, with hindsight, have been tackled more effectively. The emphasis has to be on arriving at better ways of investigating or collecting evidence which can be used in the future, rather than criticising what has been done.

A more mature form of this attitude shows when children themselves take the initiative in reflection on what they have done and realise the pros and cons of various alternatives. The actions of children which indicate this attitude include:

- willingness to review what they have done in order to consider how it might have been improved
- considering alternative procedures to those used
- identifying the points in favour and against the way in which an investigation was carried out or its results interpreted
- using critical reflection of a previous investigation in planning and carrying out a later one.

53

References and recommended reading

Driver, R. Guesne, E., and Tiberghien, A., 1985 *Children's Ideas in Science*. Open University Press, Milton Keynes.

Elstgeest, J. and Harlen, W., 1990 *Environmental Science in the Primary Curriculum*. Chapman, London.

Harlen, W. (1992) *The Teaching of Science*. Fulton, London

Harlen, W. 1985 *Teaching and Learning Primary Science*. Chapman, London.

Harlen, W, (Ed) 1985 *Primary Science: Taking the Plunge*. Heinemann Educational, London.

SPACE Research reports: *Evaporation and Condensation*, 1990 *Growth*, 1990. *Light*, 1990. *Sound*, 1990. *Electricity*, 1991. *Materials*, 1991. *Forces*, in preparation. *Energy*, in preparation. *Earth and Atmosphere*, in preparation. *Genetics and Evolution*, in preparation. *Earth in Space*, in preparation. *Human influences in the Earth*, in preparation. *Processes of Life*, in preparation. *Variety of Life*, in preparation. Liverpool University Press.

Professor Wynne Harlen OBE is Director of The Scottish Council for Research in Education.

(This chapter is based on Chapters 2 to 5 of The Teaching of Science, David Fulton Publishers, London, 1992)

Scientific Investigation

Rosemary Feasey

4

A pragmatic view of primary science is that it consists of a set of activities through which children develop attitudes, processes, skills, knowledge and understanding. Most activities in primary science fall into one of the following categories;

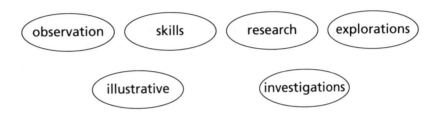

All of these activities have a place within primary science, collectively they provide a menu from which teachers can choose, each offering something different. However, although all are important within the National Curriculum for Science, one type of activity, 'investigations' carries greater weighting in Key Stages 1 and 2 than each of the others. Fifty percent of primary science should be devoted to the development of Attainment Target 1 (Sc1) which, logically, means that half of the time allocated to science or activities should be investigations.

In order to understand the nature and purpose of investigations at the primary level we need to analyse the range of activities and the functions they serve within primary science, thus bringing the differences into focus. For further discussion, see Aubrey. C (1992).

Observation   *Observation tasks enable "pupils to look at objects or events in a 'scientific way'".* Gott R., Duggan S. (1992)

Observation is an important element of primary science and can feature either as an activity in it's own right or as part of other activities. Observation is a process not a skill; it is concept driven. We make sense of what we observe in terms of existing knowledge and understanding. However that is not to suggest that the teacher cannot develop children's observation. Indeed it is important that teachers demand that children observe objects and phenomena through 'science spectacles'. Without this, observation in science is in danger of becoming a language, maths or art activity. The teacher can help to develop children's observation by:

- demanding that children use scientific knowledge to make sense of observations;
- encouraging children to make appropriate use of their senses;
- developing children's ability to use and choose equipment to enhance observation;
- developing children's ability to note similarities and differences;
- developing children's ability to focus on salient points or events.

Skills This type of activity is aimed at training children to become competent in such things as producing graphs or using a thermometer. The most useful time for teaching children any skill is when the child needs to use it. One of the most frequent problems in science is the inability of children to transfer skills, particularly mathematical (graphs, measurement) to science. Often children develop skills in isolation or inappropriate contexts and are unable to recognise when, for example, to employ graphs or measurement. Being skilled in using a piece of equipment or producing a graph is not the only demand that should be made on children. Teachers should develop children's ability to recognise for example when equipment or a graph should be used and the most appropriate kind.

Research There are a number of aspects of science which by their very nature do not lend themselves to 'hands on' tasks. Facts such as the distance the Sun is away from the Earth, require children to be able to research information using a range of resources from books to videos. Research requires the use of skills from other areas of the curriculum, for example language, where children use a contents page or an index. However, many children merely copy facts *ad verbatim*, without making sense of what they have read. Providing children with an audience or a specific type of recording such as a newspaper article can force children into making sense of information in order to explain it to others.

Illustrative Within the primary context these activities are invariably those which involve children carrying out a set of recipe-like instructions. The intention is to lead children through a task to a defined outcome, usually a specific concept. Unfortunately a consequence of this type of activity is that it denies many children the opportunity to work at their own level and use their own knowledge and understanding. However, it is most powerful when used to teach a concept. Illustrative tasks should not be confused with investigations, since there is little or no scope in the former for children to be involved in the decision-making process which is central to investigative work.

Exploration

MD '92

Activities in this category provide opportunities for children to interact with objects to try to make sense of them; they could be called 'try it and see' activities since essentially that is what is happening. Interaction with the object should be viewed in terms of children having a mental construct and trying it out to see if it is correct. In the light of this interaction, their original idea might be changed, reinforced or lead to a new set of ideas for exploration. To a casual observer a child's exploration might look unstructured; an *ad hoc* series of actions. However children invariably have a particular idea which they try out in a deliberate manner. In many ways this way of working is a natural precursor to the development of more formal investigations. These activities are common in Key Stage 1 where interaction and the opportunity to manipulate their environment are important parts of science for young children.

Investigation

The term investigation is now more clearly defined than it has been at any other period in the history of primary science. Until the NC, the word 'investigation' referred to a wide range of activities which closely resembled the Oxford Dictionary (1986) definition to 'find out'. This literal interpretation appears to have been given to all activities where children engaged in 'hands on experience'.

> *Since the advent of the NC, the term investigation is defined as "The kind of problem for which the pupil may not see an answer or recall a routine method for finding one" Gott R., Murphy P. (1987).*

In other words, the solution to the problem is not obvious and whilst the pupil might speculate or hypothesize on what might happen or on what the solution might be, s/he will need to carry out an investigation in order to produce evidence to support, or otherwise, the initial hypothesis.

> *"A feature of investigative work is that pupils are required to work on their own initiative; they must make their own decisions. These decisions reflect aspects of what the pupils see as appropriate to the problem in hand including their interpretation of the concepts involved. In addition, pupils will need to develop their investigative skills and, more importantly, their ability to put those skills together into a strategy for a complete task. They must make the key decisions about what to change, what to measure and what to keep the same for a fair test. Since investigations use concepts, investigations are likely to be most*

*effective when those ideas have already been intro-
duced and explained or when children have some basic
understanding through their everyday experience.'*
Foulds K., Gott R. Feasey R. (1992)

The knowledge base in investigations has several aspects. One is procedural knowledge such as the skill of using a ruler and processes such as recognising the need for a fair test, combined in an overall strategy which will help towards a solution. A second aspect, that of conceptual knowledge of scientific ideas, comes into play when recognising the problem or appreciating the nature of the question and in interpreting, but there may be occasions where the needs of the children necessitate an emphasis on one particular element. In one investigation the teacher might decide to focus on the use of tables. During another, the teacher might decide to focus on challenging children to use their knowledge about plant growth to make sense of the results of an investigation into the effect of different amounts of light on a plant.

The function of investigations within the curriculum should not be to 'teach' specific concepts but to provide opportunities for children to use their concepts in a practical and relevant context. Investigations will provide opportunities to refine and develop understanding in the other attainment targets.

Having defined the different types of activities it becomes clear that investigations are not just any kind of practical work. It is probably easier to define investigations in terms of what they are not rather than what they are.

Investigations are *not* about:

- teaching isolated skills;
- developing isolated processes;
- teaching concepts;
- teacher directed activities.

Investigations *are about using and developing* concepts, skills and processes in a way which will assist children in finding the solution to a problem or question or in following an idea.

Teacher Perceptions of AT1

Research by the Exploration of Science Project (carried out in 1990-1) into teacher perceptions of Sc1 1 indicates that despite the publication of the NC for Science, there is some confusion as to the nature and intention of practical work which colours the perception of many teachers throughout Key Stages 1-3. Teachers nationwide completed a questionnaire which asked them to indicate their perceptions of the following;

- the purpose of practical work
- the purpose of investigations

Having completed the questionnaire teachers were then asked to provide three samples of work which were perceived by teachers to be investigations.

An analysis of the data allows the tentative conclusion that teachers have mixed perceptions of the nature and purpose of investigations which affects the reality of investigations in the classroom. Yet teachers are picking up some of the messages about investigations but as yet are not totally *au fait* with the philosophy and its translation into the classroom.

The following summarises some of the main points from the research.

- At KS 1 many teachers see the aim of practical work as being the development of observation. When asked to suggest the purpose of investigations, the majority responded in terms of developing skills and processes. However the samples of work indicated that a large percentage of activities which were perceived to be investigations were in fact observation activities.

- At KS 2 there was a more even distribution in terms of the aims of practical work between concept development, raising and answering questions and observation. When asked about the purpose of investigations there was a move towards the development of skills and processes. However the sample material was dominated by teacher-directed activities, which are illustrative activities and not investigations.

The main inference from the data is that there is some confusion about the nature and purpose of investigations. This begs the question as to why there should be such confusion. There are several possible reasons for this. Over the years teachers have been introduced to a range of different views on the teaching of science from Nuffield to the skills/process approach.

> *"It is important to appreciate the context in which teachers received and placed their personal interpretation on these different views. Given that so many teachers lack confidence in science it is not surprising that many chose to take only that part of any view with which they felt some sympathy."* Aubrey C. (Ed.) (1992)

Some teachers teach skills, others taught concepts, whilst many develop the process approach or those parts of it with which they feel confident. There are of course those who have been more eclectic in their approach and taken parts from each of the viewpoints. The result is a mixture of responses to the nature of science and to investigations.

We should not be surprised to find that there are different understandings of investigations. In the form defined by the NC, they are relatively new to primary science. Teachers are at the beginning of a learning curve in terms of making sense of the nature of this type of activity. Their response is often determined by their own perceptions of science and their own confidence, which leads teachers to adopt the most familiar and comfortable aspects .

Such an insight into teacher perceptions is important since it provides some indication of the way in which teachers might respond to the Orders. It suggests that many teachers at KS 1 place emphasis on observation to the detriment of other aspects such as the introduction of simple investigations. At KS2 the suggestion is that teachers still offer recipe-like activities as investigations or teach children to hypothesise, record etc. in isolation and expect children to put them together rather like a jigsaw but without ever having seen the whole picture.

What can we expect of children at KS 1 and KS 2?

Level 1

Observation is central to this level; the teacher needs to encourage children to observe their world wearing 'science spectacles'. Children should be encouraged to talk about their own understanding and make connections between what they observe and what they know. It is through the use of effective questions that the teacher can probe children's understanding or focus attention on salient points. A wide range of teacher questions is essential in order to provide a useful model for children. At the same time the teacher needs to encourage children to ask their own questions and present their own ideas.

Level 2

The levels in Sc1 are cumulative, not in isolated steps. Children should now be able to find answers. At this level many activities will be explorations where children have an idea and try it out. However the teacher should begin to introduce the idea of simple fair tests as a precursor to investigations at level 3. In terms of recording and communicating children should be able to provide oral or written descriptions which are sequential. They should also be able to use a simple table and be introduced to bar charts.

Level 3

At this level expectations are more rigorous. Children should be able to suggest ideas, questions etc. which can be tested. This demands that children understand the idea of a fair test and appreciate what kind of questions or ideas can be tested. Children should recognise that unless they carry out a fair test their results will not be 'believable' (however recognising the fairness of the test can come at any point, beginning, middle or end of their investigation). This is a difficult concept for children. It is about validity of evidence i.e. have they carried out their test in such a way that allows them and others to have confidence in their results? This demands that children generate data which should be numerical in nature, hence, precise standard measurement will play an important part at this level. Having generated and considered their results children should be able to answer their original question.

Level 4   The differences between levels three and four are subtle and relate to the way ideas are generated and the use children make of evidence. Level 4 demands that children

> *"Ask questions, suggest ideas, and make predictions, based on some relevant prior knowledge, in a form which can be investigated."* N.C.C. 1991

This statement requires children to use their scientific knowledge to generate specific ideas which they can test. There is progression in terms of fair testing; level 4 demands that children plan a fair test from the beginning. Central to investigations is the need to generate and handle numerical data and at this level it correlates with the requirement to use appropriate measuring equipment. Children are then required to use the data to draw conclusions based on patterns in results. Progression in terms of data handling requires children to use tables as organisers and graphs to represent data.

Level 5   At this level children are expected to generate a hypothesis based on information and ideas which have been taught. It should indicate that they have some understanding of cause and effect. Children are expected to plan and carry out a fair test which displays an appreciation of how numerical data will give useful results. The teacher should challenge children to decide what measurements they need, how many they need, if they need to repeat any and to calculate an average.

At this level the pupil's ability to be critical of the way in which the investigation was carried out is very important. They should ask themselves whether they are confident in their results, and if not, which aspects they would change if they were able to repeat the investigation.

The following example indicates progression in Sc1 1 through and across KS 1 and 2 in the context of plant growth.

Level 1:
What happens to
the seed when it grows?

- Working with a group the teacher could engage the children in observation of a seed and a plant, discussing how the seed grows into the plant. This would enable the teacher to access pupil ideas about plant growth.
- Children then plant the seeds discussing:
  - (i)   how to plant them;
  - (ii) what plants need to grow;
  - (iii) what they think will happen to the seed as it grows;
  - (iv) how to care for seeds and young plants;
- Children observe and record the growth of their plants.

Level 2:
How can we find out what
seeds need to grow?

- With the support of the teacher children offer their own ideas such as seeds need water, light, soil.
- With support children offer strategies for trying out their ideas for example, planting seeds and watering some but not others.
- Although not required for assessment purposes at this level, the teacher should begin to introduce the idea of a fair test.
- Children regularly observe the two sets of seeds, keeping a diary of observations, written and/or drawn. Where appropriate, observations should also be quantified using non-standard or standard measurements.
- Using their experience of the activity and the data children should make generalisations about plant growth.

Level 3:
Which is the best
place to grow seeds?

- Using everyday knowledge about plants, the class and teacher discuss the requirements for growth. Children are invited to ask a range of questions about growing plants; from this, one or more are chosen for investigation.
- Children decide on the best way to answer their question.
- Children choose their own equipment and materials.
- Children decide to place seeds in light, shady and dark places.
- Decisions about a fair test are made as they carry out the investigation planting the seeds in the same way, watering at the same time and same amount etc.
- Children decide to measure the growth of seeds at regular intervals and keep a diary to note observations which cannot be measured.
- The teacher encourages children to represent data on growth as a bar chart which, used in conjunction with their diary, enables them to draw conclusions and answer the original question.

Level 4:
How much light do
plants need to grow?

- The teacher asks children in a group or individually to state (oral or written) what they know about plant growth and then to ask questions about what they would like to know. Some children decide to investigate 'Does the amount of light affect how well a plant grows?'
- A fair test is planned at the beginning which includes growing the same kind of plants, controlling the temperature, amount of water etc.
- Children recognise that the plants need to be in dark, light, and dim conditions; some children use a light meter to help them create an environment in between light and dark.
- Children select their own equipment, choosing the most appropriate from a range offered by the teacher. Children measure plant growth at regular intervals over a set time. Children realise that qualitative as well as quantitative observations are required and keep detailed sketches and photographs.

- A table is used to record growth and this data is represented as a graph which enables children to recognise patterns more easily.
- Using the range of data i.e. sketches, tables and graphs, children draw conclusions about the effect of different amounts of light on the growth of the plant.
- Children report their conclusions to others and are able to respond to questions about their investigation.

Level 5:
How does the amount of
fertiliser affect plant growth?

- Children have been involved in learning about plants and the use of fertilisers for enhancing plant growth by gardeners and farmers. They decide to carry out an investigation to find out if the amount of fertiliser affects plant growth.
- Children decide to plan a fair test which involves the use of different amounts of liquid fertiliser but using the same amount of water, same growing conditions etc., and the time needed to run the experiment.
- Decisions about the range of quantities is based on the maximum amount suggested by the manufacturer. Children decide that the range will be no fertiliser, half the maximum, the maximum and double the maximum. The children think that this range should produce significant differences.
- The children appreciate the need to record both qualitative and quantitative observations including height, weight, quality of growth, number of leaves and average leaf size. Children make decisions as to whether the data will be valid and provide results which they will be able to use to draw conclusions.
- The range of data is then used to draw conclusions but children are aware of the limitations of their data and other interpretations, for example that one of the plants might naturally be a stronger plant than the others and affect the results.
- Children present their results which include a word-processed report. This includes a critical review of their investigation indicating the most successful aspects and those elements which could be improved if the investigation were repeated.

The Role of the Teacher in Investigations

Central to children being able to achieve these levels is the role of the teacher. Naime Browne (1991) asks

> *"Why have we been willing to leave science to luck whilst maintaining that other areas of the curriculum, such as literacy and maths require higher teacher input?"*

A number of reasons could be responsible for this disinclination to intervene; firstly the belief that children should discover for themselves still has something of a stranglehold on primary science. Secondly, lack of confidence in science means that teachers are reluctant to intervene because they are unsure how to handle the situation or questions from the children or they are unsure of the objective. To develop children's ability in carrying out investigations a shift in attitude towards teacher intervention is necessary. Alexander *et al* (1992) raise the issue of the teacher as a source of knowledge and comments on the

> *"persistent and damaging belief that pupils should never be told things, only asked questions"*,

suggesting that there are occasions when it is necessary to teach children by imparting information.

Teachers need to clearly identify learning outcomes. Appropriate intervention strategies must be employed to help children reach these outcomes. Teachers should also see themselves as a resource and feel free to impart certain knowledge and understanding to children, or to intervene and ask children to clarify their ideas, explain procedures etc.

Planned intervention is essential. Research into teacher questions by Wragg T. (1992) indicates that much of teacher intervention relates to management issues rather than the subject being taught. The ability of the teacher to ask suitable questions and the quality of intervention is dependent on a teacher's understanding of the nature and function of investigations and their knowledge and understanding of scientific concepts. Where personal understanding is high, intervention is more likely to be relevant and successful.

Research into children handling investigations carried out by the Exploration of Science Project sheds light on enhancing children's performance at KS 1 and 2. The outcomes of this research can help to provide some indication of the timing and nature of intervention and the roles teachers might adopt.

Introducing investigations Since investigations are intended to use children's knowledge and understanding then it would seem obvious that the best starting points for investigations are those raised by children themselves. This does not preclude teacher questions but motivation is probably higher when children have ownership of questions or ideas. The very action of allowing pupils to answer their own questions validates them and indicates to children that their questions are valued. However for children to be able to ask questions they require the teacher to be a good model for effective questions. Questions raised by children must be at their own level of knowledge and understanding, rather than at the teachers.

However, inviting children to answer their own questions requires careful planning and a defined outcome, otherwise the range of questions offered might be too wide and unprofitable in terms of potential learning. By narrowing the range of questions it is more likely that the teacher will be able to support the children effectively.

Before children embark on planning their investigation it is important that they are given the opportunity to analyse the question and indicate their understanding of what they think they are trying to find out. Indications are that children frequently carry out an investigation which bears little or no relation to the original question. This suggests that effective teacher-intervention would be to challenge children to explain what they think they have to find out.

Planning Planning is a complex procedure, very young children find it difficult to plan ahead. If asked to explain what they would do to find out which car went the furthest, they might suggest that they raced cars against each other but would probably be unable to add detail. Young children need to interact with materials and equipment to move from one part of an investigation to another. It is this interaction which often suggests the next step for children. In this respect children are reactive rather than proactive in investigations. With experience children are more able to include detail in their planning but still rely on interaction to help suggest the next step or refinements. However as children begin to develop their ability to carry out more structured investigations, giving them outlines is useful. The teacher should ask children questions which focus attention on the salient points of investigations, for example;

- what are you trying to find out?
- what are you going to measure?
- what do you need to change?
- what do you need to keep the same?
- how are you going to record results?

Fair tests Data from the Exploration of Science Project (1992) indicates that children at KS 1 often treat investigations as competitions and see the results in terms of winners and losers. This might reflect the need of younger children to relate investigations to some aspect of their own lives. Teachers might wish to take their cue from children and in the early stages of developing investigations introduce these activities as mini-competitions. The research suggests that children at KS 2 are *au fait* with the idea of a fair test. This was one of the most successful parts of the investigations. Why this is so might be that a fair test is the aspect teachers feel most confident with in terms of intervention in investigations.

Generating and handling data

This aspect of the Project's research indicates that the generation and handling of data was the least successful part of all investigations. Many children did not generate data at all, whilst those children who did rarely used it. The focal point of an investigation should be the collection of data which enables children to support or otherwise their hypothesis or answer a question. Children do not appreciate the power of data, particularly numerical data.

In many respects this could reflect the present position of teacher understanding of investigations. Many teachers equate investigations with the idea of a fair test, and, as the research indicates, have successfully developed this idea with children. However, teachers are less familiar with the importance of evidence, and as a consequence many children involved in the research carried out what can only be described as 'truncated investigations'. They carried out the fair test element but either did not generate data or where they did failed to use the data to interpret the evidence and to draw conclusions.

This has implications for science and indeed for mathematics. Teachers need to help children to appreciate the power of evidence. It is the quality of the data that enables children to make useful inferences and draw conclusions. Without data their conclusions are subjective. Equally there needs to be a move, much earlier than we have at present in KS 1, towards collecting numerical data. This is not as complicated as it would suggest. All it really means is that teachers demand that children place a number value on their results. It allows children to make comparisons, search for patterns and predict with some justification what might happen. At KS 1 this might mean that where children have raced toy cars instead of saying the blue car went furthest stating that it went 9 tiles whilst the red car went 6 tiles. Immediately, questions such as "why did one car go three tiles further than another?", "put them in order, what do you notice, did the biggest go the furthest?" can be asked.

By the end of KS 2 the expectation should be that children are able to do the following;

- plan to collect 'useful data'
- decide what kind of data, how often to collect it, whether to repeat measurements.
- appreciate the importance of numerical data
- be able to note patterns in data
- make inferences
- draw conclusions
- consider whether they have confidence in their data

Recording

The research data indicates that the standard form of recording at KS 1 is pictures and simple sentences. At KS 2 the overwhelming number of children recorded investigations in the form of a written account. Analysis of the accounts raised a number of issues;

(i) accounts were descriptive in nature rather than analytical or critical.

(ii) accounts contained information about equipment used and what children did, but not about conclusions they drew and why they thought certain things happened.

(iii) results were often in the form of lists or prose rather than tables, an inefficient method of recording numerical data which does not allow patterns in data and anomalous readings to be easily recognised.

Had children appreciated the usefulness of tables as organisers and been skilled in their production and interpretation then more children would have used them as part of their investigations.

An understanding of the place of tables in investigations is not yet fully appreciated. If one acknowledges that one central tenet of investigations is the generation of numerical data then tables have the following uses. Tables can:

- encourage children to set out data in an orderly manner;
- organise data into a useful format;
- sequence action;
- encourage accurate observation;
- define the beginning and end of data.

Indications from the research are that generally children appear to have little idea as to why they are recording and producing accounts. There is no sense of purpose or audience, consequently children write narratives which are unhelpful in terms of making sense of the investigation or for assessment purposes.

The role of the teacher in this aspect would be to offer support by asking children to consider what the person reading the account might need to know. Equally important is to ensure that those children who have difficulty producing written accounts are supported in some way. This might take the form of encouraging oral feedback or the creation of strip cartoons where pictures are accompanied by sentences.

Feedback   Feedback is an essential part of investigations. This is where the children can make sense of their learning through discussing their investigation and data. In verbalising what they have found out and making sense of data the teacher can have access to what children know, tease out understanding and help to refine and develop understanding. As children's ability to carry out more sophisticated investigations improves so should their ability to communicate their findings and critically evaluate their investigations. It is during feedback sessions that children are given the opportunity to give coherent presentations to an audience and receive and reply to comments and questions.

Conclusion

The inclusion of Sc1 in the National Curriculum has introduced to many teachers a new approach to teaching and learning in science. It will take time for teachers to respond to the demands of this aspect of the science curriculum. Equally this area requires more research and development in the classroom followed by dissemination of the findings. Research by the Exploration of Science Project provides some insight into present practice and suggests areas in which more attention is required if both teachers and children are to move forward in this aspect of science. The most positive finding of the research was the high motivation factor associated with investigative work. Over 3000 investigations were carried out by children of varying abilities including children with special needs. All the children were able to offer something, albeit in varying degrees. Investigations enrich the science curriculum, they offer children a venue for using their knowledge and understanding, they are highly motivating and if offered at the correct level allow the majority of children access to and success in science.

References

Alexander R., Rose J., Woodhead C., (1992) *Curriculum Organisation and Classroom Practice in Primary Schools* – A Discussion Paper D.E.S.

Aubrey C. (Ed) (1992) *The Role of Subject Knowledge in the Primary Curriculum* Falmer Press.

Browne N. (1991) *Science and Technology in the Early Years* O.U.P.

Foulds K., Gott R. Feasey R. (Exploration of Science Project) (1992) *Investigative Work in Science* – A Report Commissioned by National Curriculum Council

Gott R., Duggan S. (1992) *Why Investigations?* Internal Working Paper, Exploration of Science Project, University of Durham

Gott R., Feasey R., Foulds K., (1991) *Science Explorations* N.C.C.

Gott R., Murphy P. (1987) Assessing Investigations Ages 13 and 15 *APU Science Report for Teachers:9* DES 1987 APU Assessment of Investigations at ages 13 and 15

Swannell. (ed) (1986) *The New Little Oxford Dictionary* O.U.P

Wragg T. (1992) *Ain't Misbehaving* (Article) Times Educational Supplement 22.5.92

Rosemary Feasey is a Lecturer in Primary Science at the University of Durham and co-director of the Exploration of Science Project. She was formerly Deputy Head of a Primary School and Advisory teacher under the ESG Project.

Science for All Pupils
Science and 'Special Needs'

Jeanette Sutherland and Dominic Boyes

All children will have at some point in their school lives some form of what is currently known as Special Educational Need. It could be that a child has a physical disability, a difficulty in making relationships, a family break-up or bereavement, a problem with vision or hearing, learning difficulty or one of communication. It may be a problem of behaviour or emotion. It could be that a pupil's attainment is so high that he or she is not extended. It may be a long term significant need or one which is a problem for just a day. It may be a broken wrist. As teachers it is our responsibility to recognise this need and make efforts to understand and address it.

The 1988 Education Reform Act requires that all children regardless of circumstances should receive the National Curriculum.

> *'At the heart of the process is the individual/child who is entitled to the same opportunity to receive a broad, balanced, differentiated curriculum regardless of race, gender, disability, or geographical location'* (NCC 1989)

If it is argued that Science is good for children it must be the case that this applies to all children. All children have the right to curriculum initiatives. All children have needs that are individual, special and ever changing. Science enables all children to be integrated and equal. There is therefore the potential for equality of opportunity.

There is no need in this chapter to elaborate on the reasons why science is so crucial for all the children of the land. Curriculum Guidance 10 from the NCC deals with teaching science to pupils with special educational needs. It maintains that every pupil....

> *'...... should have the opportunity to learn science. Activities in science have characteristics which will help pupils with SEN achieve success'* (NCC 1992)

It goes on to list five reasons why this is so:

- They are about first hand experience
- Knowledge and skills can be developed in small steps through practical activity, so helping concentration

- Science activities can capture the imagination and may reduce behavioural problems
- Working in groups can encourage participation and inter-personal communication
- Working on a variety of activities allows pupils to share their strengths and help each other.

It is surely the case that these reasons hold true for all pupils. They are beneficial for children of all abilities; physically, emotionally and academically. They are relevant for the so called 'gifted child' as well as a pupil who may be undertaking a curriculum suitable for youngsters with a severe learning difficulty. They are appropriate for youngsters who have challenging behaviour and those pupils for whom access is a challenge.

It is also the case that effective methods employed to enable pupils with special educational needs to achieve meaningful success can be used to improve the learning experience for all children and young people.

> *'What is good practice in relation to special educational needs is good practice for all'* (NCC 1989 2)

> *'The main features of practice which resulted in work of at least satisfactory standard among pupils with special educational needs also constituted good practice for all pupils'* (DES 1989)

There must therefore be a healthy symbiosis between Science and Special Educational Needs. How does one facilitate the opportunities for success using both? How does one enable the pupil to receive his or her entitlement? What is the best way in which a teacher can maximise the opportunities for this entitlement?

The major variable that can be affected by the individual teacher is the delivery of the curriculum. The crucial elements of this are differentiation and access.

Differentiation

Differentiation within the curriculum is how the content, teaching methods, resources, curriculum objectives and learning activities are varied to cater for the diversity of experience of the children. It encourages success not failure. It concentrates on what children can do. For the less able the activity is broken down whereas for the more able it is extended. An example of this can be found in the *Science Non Statutory Guidance C11: 'Making and Investigating a Windmill'* NCC 1989. The objectives are the same. All the children are learning about forces. Differentiation is introduced by either task or outcome

Differentiation by task   Differentiation by task is done by analysing the task and the objective so as to ascertain what is expected of the child in terms of concepts.

These are then considered in relation to the child 's previous experiences and capabilities. If necessary, the task is redefined into achievable goals.

The task goals and expectations are then clearly and appropriately presented to the group or individual. In some cases it may be appropriate to fully break down the task into small achievable steps. The child would then work through these and move towards the final goal. Various tactical methods may be needed to suit the situation and one model for this is explored later in the chapter.

An example of differentiation by task is the activity already mentioned 'Making and Investigating a Windmill' from the *Science Non Statutory Guidance*.

Differentiation by outcome   Here a common task is undertaken which has a variety of possible responses or outcomes. It enables all learners to demonstrate what they know, understand or can do at their own level. The outcome of the task informs both the child and the teacher as to:

- What the child has done
- The attitude of the child on that particular occasion.

The degree of direction given by the teacher may depend on the situation and the intended outcome. Teachers must be fully aware of the problems children may experience. An example of differentiation by outcome would be setting a task to classify biscuits. (eg from shape and colour to calorific value and composition).

For a more expansive definition and description concerning differentiation by task and outcome please see *'A Guide to Teacher Assessment'* SEAC 1989.

Access   Having differentiated and ensured appropriateness of the task there is the essential need to give all children equal access to it. It would be unfortunate to provide an excellent learning environment only to restrict the pupils involvement in it. Equally it would be a waste of time to access a pupil into something that was totally inappropriate and incomprehensible to the pupil.

Access may take different forms and will be dependent on the individual needs of the child. Children with physical disabilities may need technological aids to communicate. Children with hearing impairment may need more pictorial cues and simpler language. Children with reading difficulties may need written work presented in a simpler form or orally. If there is full access a child may be integrated within the class group and therefore there will be an equality of opportunity.

There are various factors which affect the success of teachers in implementing a broad, balanced curriculum for all pupils. These factors can be grouped into three main categories: those relating to individual children, as detailed in the introduction and which are out of the teacher's control, those relating to teaching style and environment and those relating to the choice of the content vehicle used to convey the subject being taught.

Teaching style It is clear from the National Curriculum document, particularly Sc1, that children are expected to take an active role in the planning and carrying out of investigations. The role that the teacher adopts to allow this to happen are many and varied. A range of teacher roles, aimed at developing a learning environment in which pupils are encouraged to be independent and take responsibility for their own learning can be found in the NCC's *Non Statutory Guidance for Science*. For example:

Role	**Example**
Enabler	Facilitates the learning opportunities which are the objectives of the lesson.
Manager	Coordinates all class activities and organisation.
Presenter	Sets the scene, clarifies the processes involved and gives information.
Adviser	Listens, suggests alternatives, offers references and encourages.
Observer	Studies the processes and gives feedback.
Challenger	Comments critically on procedures and outcomes.
Respondent	Answers questions
Evaluator	Assesses progress against learning objectives.

A framework within which a child centred approach to learning in science can evolve was put forward by the *'Children Learning In Science Project'* ('CLISP' University of Leeds 1987). This is based on a 'constructivist' theory of learning which suggests that all pupils bring their own 'models' or preconceived ideas to any new learning situation, based on their own experiences and knowledge; these models will be at different stages along a concept line. CLISP recognised that it is important that children have opportunities to recognise and reflect on their 'models', realising that others may have different models to explain the same phenomena, and to challenge, test and if appropriate modify their ideas.

Teachers must base their planning on the pupils' existing models and their position on the concept line. The constructivist approach requires that the teacher be other than a bestower of knowledge. It means that the teacher must shift attention more frequently from the whole class to the individual pupil, resulting in greater awareness by the teacher of individual needs and differences.

Learning Activities Having identified a teaching style which allows for differentiated learning, suitable learning activities are now required. Before any planning of learning activities takes place it is suggested that the following points are considered:

- Children will master a concept which they easily relate to and which bears the most relevance to the concept they have just studied.
- Studying a suitable 'content vehicle' allows pupils to travel along the concept line at their own pace and reach a deeper understanding of the world around them.
- First hand experiences brought to the attention of all pupils the concept journey to be started by giving all pupils an equal opportunity to step on to the relevant concept line.
- Different pupils travel along the concept line at different paces, often the more 'able' travelling the furthest and the quickest.

The Humberside model One can see that the choice of a 'content vehicle', ie. the topic content you choose to base your learning activities on is very important. It was on these foundations that a group of Humberside teachers developed the following model for differentiated science. It is not claimed that it is the only way of 'meshing' individual needs with the requirements of the National Curriculum but it has been used successfully to plan a variety of content areas, one of which will be detailed later.

The Model

- Select from the programmes of study
    Read through the Programme of Study for the appropriate Key Stage.
    Select a section on which to base the pupils' work.

- Identify the key concept
    Read the chosen section of the Programme of Study and identify the basic scientific idea underlying that section and towards which the children will be working.

- Determine the learning objectives
    List the 'sub-concepts' (the steps on the way) leading to understanding of the Key Concept.

- Choose the content vehicle

    Decide on the subject matter to be used to extend the pupils' knowledge and understanding. This should involve something from the pupils own experience.

- Select a common experience

    A common experience is needed to focus the pupils' attention on their common conceptual goal.

- Consider possible learning activities

    Although advocating pupil ownership of the investigations they undertake, it is recognised that there is a need of some pre-planning by the teacher of the way these investigations are likely to proceed. The teacher can usually predict a series of investigational activities which pupils at different points along the concept line will wish to carry out.

- Consider issues of access

    Considering the range of activities in which the pupils are likely to be involved, do any special arrangements need to be made to ensure that all pupils can take an active part in the learning activities?

All of the above are learning activities which occur before the learning session. The remaining points in the model take place when the children are present.

- Present a common learning experience

    Present the pupils with a common experience related to the Key Concept which will stimulate pupil discussion.

- Allow group discussion

    With appropriate intervention from the teacher, the pupils should be allowed to discuss the common experience in small groups and plan activities to test and extend their ideas. Intervention is necessary in order to determine the point along the concept line from which the children are starting, enabling teachers to map the development of understanding of the Key Concept as the learning activity progresses.

- Allow group investigation

    Groups of pupils should be allowed and helped to carry out investigations they have planned. Teacher intervention is often necessary for a variety of reasons. For example, where pupils have planned an investigation which has a potentially hazardous aspect the teacher must provide safety guidelines for the group to follow or suggest an alternative route.

- Encourage group conclusion

    Pupils should be encouraged to consider the result of their investigations and the implications for their original hypotheses and understanding.

By thorough planning for differentiation using content vehicles familiar to children and allowing child ownership of the learning activity this offers a sound way of working. As HMI comment...

'Good lessons were associated with high pupils expectations, sound preparation, motivating work and relevant starting points'. (H.M.I. 1991)

The Model in Action

To aid understanding of the model one section of the Programmes of Study from Key Stage 2 has been taken through each stage of it.

A section from the Programme of Study is selected: KS2 'children should explore chemical change in a number of everyday materials'.

This section is basically asking us to look at chemical changes experienced in everyday life. This is the Key Concept. In order to understand chemical change, children will need to have grasped several concepts which precede and contribute to this one:

1. Classification of materials
2. Experience change in materials
3. Recognise change in materials
4. Recognise that some changes are reversible and some are not
5. Identify chemical change

An idea of various possible starting points that children will have in a 'typical' teaching group has now been established.

An appropriate content vehicle might be *'Chemical changes involved in food preparation'*.

A problem or a question now needs to be posed to tie all the starting points together and which is open ended enough to be relevant to all pupils. In this case *'what happens when you burn toast?'*

In an ideal world that would be the end of content planning but in reality, in order to have ready the resources that may be requested, the teacher has to think of possible approaches that the class may take towards the investigation (Possible Leaning Activities). In this case these may be:

1. Make toast
2. Observe the effects of heat on different foods.
3. Look at properties of food before and after heating
4. Look at reversible and irreversible changes in food eg. can you uncook bacon?

5. Classifying these changes by result
6. Quantitative work on the above.

The planning has now provided the children with a differentiated curriculum and it is at this point that considerations of access need to be made. For example a child with a visual impairment may need a talking thermometer or fill indicator for measuring out hot water when making jelly. It is worth pointing out that these sorts of considerations will not need to be re-made every time as many access solutions will be common to a lot of situations. It will probably be the case that access issues for pupils will have already have been resolved as a whole-school approach, as it would be exceedingly unusual for a child to have special needs only during science sessions.

As the children tackle the problem set, they are asked to go through certain steps towards confirming, moderating or altering their existing concepts.

Each group will be asked to state their existing ideas and ways in which they can be investigated. For example a group may decide to look at toast and subsequently other foods before and after toasting. This will probably be a very qualitative investigation with few variables controlled. Another group, further along the learning continuum, may want to investigate how much heat is required to burn toast and compare this results with those for similar quantities of other foods – a far more quantitative investigation with many more variables controlled.

The children will then be asked to carry out their investigations and discuss their findings, thereby drawing conclusions and revising concepts. This is not done in isolation and requires teacher intervention all the way through in the form of questioning, responding to questions, teaching new skills – for example the proper use of the meniscus when measuring liquids, organising equipment, advising on methods of achieving the groups' aims and of course assessing the levels of attainment for the group members.

Summary

In the 1988 Education Reform Act there is an expectancy that you can achieve differentiation within the curriculum for all pupils. All children have the same legal 'entitlement' to a broad and balanced curriculum. The National Curriculum has the potential for teachers to deal with the full range of individual needs. Opportunity now exists to place any pupil at their own appropriate level in the wider curriculum, irrespective of the 'Special Educational Need' they may have at that particular time. The crucial elements of this opportunity are Differentiation and Access.

The opportunity is enhanced when there are the following factors at work:

- There is a whole school approach

- There is positive team work.

  There may be numerous agencies and professionals working along side the youngster with Special Educational Needs. Interdisciplinary working is essential. The team approach willl enable collective and collaborative working and therefore will instil confidence in all those involved. It is essential that there is a holistic view of the child and that all support is provided in an integrated manner.

  'Satisfactory differentiation of learning tasks and resources used have frequently been achieved through collaborative planning by class or subject teachers and designated specialist staff foe special educational needs.' (DES 1989)

- There is integration.

  In any class a child with special needs must be fully integrated with their peers. It must be realised that it is the responsibility of the teacher to facilitate this integration. The pressure should not be on the pupil to conform to the rest of the class, their needs miraculously merging with those general needs of the majority. The class and school need to change. The crucial factor is that all children should be presented with appropriately differentiated activities which have been made accessible for the pupil. There is only true integration when there is an equality of opportunity for all children. That opportunity should include experiencing success and enjoyment in science.

References

NCC 1989 Curriculum Guidance 1: A framework for the Primary Curriculum

NCC 1989 Curriculum Guidance 2: A curriculum for all

NCC 1992 Curriculum Guidance 10: Teaching science to pupils with special educational needs

NCC 1989 Science: Non Statutory Guidance

A survey of pupils with special educational needs in ordinary schools: DES HMI 1989

Science at Key Stage 1 and 3: DES HMI 1991

A guide to teacher assessment: SEAC 1989

Children Learning in Science Project [CLISP]: University of Leeds 1987

Acknowledgement   The authors would like to acknowledge the contributions of their Humberside colleagues.

Jeanette Sutherland has taught for nine years in the primary phase. She was seconded as an advisory teacher for primary science and technology where she became involved in the county initiative on special needs education.

Dominic Boyes has worked in five special schools in Humberside. He has always had an interest in science education which culminated in working with Humberside colleagues on access for children with special needs.

Science for All Pupils
Teaching science for equality: issues and opportunities in a multicultural society

Esme Glauert and Steve Thorp

What are the Issues?   In their discussion paper on 'Race, Equality and Science Teaching', the ASE Multicultural Education Working Party states:

> *'The Working Party believes that the issues of racism and access to the curriculum for all children in a multicultural society need to be addressed as a matter of urgency. By its very nature, racism aims to devalue specific groups of human beings based on the colour of skin and/or cultural and social background. If an entitlement to a balanced and relevant science curriculum..is to be taken up by every child, there must be recognition that in establishing equality of opportunity, racism will always have a negative effect on children's learning, achievement and attitudes towards others'*
> (Thorp, 1991)

This explicitly recognises that racism is not simply a theoretical and political concept but is a practical reality which affects the life chances and the viewpoints of children in our primary schools. From a very early age children begin to learn about how they a re-valued by each other and by society. This places a responsibility on teachers and schools to recognise how racism 'operates' on children, and what they can do to challenge its causes and effects.

Primary teachers rightly stress the importance of valuing and building on the experiences of children and this is particularly important where racism is concerned. Many children, black and white, will bring from their homes and communities experiences of racism – whether this is direct experience of abuse or harassment or exposure to racist language and attitudes from adults around them. Unless teachers are prepared to acknowledge and address these issues explicitly in classrooms, thus building a climate in which each child feels valued, effective learning in science or any other area of the curriculum cannot take place. It should be recognised that schools are also places racism is experienced (see Troyna and Hatcher, 1992; C.R.E. 1989) – playground name-calling, an eurocentric curriculum, inappropriate resources, poor home-school and community relations etc. It is therefore vital that racism is not just addressed in individual classrooms but by the whole school community at a management and policy level.

Although there has been much written and said about 'access and entitlement' to a 'broad, balanced and relevant' curriculum, the key question is whether these stated opportunities are taken up by each child. Since the publication of the *Swann Report* (House of Commons, 1985), there is a growing body of evidence to show that many children, including those from some minority ethnic groups are not achieving their full potential, particularly in formal assessments.

There is clearly a variety of factors which may contribute to this – but many of them will have their foundation in racism or in racist assumptions whether obvious and overt or more implicit and subtle in their effects. For example, experience of Key Stage 1 SATs (Donald, 1992; Dutta, 1992) have shown that 'access' to a science assessment may be severely curtailed if:

- the task is heavily language based.
- bilingual support is not available.
- the context of the SAT makes assumptions about children's' previous cultural experiences.
- the teacher makes negative assumptions about the child's aptitudes or abilities.

In a wider context, socio-economic factors have long been shown to have considerable impact on achievement. Discrimination in jobs, housing etc. against minority groups in society means that children from these groups come to school already disadvantaged by society. The effects of bias and low expectations in school simply enhance the effect.

For white pupils in schools the impact of racism is equally important, if more difficult to quantify (Gaine, 1987; Carrington and Short, 1989). Nevertheless, while research shows that white children will reflect the racist attitudes and behaviour they encounter in society, they are often also committed to egalitarian and anti-racist viewpoints (Troyna and Hatcher, 1992). If children are not given the opportunity to critically explore these contradictions, and to address power relationships and inequalities, they will be ill-prepared for adult life in a complex and interdependent world society.

Science can offer valuable opportunities for addressing racism and its effects – through the processes which should involve a critical examination of evidence and analysis and discussion of differing viewpoints, and by ensuring that the contexts through which science is learnt offer a challenge to the eurocentric notion of science as a western, objective and value-free area of study. Indeed science itself has often promoted racist ideas, providing the justification for discriminatory practices and racist viewpoints (Gill and Levidow, 1987). In the past this has involved the 'proving' of black inferiority by a range of physiological and psychological theories (Gould, 1984; Rose et al. 1985). More recently the application of 'western' science and technology has been viewed as the 'touchstone' of development and progress. However, in cases such as the 'green revolution', science has offered solutions to problems such as world hunger, which ignore local expertise and environmental and socio-economic factors, and which have sometimes benefited western industry more than the people it was supposed to help (Shiva, 1989).

Teaching and Learning for Equality

The ASE Multicultural Education Working Party, in their INSET manual, suggests that teaching and learning promotes equality when:

- *a variety of strategies are used;*
- *children's own experience is valued and built on;*
- *children are enabled to develop autonomy and responsibility for their own learning;*
- *ideas and assumptions are challenged;*
- *strategies are collaborative, not competitive;*
- *control of learning is shared between teachers and pupils.*
  (Thorp, 1991).

As stated in the section above, the accepted tenet of primary practice of valuing and building on children's experience is a crucial starting point for creating a climate of equality in the classroom. This involves more than just a child-centred' approach in teacher's curriculum planning, but means a commitment to a democratic classroom where all children feel that their opinions are valid and their actions have some positive influence. This will mean that children and teachers are asked to examine critically their assumptions about science, about 'race' and about equality and to learn to listen to and respect each other. With primary age children, development education and world studies approaches are particularly appropriate and a number of resources are referenced below (eg. D.E.C.,1992; Fisher and Hicks, 1985; Hicks and Steiner, 1989)

An active and collaborative approach to learning is essential when 'teaching for equality'. First, they enable children to discuss concepts such as justice, inequality and racism in an open and non-threatening forum. Secondly, discussion particularly promotes 'access' for bilingual learners by actively involving them in 'speaking and listening' activities, and enabling them to negotiate the terms of the learning task in English or in their mother tongue. Third, it makes learning in science more relevant and immediate to all children, enabling them to construct their own meanings and apply their own experience to the task or concept.

With children of all ages the way in which such collaborations are set up are important. There needs to be a clear framework of expectations for children and teachers alike, so that the teacher will intervene both to ensure that a group is on task, but also, crucially, to ensure that 'equality' is being practised within the group and that all children are able to participate actively. The way in which children are grouped also needs to be considered with regard to their access to the curriculum. Careful planning and evaluation, involving the children, will also enable teachers to judge how effective an activity has been in contributing to this 'climate of equality' as well as how each child is achieving individually.

A variety of strategies will be required at several different levels in the classroom to promote access and to enable children to demonstrate achievement.

- Using different resources as stimuli for an activity or discussion;
- encouraging a number of ways in which a task can be carried out and reported;
- assessing pupils in ways which show what best they, as individuals, 'know, understand and can do'.

Once again, bilingual children may particularly benefit from such approaches, as flexibility in the linguistic forms encouraged in the classroom gives greater opportunity to take up a genuine entitlement to the science curriculum (Shan, 1990).

Equality and Science

The science process itself, as currently defined in education, can also be a positive tool for equality – although there are also possible problems with the approach. As a practical 'hands on' experience in the primary classroom, science promotes the active and collaborative approaches described above, and provides motivation for children of all backgrounds. The processes of hypothesis, observation, interpretation etc. also encourage children to question and to value their own, and each others, viewpoints on an activity. It thus provides a focus for the development of positive individual and group identity and collective exploration. However, it is important that a 'process model' of science is not adopted uncritically , and that it is recognised, at all times, that science is not neutral and value free and that it exists within social, environmental and historical contexts.

The work of research projects such as SPACE and CLIS have stressed the importance of talk and language development in the learning of science. Language enables learners to clarify ideas and develop thinking in science. As stated above, collaborative activities promote both this approach to learning and science and equality of access for all children. Conversely, science itself offers many opportunities for language development and this is particularly important for those children for whom English is not the mother tongue. The promotion of the use of a child's mother tongue alongside English in the classroom is crucial for his or her self identity and conceptual development, but there are other implications of a positive, multilingual approach in all classrooms.

For the black bilingual child such an approach can be genuinely anti-racist – as for many, one manifestation of racism in society may be the undervaluing or, in some cases, ridiculing of their home language. This has major implications in school where teachers expectations of bilingual pupils are negative – based on a false preconception about the nature of learning which sees a 'need' for a child to learn English first, before gaining access to the rest of the curriculum. For the pupil, seeing their language valued in the environment of the school, in displays and in resources, and being encouraged to use their mother tongue positively in their learning can go some way to challenging such racism, and is likely to lead to enhanced achievement. Equally, seeing other languages than English regarded positively in school, will promote respect and enhance the cultural awareness of other pupils. A commitment to equality requires equal status for the linguistic experiences and capabilities of all children, whilst recognising their right to fluency in the main 'language of achievement' in society – English. As well as placing a responsibility on teachers and schools, this should also mean that standard (and teacher) assessments – in whatever form – are free of cultural and linguistic bias and that the resources are available to ensure full access to the tasks. A child taking a science SAT should be assessed in science, not on their current capability in the English language.

Curriculum Contexts and Opportunities

The real challenge to primary teachers is to offer to all the children in their classrooms learning experiences which provide full access to, in this instance, the National Curriculum for Science – and which, therefore, value and build on each child's experiences in home and community, challenging preconceptions and exposing injustices. Only then will children be able to practice the active and positive 'citizenship' which sees them taking responsibility for the well-being of themselves, their families and communities and the environment.

Science has a key role to play in developing the global skills, concepts and understanding required by children to address the complex inter-relationships between environmental awareness, local and global 'development' and economic and social justice (see D.E.C 1992).

The traditional 'multicultural' classroom approach regards 'diversity' as the key. Hence the teacher builds in cultural diversity into her planning of a topic or unit of work, and into the classroom environment. The home corner may have a selection of cooking utensils, dressing-up clothes reflect cultural diversity, cooking and food topics cover 'different' foods, religious festivals are studied and celebrated as part of a cross-curricular approach. Many schools have been able to build in such approaches with great success, creating a rich and welcoming environment for all children which celebrates and draws on the cultural diversity found in Britain today. However what must be questioned is whether such a stress on 'cultural diversity', however positively put into practice, can begin to prepare pupils for the complex issues which face them as citizens of the future, or can provide genuine equality in education (see chapters in Peacock, 1991 for approaches to this issue). We would argue that, despite a growth in such approaches in the last two decades, there has been little change in patterns of achievement of minority ethnic groups, and racial harassment of black children and communities continues to be a major problem in school and society.

Consider the case of Julie: Julie is ten-years old and was born in Britain, although her parents originally come from Jamaica. Her parents are both active in local Afro-Caribbean organisations, and Julie attends a Saturday school run by the community, as well as her junior school. At Saturday school she hears stories about the achievements of black people in history and the links that black people all over the world have with Africa. One day the teacher tells of the Dogon people of Mali, who have been studying and charting the stars and planets for m any centuries. She learns that the ancient Dogons knew about distant stars which were not charted by Western scientists until modern times. At school her class is doing a topic on 'The Earth in Space', and have been using a telescope and finding out how it works. She is very excited about the Dogon story and wants to tell the teacher about how these people charted the stars and planets without any modern telescopes. She hopes that her teacher will be interested and will help her find out more about it.

There are a number of questions raised by Julie's experiences which a traditionally planned multicultural approach could not hope the address, for example:

- Do teachers recognise the need for black children to associate themselves with positive images of black people in history and around the world? (van Sertina, 1986);
- Do teachers use examples such as the Dogon to allow children to question the Western concept of technology driven science as the only path to human knowledge?;

- Do schools value and build on the community based activities of their black students, such as attendance at Saturday schools and home-language classes?;
- Do topics allow issues such as racism and inequality to be confronted by getting children to tackle issues like why many black achievements have been hidden in history?.

Teachers need to be imaginative about the context in which they set science activities and should ensure that issues such as addressing racism and global issues appear in the initial learning objectives set for a topic or a unit of work.

In practice this means that, in order to provide equality, science teaching should:

- be relevant to all pupils regardless of class, gender and ethnicity;
- reflect and build on the experiences of all pupils;
- portray science as an everyday human activity;
- place science in cultural, historical, social, political, environmental and economic contexts;
- be global in nature and portray positive images of people and places;
- should challenge racism and the false science which defines "human race";
- should challenge deterministic arguments – particularly with regard to human behaviour and characteristics;
- should challenge all forms of stereotyping and discrimination.

This may seem like a tall order, but it is entirely consistent with good practice approaches in primary teaching generally and the teaching of science in particular. For example, a series of science activities can be based around a story set in another part of the world and provide positive images of the people described. Young children quickly identify with the characters and their everyday lives and feelings can be discussed. A range of language based activities can promote access, and science investigations then fall naturally into place as the children explore solutions to situations based on the story.

Alternatively, the stimulus might be a series of photographs or visual images which challenge children's preconceptions of 'development' both at home and in other parts of the world. Materials used, for example, for housing or shelter can be investigated as appropriate to their setting rather than assuming European social and climatic criteria. Where there is evidence of poverty and inequality children can be challenged to find reasons and provided with a range of alternative viewpoints with which to test their own theories on the world. This 'theme' based approach can be particularly useful when addressing 'traditional' cross-curricular topics such as 'Homes', 'Food', 'Clothing' and so on. It avoids the dangers of simplistic stereotyping by diversity and encourages an egalitarian and democratic ethos in the classroom. It is also dependent on the open and active learning approaches discussed in more detail above. In recent years many high quality 'development education' packages have become available for primary schools which take this 'theme' based approach and which in volve children in creating their own contexts and rationale for science investigations.

A further development of this approach involves working overtly from an issue – such as how a minority or indigenous group is treated and how their culture might have been misrepresented and undermined; how a technological system, such as farming, might have been imposed on a country or community for economic reasons and the social effects of this, or bringing together the human and environment al aspects of global developments to enhance children's understanding of a complex issue such as the destruction of the rainforests (eg. Lyle and Roberts, 1988)1. Each of these can be overtly anti-racist in the context set. Each can use a range of material for discussion and practical work – and each has the potential to develop, in children, a more sophisticated conceptual understanding of t he way science relates to humanity and to the planet. Further practical examples of such approaches can be found in some of the resources referred to at the end of this chapter, and in the 'Race, Equality and Science teaching' INSET manual and handbook published by the A.S.E.

Conclusion

Using approaches such as those described will certainly involve teachers in being more creative about the planning of the contexts in which they set science activities. This is important as a National Curriculum takes hold which has greatly enhanced the profile an d levels of practice of science in science schools, but which may also have the effect of stifling teachers creativity as they struggle to meet the heavy demands of an overloaded curriculum. In the Non-Statutory Guidance for National Curriculum Science, there is a recognition of the importance of careful choice of context and its strong effect on pupil performance. It also suggested that pupils should come to realise the 'international nature of science and the potential it has to overcome prejudice'. However such approaches will also require, from teachers, a clear commitment to equality and to developing their own knowledge and awareness in this area.

The relationships between science and world society, which must be explored if equality is to be realised, are complex and challeng ing to pupils and teachers alike and should be explored together. Teachers can learn much from children's experiences and knowledge, which, in sum, will be wider and deeper than their own on many levels. Not least of which will be children's knowledge and awareness of racism and its effects. Science in the classroom has great potential, in terms of the processes and teaching styles, the practical nature of the explorations and the contexts teachers use to plan the curriculum.

However we must also emphasise institutional responsibility for promoting equality in schools. Although this chapter has dealt predominantly with classroom practice, no teacher can hope to achieve change on her or his own. A policy commitment at all levels is required which is developed and shared within the whole school community. Governors and management, teachers and non-teaching staff, parents and children and people in the local and wider community, all need to be involved. There should be a real sense in which equality of opportunity and access for every child should be seen as the predominant criteria of a school's success.

Equality is therefore an essential and central part of 'quality' and contains within it an entitlement for every child – white or black – to be equipped with the attitudes, values, skills and knowledge required to live as active and open-minded citizens in the increasingly complex and interdependent world of the future.

References

Association for Science Education (1992) Policy Statement: *Race, equality and Science Teaching*

Brandt, G (1987) *The Realisation of Antiracist Teaching*, Falmer Press.

Carrington and Short (1989) *'Race' and the Primary School: Theory into Practice*, Windsor, NFER-Nelson.

Commission for Racial Equality (1989) *Learning in Terror*, London, C.R.E.

Development Education Centre (1992) *Why on Earth: an Approach to Science with a Global Dimension at Key Stage 2*, Birmingham, D.E.C.

Donald L (1992) "Key Stage 1 SATs and Science for Bilingual Pupils – Some Observations" in Deshpande, P., Edwards, C. and Thorp, S (eds) *Race, Equality and Science Teaching – A Teachers' Handbook*, ASE.

Dutta, K (1992) *'The SATs Experience: an individual teacher's perspective'*, Multicultural Teaching, Vol. 2, No 2.: 24-27.

Fisher, S. and Hicks, D. (1985) *World Studies 8-13: A Teachers' Handbook*, Edinburgh, Oliver and Boyd.

Gaine, C. (1987) *No Problem Here: a Practical Approach to Education and Race in White schools*, London, Hutchinson.

Gould, S.J. (1984) *The Mismeasure of Man*, London, Pelican.

Gill, D. and Levidow, L. (1987) *Anti-racist Science Teaching*, London, Free Association Books.

Hicks, D. and Steiner M. (1989) *Making Global Connections: A World Studies Workbook*, Edinburgh, Oliver and Boyd.

House of Commons (1985) *Education for All – The Report of the Committee of Enquiry into the Education of Children from Ethnic Minority Groups* (The 'Swann Report'), London, H.M.S.O.

Lyle, S and Roberts, M. (1987) *Rainforest Child*, Greenlight Publications.

Lyle, S. and Roberts, M. (1987) *Tomorrow's Woods*, Greenlight Publications.

Peacock, A. (ed) (1991) *Science in Primary Schools: the Multicultural Dimension*, London, MacMillan.

Rose, S., Kamin, L. and Lewontin, R. (1985) *Not in our genes: Biology, Ideology and Human Nature*, London, Pelican

Shan S-J. (1990) *'Assessment by Monolingual Teachers of Developing Bilinguals at Key Stage 1'*, Multicultural Teaching, *Multicultural Teaching, Vol 9, No 1*.

Shiva, V. (1989) *Staying Alive, Women, Equality and Development*, Zed Books.

Thorp, S. (1991) *Race, Equality and Science Teaching – An Active INSET Manual*, ASE.

Troyna, B. and Hatcher, R. (1992) *Racism in Childrens' Lives*, London, Routledge/National Children's Bureau.

Van Sertima (ed) (1986), I. *Blacks in science – Ancient and Modern*, USA, Transaction books.

Esme Glauert is currently an advisory teacher for science in the London Borough of Hackney. She has taught in Inner London schools for 12 years and has a continuing interest in equal opportunities in education.

Steve Thorp has worked as an advisory teacher for multicultural education in both primary and secondary schools in Northants for the last five years. He is editor of the ASE's "Race Equality and Science Teaching" publications. He has contributed extensively to journals on all aspects of equality in education.

Science for All Pupils
Gender Issues in Science Education

Barbara Smail

Why Worry about Gender and Science in the Primary School?

Discussion about the effects of gender in education has focused mainly on the secondary school and on the tendency for young women to opt out of physical science, computing and technology at option time. Not very long ago, it was assumed that this pattern of option choice reflected differences in the innate abilities of women and men, but that explanation has come to seem less convincing as under some conditions girls achieve as well as boys. For example, in Eastern Europe more women take these subjects in the upper secondary school than in Western Europe.

Now, with the advent of the National Curriculum, it is tempting to assume that, giving girls and boys equal access to all areas of a compulsory curriculum, we will see a large increase in the numbers of women entering the traditionally male fields of science and technology. But, in order for this to happen, the science and technology diet provided by schools must be equally appealing for both sexes and women as well as men must see careers in science and technology as appropriate for themselves.

So, why should primary teachers be concerned? Surely, they work very hard to treat each child as an individual and to give both girls and boys a good all-round basic education? Careers and options for A level are far in the future for their pupils. What more can they do?

There is plenty of research evidence to show that attitudes to learning about science form at an early age (for example see Harvey 1977). By eight or nine girls and boys differ in the interest they show in areas of science and technology; the girls prefer to learn about biological science topics, the boys prefer to study physical science. The GIST survey in Greater Manchester (GIST 1982) showed an even greater divergence of interest and experience by age 11 and the Assessment of Performance Unit (APU) substantiated in a national sample of 11 year olds the large differences in experience and attitudes between girls and boys as shown in Tables 1 and 2 below.

Table 1 Most popular science topics for 11-year olds (GIST) project results

Girls		Boys	
Question	**%**	**Question**	**%**
What food is good for you	73 (56)	How motor cars work	78 (30)
How children develop	70 (52)	Computers	73 (47)
Our eyes and how we see	65 (51)	Volcanoes and earthquakes	71 (48)
What makes a rainbow appear	63 (47)	Stars and planets	71 (46)
How a record is made	63 (60)	How machines work	67 (26)
Germs and illnesses	60 (36)	How transistor radios work	66 (31)
Animals in the jungle	60 (60)	Nuclear power	64 (25)
Our ears and how we hear	58 (41)	Acids and chemicals	63 (56)
How our muscles work	58 (59)	How a record is made	60 (63)
Acids and chemicals	58 (63)	Animals in the jungle	60 (60)

These are 11-year-olds on entry to secondary school. Figures in brackets are percentages of the *other* sex answering 'I'd like to know more'.

Table 2 Differences in the percentages of 11-year old boys and girls reporting to have 'quite often' engaged in particular activities at home or otherwise out of school

Activity	% pupils		Discrepancies in favour of
	boys	**girls**	**girls boys**
Make models from a kit (Airfix)	42	6	
Play pool, billiards or snooker	59	30	
Play with electric toy sets	45	16	
Create models using Lego, etc.	50	23	
Take things apart to see inside	38	18	
Go fishing or pond dipping	30	13	
Watch birds	30	27	
Sow seeds or grow plants	30	34	
Look after small animals/pets	52	57	
Collect/look at wild flowers	8	27	
Weigh ingredients for Cooking	29	60	
Knit or sew	5	46	

From 1984 APU national survey data – approximately 600 pupils were sampled.

Do these Differences Matter?

Attitudes to science at 11 have been shown to predict involvement in science education and scientific occupations later on (Brown 1976). If children do not develop positive attitudes to science and technology in the primary years, there is little evidence to suggest that they will acquire them in secondary school and beyond! Girls who are not interested in physical science are cut off at an early age from a wide range of careers. All scientific occupations demand a broad and balanced science education. By preferring the biological to the mathematical, mechanical and electrical aspects of science, young women are moving towards traditional women's occupations which are often low paid and low status.

But all women are affected by the changes which science and technology are bringing about in the world around us. Without a confident grasp of basic scientific ideas, women of the future will be unable to take part in debates about key issues involving health, the environment and the uses of technological developments.

Before we change our approaches to alter these traditional attitudes and patterns of choice, we need to consider what the teachers and the children bring to the situation. In talking to teachers about the problem, they identify the following factors which need to be approached:

- Teachers' own experience of science education
- Childrens' attitudes derived from parents, television etc.
- Current social interactions and practices in primary school

The next three sections look at these in turn to draw out the areas in which teachers need to become more self-conscious and aware of their own behaviour.

Primary Teachers' Perceptions and Experience of Science Education.

In INSET courses for teachers on gender and science, I have been interested to explore teachers' own experiences of science education as the starting point for discussions about teaching science in a girl-friendly way. Insights from our own experiences often suggest new directions and approaches.

Firstly, the statistics and everyday observation tell us that the majority (75%) of primary teachers are women. Most have experienced no science education beyond 16. According to the International Council of Associations for Science Education (ICASE),

> *'less than half of all primary teachers have studied science beyond 13 and less than 10% of teachers of 10 year olds have science as their main subject in teacher education.'* (Times Educational Supplement 1989).

'A' level qualifications in science, if any, tend to be in biology.

One of the groups I talked to reported that they enjoyed biology because the work was based on discussion and their own research. There was a more artistic side to it and it was more relevant. Teachers in training agreed that the key to enjoying science for them was an enthusiastic and encouraging science teacher. They liked the practical work, finding out, investigations and discovering. One group which contained both male and female PGCE students, some of whom had science degrees, had found science in school fun and fascinating. They had also liked drawing diagrams, recording information and the maths content of science. One woman in this group was anxious to point out that she had been at an all-girls school with exclusively female science staff.

All the groups had no difficulty in defining the negative aspects of their own experience of science. They complained of poor teaching, confusing explanations, rote learning and experiments which did not work. They disliked being given a recipe and the fact that there often seemed to be only one right answer.

Several women teachers said they'd felt intimidated by their science teachers. One had been told that she was no good at maths so couldn't do science. Another said she'd always feared accidents when using equipment.

In talking about making their option choices, the groups identified a feeling that girls were pushed towards languages and boys towards science. They felt that the few girls who did science were the most able and that other girls were not taken seriously.

While aware of the shortcomings of their own science education, all were anxious to stimulate interest and enthusiasm in their pupils. These findings have powerful messages for all primary school teachers, faced with the task of teaching science and technology in the National Curriculum. Clearly, their teaching should be enthusiastic, investigatory and provide adequate explanations at the children's level of understanding. Primary teachers value the aesthetic side of science and can make use of this in the communication of results through art, drawing and poetry.

Stereotypes of Science through Children's Eyes

A further potential barrier to positive attitudes to learning science arises from the notions children gain from their environment, from parents, television etc. Some of the data used here was collected during the GIST 11 year-old survey. The rest was provided by a school in South Wales after a visit to *Techniquest*, the hands-on science centre in Cardiff.

In the GIST project, the children were given the following cue:- *Imagine you are a reporter going to interview a famous woman scientist. Describe your interview. What is the scientist like? What does she say about her life and work?*

The first three quotations are from girls and show clearly a number of their concerns about a possible scientific career:-

> *I don't have much time to spend with my family. I enjoy science. The science experiments are quite hard. The scientist said you can never know everything about science. Everybody needs to know science.* F

> *When I met her she told me about her life. When she had time off she would always go to the laboratory. She told me about her new experiment. She has a family but sometime she has too much work to see to them. She has liked science since she was about 10, when at her school she started doing experiments and she just went on from there. I learnt a lot from Mrs Kelly.* F

The scientists name was Mrs Smith, this sounds like an ordinary name but it's not. The scientist was tall and thin and very strict but she liked working on science. F

The girls' ideas about becoming a scientist demonstrate that they see it as difficult and worry that it might be too demanding and take them away from family life. They also show the unflattering stereotype of the women scientist's appearance. On the other hand, some of the boys had quite positive ideas about women in science and their contribution:-

My interview would be that she would say its a good living, it is a good and exciting job, you have to be quite brainy. She's got black hair, brown eyes, white skin, good looking, brainy, you can understand her when she is talking. M

She is famous, she made lots of people better with Interferon. If it was not for Interferon, people would die. She is tall, brainy, clever and saved peoples lives. I think she should get a lot of money, for doing experiments that succeeded.

The lady who has saved many lives is Miss Luisa. M

The ethical issues in science are a concern for the children who visited *Techniquest*, especially the question of experiments on animals. These children also show a strong tendency to think of scientists only as men.

A scientist is a person who mixes dangerous chemicals with other dangerous chemicals. Sometimes he discovers things which are good and help people who are ill and who have incurable diseases, until he finds something which will cure this disease, but sometimes he discovers bad things which could kill somebody.

Science is nearly everything around us. Science is finding out about things. Science is discovering things and trying out new things e.g. sending a man to the moon. Science is finding out more about space and the stars. I think that a dog was sent up to space first, I do not think that they should try science out on animals as the animals live less years than we do so why should they be tested on. Science effects our lives a lot. F

A scientist is a man who discovers cures for illness's and does experiments to find out different chemicals to improve human life. The thing I don't like about scientists is that they use their experiments on little animals like guinea pigs and rats etc. Mind you, what else is

there to experiment on? If the scientists didn't use their experiments on animals, they'd probably use volunteered humans. A scientist would most probably be found working at a university. But a top scientist would most probably never be found by quite a lot of people, only the people who the top scientist works for. I think the best thing the scientists have ever made is medicines because they've saved millions and millions of lives. Science is a way of finding out about life around us and experimenting on cures and things. Science is a very important thing in our lives. F

The children who visited *Techniquest* had met and talked to a male scientist during their visit and perhaps this had influenced their perceptions. Many of the guides to the exhibits there are women, but they had not been classed as 'scientists' by the children. Challenging the stereotype that all scientists are male presents difficulties. In the GIST project, the children saw on average 4-6 women scientists over an 18 month period in their own classrooms, but, questioned a year later about these visitors, few remembered that all the visiting scientists had been women!

Current Practice and Gender in the Primary Classroom

Children as young as five and six years old have well-developed gender identities and see activities as exclusively the province of women and men, boys or girls (Smithers & Zientek 1991). For example, the children in this study saw 'making car repairs' as almost exclusively a male activity while 'washing clothes' was almost exclusively a female activity. Using similar methods, 'being a scientist' was the most gendered of all the occupations included, with a majority of children saying it was only for men.

The teachers of these children were in the main aware of gender stereotyping and reported that girls and boys were attracted by different activities. The girls preferred painting, drawing and colouring, writing stories, the home corner and dressing up, while the boys preferred building and modelling with Lego and other construction kits, being active, using and creating space and football.

Although the teachers knew that these behaviour patterns were potentially disadvantaging the girls, (the connection between working with materials to make three dimensional models and so called 'spatial ability' and achievement in science and technology has been pointed out by many authors (Kelly, 1981) they found it difficult to believe that they could or should try to change them.

In other classrooms teachers have begun the process of change. Browne and Ross (1991) found that even when both girls and boys played with Lego, they used it quite differently. On starting to play, the boys 'immediately and without discussion' gave the windows, doors, baseboards and larger bricks to the girls and the wheels and rotatable connections to the boys. The boys set about making cars, aeroplanes and guns while the girls built houses and used play people to inhabit them.

The *'Design It, Build It, Use It Collective,'* a group of primary teachers in Brent developed strategies for giving access to technological literacy for all pupils(Pandya in Browne 1991). They advocate that construction activities become part of 'work' not just something that the children can choose to do after work is finished. They stress the importance of valuing children's models, not saying 'break that up and put the pieces away now that it's almost home time'! As part of the more formal curriculum, not an optional extra, both girls and boys used construction kits in a wider variety of contexts. Girls will make wheeled vehicles and boys will build houses when the task is set by the teacher as a problem-solving exercise. One example of this kind of task used by the Collective is 'There is a fire in one of the nearby houses. Make a fire-engine with a long ladder and build the house that is burning'.

It was particularly upsetting to see in 1992 at a science investigation event organised by the ASE and the British Association, a team of eight 10 and 11 year olds (four boys and four girls) divide along sex lines. The boys went off with the equipment to do the investigation, the girls set about making the poster which was to report the results! When questioned about this the children said they'd decided to do it this way because that was what each was 'good at'.

The Girls who become Scientists

Given the power and extent of the traditional socialisation of girls in the family and in school, it is interesting to consider the experience of women who become scientists and engineers and try to find commonalities in that experience. Studies have consistently identified a closer relationship between potential women scientists and their fathers than between the girls and their mothers. Many women scientists report that science appeals to their aesthetic sense – to them the patterns found by science in the natural world have beauty and wonder.

A study of girls in the GIST project who were among the 25% of 11 year old girls who were still interested in physical science revealed similar tendencies (Smail 1984). The girls often helped father with car repairs and DIY jobs. One girl shared her father's hobby of renovating old clocks. In contrast to the 11 year old girls who were interested only in biological science, those with physical science interest tended to assign gender to activities less frequently. They saw all activities from ballet to football, from fighting to wearing make-up as suitable for both girls and boys. Moreover, they tended, regardless of measured achievement, to see themselves as good at maths. The Secondary Science Curriculum Review team (Ditchfield and Scott 1987) identified developing girls' self-confidence and self-esteem as a crucial feature in encouraging girls' involvement in science and technology. It seems that only the most self-confident and secure young women, with considerable support to cross the gender divide in activities at home, can overcome the barriers to their success in science and technology in school and society.

Gender and Assessment

Assessment is a complex task and is made more complicated once it is realised that the experiences on which assessment is based are not necessarily common to all and are influenced by class, race and gender. Basing explorations around the 'pressure in car tyres', 'mowing a lawn' or 'wearing special clothes when it rains' has been criticised because not all children will have had these experiences. In theory, the programmes of study and attainment targets laid down by the National Curriculum will provide a common background of experience in the classroom on which to base assessment, but this framework may be reinforced by what happens at home or run counter to it. If certain groups are not to be discouraged prematurely, the assessment of each child's progress in developing science and technology skills, processes and attitudes must focus on the individual and take into account home factors.

We must always ask ourselves whether the child has failed on the task because s/he lacked the knowledge, skill or understanding which is being tested or whether the failure is for other reasons. For example, some pupils may not express themselves well in writing but may perform much better if the test is oral, and vice versa. Others may not interpret the question in the same way as the teacher or other pupils.

In work for the APU, Patricia Murphy (1990) has described how girls and boys may make different interpretations of the meaning of a question. For example, when asked to 'design a boat to go around the world', boys concentrated on designing the engine, sails, rudder and shape of the hull, while girls focused on the interior design of the boat to provide food and shelter during the voyage. Both interpretations are equally valid, but may not be equally valued in the context of assessing the 'science and technology' which the children have learnt. Murphy also points out that APU results 'show that irrespective of what criterion is being assessed questions which involve such content as health, reproduction, nutrition and domestic situations are generally answered by more girls than boys. The girls also tended to achieve higher scores on these questions. In situations with a more overtly "masculine" content eg. building sites, racing tracks, or anything with an electrical content, the converse is true'.

Finally, there is the possibility that the teacher is biased in favour of girls or boys. Margaret Goddard-Spear (1989) gave teachers the same piece of work labelled with either a girl's or boy's name and showed that they assessed it more favourably if they thought it came from a boy. They thought that boys' work was more likely to be accurate and show depth of understanding, whereas girls' work was judged to be more concerned with appearance rather than correctness. In the same study, secondary science teachers, both male and female, said that they preferred to teach boys.

Conclusions

In this brief review of the factors operating to reinforce gender stereotypes among primary school children with respect to science and technology, we have identified a number of key areas for attention and action by teachers.

Firstly, women teachers themselves need to develop their own self-confidence and self-esteem in the physical sciences and technology. This can be fostered by sensitive help from those who train and supervise teachers. Bringing other adults with these skills into the classroom, particularly if these 'scientists' are male, gives the wrong message to the girls about women's competence to succeed in these fields. Although it is difficult to consciously monitor our own and children's 'taken-for-granted' behaviour in the classroom, there are strategies which can be used to reduce the effects of gender stereotyping. The social context of science and technology provides opportunities for practical work and for discussing issues which will interest both girls and boys. The use of artistic methods of communicating the results can reinforce learning in science and technology.

Girls who eventually enter non-traditional fields tend not to see the boundaries between 'girls' activities and boys' activities' and whatever the teacher can do to reduce the division between the two groups will be helpful – imagine the justifiable outrage if children were lined up in corridors and playgrounds according to their social class, race or religion. The girls' confidence in maths is allied to their performance and enthusiasm for science. The assumption that girls' underachievement in maths and science is a natural phenomenon equivalent to boys' underachievement in reading and language skills should be challenged.

Assessing achievement is a minefield for the unwary! Questions need to be carefully framed so that they are not open to several interpretations. The tasks should be based upon experience which is common to all children and care should be taken to eliminate any bias in the teacher in favour of one sex or the other.

To put all this into effect, teachers need more time to reflect upon the everyday happenings in their classrooms. With planning, the changes needed can be brought about, for teachers have considerable power to effect the learning experiences and the futures of all children. To develop the scientific and technological potential of the next generation finding the time to change is essential.

Checklist of Actions

As a primary teacher seeking to provide equal opportunities in science and technology for all children, do I...

- *Encourage* flexibility of behaviour and roles for girls and boys?
- *Never divide* the class along sex lines for:- team games; quizzes etc; to leave or enter rooms; for discipline purposes; for science and technology projects?
- *Praise* girls for good ideas as well as neat work? Praise boys for neat work as well as good ideas?
- *Provide opportunities* for girls to play with construction toys e.g. Lego, Meccano? Do I introduce these toys in a non-stereotyped context, if necessary removing the manufacturers' packaging if this shows girls or boys only?
- *Investigate* with the children how things work? Even if I don't know all the answers, do I plan the situation so that the girls find out some of them!
- *Provide role models* of women and men doing non-traditional jobs, e.g. male nurses, policewomen, women scientists and engineers and women working in wood or metal, men caring for young children?
- *Vet* reading materials for bias and never divide library books into girls books and boys books? Do I look particularly for science reference books which show girls and women doing science?
- *Encourage* girls to investigate physical science topics as well as biological topics and encourage boys to investigate biology as well as physical science and technology?

- *Encourage* mathematical and computing confidence in both girls and boys?
- *Teach* about changing attitudes to *male* and *female roles* through theme work, history and drama?

References

Browne, N (ed) (1991) *Science and Technology in the Early Years*. Open University Press.

Brown, S.A (1976) *Attitudes in Secondary School Science*, Stirling Educational Monographs, No 1.

Ditchfield, C. and Scott, L (1987) *Better Science: For both girls and boys*. Heinemann/ASE

GIST (1982) *Girls into Science and Technology: the first two years*. School Science Review, 63, pp 620-630.

Goddard-Spear, M (1989) *Differences between written work of boys and girls. British Educational Research Journal Vol 15, No3*.

Harvey, T.J. (1977) *Science in the Primary School*. School Science Review Vol 57. No 201.

Kelly, A. (ed) (1981) *The Missing Half. Girls and Science Education*. Manchester University Press

Murphy,P. (1990) Gender and assessment in science, in Murphy, P. and Moon, R.(eds) *Developments in learning and assessment*. Open University Press

Pandya, U. (1991) *Design It, Build It, Use It,* in Browne, N ed. 1991 ibid.

Smail, B. (1984) *Girl friendly Science: Avoiding sex bias in the curriculum,* York: Schools Council/Longman.

Smail, B. (1984) *Factors affecting 11 year old girls' interest in science*. MEd. Thesis – University of Manchester

Smithers, A and Zientek, P. *Gender, Primary Schools and the National Curriculum*. (1991) NASUWT/The Engineering Council.

Times Educational Cited in Browne 1991 ibid Supplement (1989)

Barbara Smail taught chemistry at a girls' Comprehensive school before becoming Research Fellow and Schools Liaison Officer for the Manchester based Girls into Science and Technology Project (GIST). She is now Education Manager for the British Association for the Advancement of Science. She is responsible for the youth activities of the association, which include the Young Investigator Awards

Science for All Ages
Key Stages 1 and 2

Alison Bishop and Richard C. Simpson

In this chapter our main concern is science in the primary school at Key Stages 1 and 2. However, because the basis for much future development happens in nurseries, our approach is to focus on science in the nursery and the early years' classrooms. We will then examine development, progression and continuity to KS2. This approach also reflects our view that experiences in science in the earliest years are vital for girls as well as boys. The ideas and attitudes which are formed here will have a profound influence on the decisions girls make with regard to science in later years.

We offer a series of illustrative science encounters for children which we have found to be effective learning strategies, with some comments on the way children learn science.

We are convinced that children of any age are perfectly capable of practising the skills identified in Sc1, providing the task is set in familiar terms. Activities at KS1 and 2 and in the nursery, involve practical experiences within the context of class, group and individual work, and often involve adults from the local community. But the skills of investigation must be linked closely to an understanding of the child's initial ideas, and any change or development of these ideas must make sense to the child. Investigation for the very young child must be grounded in the exploratory play situation where the child's own individual experiences are stressed within the task.

Practical activities provide a lot of motivation, another strong motivator is story. It is worthwhile, especially at KS 2, to tell stories of the lives of scientists and their discoveries which include women scientists and those from other cultural traditions.

Water in the Nursery

An area such as water play must ensure that the child is being offered a progressive series of problem solving experiences, which can be carefully monitored and planned for the individual child. A starting point could be a simple story such as the Aesop's Fable where the bird wishes to obtain a drink of water from a jug but finds the water level too low. This simple story offers to the very young child the opportunity to use materials which are simple, safe and familiar. Young children enjoy the feel and touch of the water upon their skin and will observe carefully and predict outcomes for the welfare of the bird.

Start with a series of containers of the same size and with equal amounts of water. Even the youngest child will soon shout if s/he does not consider the same amount of water is present in each container. The children can then find objects which will make the water level rise. Although some authors acknowledge the egocentricity of the nursery child, we have found that this sort of activity leads to co-operation. The opportunity must be given for children to work together in order to promote and develop their language skills; an adult can increase the complexity, quality and quantity of this talk. We have found children would remain interested and committed to this task for up to one hour. Photographs of the children working at their activities in the water trough would be useful for assessment and future planning.

Questions
It is essential that adults know when to intervene and have thought about the questions they would ask and have an idea of the kind of questions children are likely to ask. We acknowledge also the need to be flexible and realise that children themselves may ask unanticipated, complex and mind-stretching questions. Do not underestimate the ability of the three year old. In one nursery, a girl came up to the group who were trying to raise the water level in a container with some corks, and commented, 'If you go outside and get a big stone from the yard and bung it in there, the water will soon come over the top'.

The following questions have been tried and tested in the nurseries of South Tyneside. The children were putting objects into containers of water:

- Which objects make the water level rise the most?
- If you put more things in, does the water rise more?
- What happens to the water level if you force the polystyrene down and:-
  (a) keep your hand there?
  (b) let go?
- Place a measure of pieces, such as a cup full of wooden bricks, in one container. Place a measure of polystyrene pieces in the other container (with equality of container and water). Is there a difference in the level of the water?
- If we put the same amount of water in different sized containers and 4 bricks in each, does the water rise to the same level?
- If you have 3 containers – different sizes with equal amounts of water and same number of objects – what happens?

- Which things make the water rise?
  - (a) things that float?
  - (b) things that sink?
- Which things sink, which float?

Activities such as these, coupled with the strong curiosity shown by children, will obviously lead to a variety of experiences which lay down much of the foundation work for study in the area of materials and forces in later years.

The concepts explored in this work would include:

- Some things float, others sink.
- The position of floating objects in relation to the surface of the water varies.
- Shape and mass have a distinct bearing on this.
- Objects which sink displace water and raise the water level.

Key Stage 1   Further experiences with water should be provided throughout the infant school and should not cease after the reception class.

Another exploration of how water behaves could use tubes and funnels, sieves and other containers with holes and leaks which show children how water moves and flows and how, if put under pressure it can move quickly and exert force. Issues such as whether the length of the tube makes the water travel further, and how the direction of flow and speed of flow can be altered, can be discussed.

Questions to initiate discussion might be:

- What happens to the water when you stop pouring?
- Why does the water move when you start to pour again?
- What happens when you raise the height from which you pour?
- If pipes are coiled at the same level does restriction of flow occur?
- How can you stop the water from coming out of the tube?
- Is anything else moving along the tube with the water? (air bubbles?)
- If there is a bend in the tube; does it restrict the flow of water?
- If you pour water in, what happens to the water in the bend?
- When wide and narrow tubes of the same length have water poured into them via a funnel starting at exactly the same pouring time and height, which water comes through first?

Water usually flows in
a downward direction

The concepts introduced include:

- Water is a liquid
- Water usually flows in a downward direction
- Water finds its own level
- Water can break up into several flows
- Water can push on objects i.e. exert a force to hold things up (float).

These activities work towards the NC requirements in the following ways:

Sc3 Materials and their properties
PoS i, exploring everyday materials
SoA 3/1a, be able to describe the simple properties of familiar materials.
Sc4 Physical processes
PoS iii, They should explore floating and sinking...
SoA 4/1b, understand that things can be moved by pushing or pulling them
2c, understand that pushes and pulls can make things start moving, speed up, slow down or stop.

Key Stage 2 A logical progression from these early enquiries would be to develop ideas from 'crossing water'. Work could lead into boats with such experiences as:

What material makes the best boat?
Does the shape of the boat make any difference to the way it moves?
How much can a boat carry?
What happens if we load the boat on one side?
Can we stop the boats from 'falling over'? (Here, the ideas of a keel might be introduced, which produces a force whose effect is to turn the boat back upright.)

Other 'crossing water' explorations might develop from bridges and aqueducts. The poem '*The Owl and the Pussycat*' might be a good starting point to promote children's ideas about boats.
For example:

Sc3/3a, be able to link the use of common materials to their simple properties.
Sc4/3c, understand that forces can affect the position, movement and shape of an object.

Living Things It is essential in the early years that activities include a balance of both physical and biological science. Sensitivity to living things is linked closely to their care. In the case of young children, this needs to be taught. The authors remember vividly the case of the three year old, who, after watching her first ladybird in amazement and pleasure, tried to pick it up between her thumb and finger, only to watch in horror as it was squashed. Her cry of 'put it back together again' brought words of sympathy from the other children. As well as the obvious distress caused to the ladybird, children need to be taught that it can be dangerous to pick up creatures, leaves or other living things and that tools should be used at all times.

Observation

In the earliest stages of learning, observation and communication about the living things which children find in their environment are crucial. Observation skills in particular do not come easily to the young child and s/he needs to be directed to lots of practical activities in order to gain such expertise. These activities, of course, must enable children to use all of their senses, for it is only then that young children will be able to hypothesise and test out their observations. As knowledge and concepts grow, they will influence what the child observes They should be encouraged to observe the similarities between living things and look for patterns as well as noting the differences between things. Children who have the evidence of their own senses will raise questions and check their ideas against the behaviour of living things. However, they need time to discuss these ideas with a listening, attentive adult and also with other children. Explaining their ideas to others helps in the planning as well as the refining process and we have found very young children, even in nursery, will check their findings, review their activities and then develop and extend their ideas. The ethos of the classroom is crucial to this development. Some of the best work seen with regard to the study of living things takes place in inner city schools where teachers have limited resources and materials and yet provide worthwhile experiences for children to interact with living things.

Life and living processes

Activities can arise from various sources but Sc2, *Life and living processes*, tends to reflect traditional biological thinking with particular reference to flowering plants and human life processes. One important aspect of any biological understanding is the concept

- *Structure of an organism is related to function.*

The following approach is somewhat different from the traditional one of considering the organs and systems of flowering plants and people and their functions.

Nursery and KS1

A trip to the shops is always a useful starting point. Here the children can buy both traditional and exotic fruits and vegetables. Buy tomatoes, apples, pomegranates, peppers as well as pineapples and star fruit. The children will need very little encouragement to handle, smell and taste the fruit and some interesting descriptions will follow. Printing with sections of the fruits and vegetables is enjoyable and leads to interesting discussions about similarities as well as differences. It is particularly useful, after the children have examined the fruits and vegetables for taste, colour and texture, to look inside for seeds. The concept that plant life begins with seeds is a useful one for the children to acquire.

Some of the seeds mentioned above however tend to take rather a long time to germinate, which can be very frustrating for young children, who tend to dig them up to see what is happening if growth doesn't appear quite rapidly. It's a better idea to use some quick growing seeds such as mung beans. These can be bought in quantity from Health Food Shops. (See also Chapter 4 for more ideas on growing seeds). Hopefully, the children will discover that plants need certain conditions before they will grow.

In order to extend their ideas to animals (i.e. any organism that is not a plant) it is useful to watch the life cycle of the blowfly. Gentles (maggots) can be purchased as bait from fishing tackle shops. These need only be kept for a few days to observe the pupa (chrysalis) then the emerging adults. So apart from the egg stage they can see easily, and with no problem of feeding, an animal life cycle.

(Egg) ——— Larva (maggot) ——— Pupa ——— Adult.

The concept that animals begin from eggs can be further explored with eggs of butterfly, chick or frog spawn. (See ASE *Be Safe* on using living organisms).

Key Stage 2 Again, considering the links between the structure and function of organisms, an interesting idea is to start with a question such as, 'How do seeds get spread?' We took 8 year old children out for a seed collecting walk in the autumn. On returning to the classroom, the children sorted the seeds into those that were brightly coloured (haws, rose hips), those that might 'fly' and those in pods. We guessed that animals might eat the seeds in pods and fruits, and established the connection that much of our food comes from seeds. We looked at wheat grains and breakfast cereals. An interesting question arose here as to whether little seeds which contain comparatively less food, grow quicker than large seeds, which contain lots of food. We next talked about dispersal; winged seeds such as sycamore and ash make terrific experimental material. We challenged the children to make a big model with card and plasticine which simulates the behaviour of the real seed, but not before they have been encouraged to look carefully and compare the seeds.

It is also useful with regard to observation skills to ask the children to draw what they see. From our experience, these questions may arise:

- Why is the leading edge of the wing in both ash and sycamore thickened?
- Cut it off to see the effect this gives or alternatively make the model without a thickened edge. Compare.
- Why is the seed at one end?

Make a model with varying amounts of plasticine on the end.

- Do each of the seeds perform in different ways when dropped? Extend the idea by investigating dandelion parachutes. Do these really behave like the made structure?
- How do seeds get into the ground after they have fallen? Try putting a drop of water on a wild oat seed. It will twist around and bury itself .

Concepts include:

- Seeds need to 'flow' away from the parent plant
- Plants may need help to disperse seeds
- Animals may be attracted to seeds by their colour.

The environment

We would further wish to stress, however, that any activities of life and living processes should be linked with environmental issues. Young children are interested in what is happening to the world around them. It is especially interesting to note that children who have undergone abnormally upsetting emotional and social difficulties in their own lives can develop respect for other living things and for their surroundings and ultimately, for themselves.

A recent experience in a nursery class is characteristic of the way young children react. Specimens of shells and seaweed had been collected (together with a supply of seawater) to introduce the children to the organisms of the seashore. Shells are a particularly good starter activity since no damage is done to the environment by collections of empty shells which can be used to develop observation skills. A group of children was organised to look at the plants and the shells. Green seaweed was placed in seawater. Forget the shells! A tiny shrimp darted out of the weed and the children got very excited, playing gently with it, watching closely what it did and greatly extending their use of language. They made some verbal comparisons with caterpillars which they had just studied (both are arthropods – jointed limbed-animals). More and more children gathered round attracted by the cries of excitement, it became virtually a class experience. One boy, who rarely settled for long at any activity, remained fascinated for a whole hour, a reinforcement of our previous experiences of the ability of young children to maintain concentration for long periods of time. It remains true that 'chance favours the prepared (open mind)' and much environmental work involves chance encounters with animals and plants.

Recent studies have shown that frequently children assess 'animal' as meaning 'creature with fur' so it is necessary to dissuade children of this by wide experiential work. 'Animal' is simply anything not a plant in the scheme of nature. Fewer children are confused by the term plant, but again, they need experiences of other kinds of plants, eg. those that do not flower.

We have tried to give a flavour of science in primary schools and stress the progression investigative work and concepts which can take place from nursery through to the end of KS2 We would reiterate our commitment to play, from the nursery throughout the early years of schooling, but would acknowledge that children can be in a situation in the classroom where they are active without being purposefully employed in the learning of science. We have therefore attempted to link the play of the child to the enabling role of the teacher to ensure the careful planning necessary to address concepts, attitudes and skills which are to be developed. Finally, we would repeat our concerns that from nursery through each of the key stages the expectations and experiences which are offered should be equally suitable for both boys and girls.

Reference   *Science in the National Curriculum* (1991) DESWO.

Alison Bishop is a Senior Lecturer in Education at the University of Northumbria where she teaches Early Childhood Studies in Science after twenty years' experience in teaching science to young children

Richard Simpson is Senior Lecturer in Science and Environmental Education at the University of Northumbria. He was formerly an advisory teacher for primary science and has experience of teaching science and technology in primary, first and nursery schools.

Science for All Ages
Key Stages 3 and 4

Terry Parkin and Jenny Versey

A Day in the Life of a Head of Science
Period 1: Non-contact

As I return from seeing the technicians, I look through the door of a laboratory. Something is wrong: there should be a Year 8 class here, but the room is silent and appears empty. The room smells of cloves. I soon realise that my first hypothesis, vampires, is wrong: it is cloves, not cloves of garlic; I am a physicist and I still cannot get this biology right. 'Toothache' I think: perhaps someone has been using the wrong brand of toothpaste.

The class turns out to be in the corner, huddled around the radiator, gently rocking from side to side. The sun is out; the room is warm; probably not then a post–LMS ploy to save money. A teacher's voice comes from the centre of the scrum.

'And what happens if we get more energy?'

The huddle begins to rock more violently. Robert detaches himself from the scrum.

'I've evaporated', he says, grinning at me over his shoulder. (Robert would be the first to evaporate I think to myself). He sits on the side bench.

'It's the coldest part of the room. I'm condensing on the window sir.' I nod sagaciously.

'And if we get more energy?', my colleague asks the group.

The huddle starts to break up, with pupils moving around the room in organised chaos. They begin to condense back onto their stools, while the teacher remains in the corner with a watch glass in her hand. Aha! Oil of cloves, particles spreading like pupils! The thoughts in the minds of many pupils seem to appear bubble-like over their heads. 'So that's what she means when she talks about particles and energy'.

However a few bubbles are clearly saying 'I really enjoyed running around the room for a couple of minutes!'. My colleague sees me for the first time.

'Hello; Year eight particles' she says, smiling, feeling that some sort of explanation is needed. Several different work sheets appear to be in use. The 'running round the room is fun' group have a table to complete. I see three headings, 'Gas', 'Liquid' and 'Solid' down one side, with blank spaces opposite them and key words at the bottom of the page for them to match to the appropriate state (Fig 1).

Energy and Particles

In Particleworld	Particles are moving	Distance between particles	Forces between particles
Gas (like steam)			
Liquid (like water)			
Solid (like ice)			
Use words like	a little a lot a bit	close far apart	strong weak

ENERGY INCREASING (left margin, upward arrow)

ENERGY INCREASING (right margin, upward arrow)

© Science Education Development Unit WSCC 1990

Figure 1 Particleworld – data sheet 6.5

A second work sheet has drawings of particles in various materials and supports a second matching exercise, drawn from a different science project, designed to consolidate understanding. Robert's group appears to have moved beyond these activities. They are attempting a range of problems on changes of state.

'Of course you can get liquid carbon dioxide' says one; 'It's mixed with drinks to make them fizzy.'

The teacher sits with this group. She has the gleam in her eye of a committed reconstructivist, and starts questioning them. A recent in-service course reminded her of some of the strategies she might use in modifying the concept models held by children.

Now that I am in the room, I take the opportunity to work with one of the groups. As head of faculty, I get twice as many non-contact lessons as most of my team of eight. We operate an 'open-door' policy and regularly drop in to each other's lessons. I drop more than most. I read some sentences to Stuart and Jane but their understanding fails. I change some of the words and use a clever (?) example.

'How do Eskimos make soup?'

'They would get some ice and melt it, then add fish or something and boil it up.'

'What would happen if their soup kept boiling?'

'It would boil away.'

'So where would the water go?'

'All around the igloo. Ah.'

We work out that the water is then a gas, and in a gas the particles move very fast and have lots of energy (good). There is a big distance between the molecules (excellent). I think Stuart and Jane have the pattern. They record their success in their personal record books and feel ready to attack another problem and select the next work sheet for this theory lesson.

This is a fairly typical Year 8 lesson. They are mostly held in purpose-built laboratories, but, because of timetabling constraints, a group occasionally finds itself in a classroom for one or two of its four fifty-minute lessons a week. Our schemes of work usually contain a scattering of theory lessons that do not really require a laboratory. This particular group gets all four of its science lessons (as two doubles) in specialist rooms. Examination groups are always in laboratories.

The scheme of work for particles is a component of our 'Energy' module and is based on a nationally available scheme. It is closely linked to the Y7 courses of our eight feeder schools and is coordinated across the key stage by the KS3 coordinator, who receives an A allowance. Our schemes are very detailed and aim to support faculty colleagues in teaching unfamiliar areas of science. They include lesson objectives, (based on our interpretation of the National Curriculum) suggested means of delivery, resources, practical ideas, homework and provision for special needs and other forms of differentiation, including work for the more able as well as the slower pupils. Once, after struggling to set 'cover' work when feeling like death (well I felt pretty rough anyway) I suggested including cover work in the schemes; it may have been my most popular idea ever.

Other secondary schools in our area have similar cross-phase systems: in one, the head of science fulfils the role of coordinator, as she believes that the quality of the cross- phase links determines the success of her KS3 results. The LEA has provided considerable support in building up these links, but priorities are moving elsewhere. This 'seed corn' expenditure has left us in a good position to develop them further, but how does this sit with the other priorities of the faculty?

Local primary schools may feed five secondaries; with coordinators in a range of subjects wanting to meet individual class teachers, we continually sympathise with the workload of primary colleagues, (even if we occasionally act as if we are the only school in the area that they send pupils to).

As the lesson comes to an end, several pupils refer to their personalised record books and note their progress for the session. Several record that they now understand particular aspects of the course, others that they need to revisit ideas, rating their progress on a 0-3 scale. These aspects started off life as statements of attainment but we found them unhelpful.

Instead, working with support staff from our special needs department, we have developed our own pupil- friendly outcomes to guide progress and to aid record keeping.

Towards the end of this half term, pupils will be expected to produce a profile in cooperation with their teacher. The profile is expected to be a positive record of achievements and we encourage all pupils to set targets for the next stage of the learning process. For about half the class, targets will be negotiated with the teacher on this occasion; the remainder will negotiate on their next profile. Typically, one profile is produced each half year, as a minimum. Two copies of the profile are raised, one for pupils, which they keep with their personal portfolio, and one for parents. The portfolio forms part of the agenda for our subject review evenings to which both parents and their children are invited: we have found that this arrangement makes these meetings most constructive.

It is ten minutes until the end of the lesson. I thank my colleague for 'allowing' me in her lesson and head for the faculty office. I pass one of our two technicians. She reminds me that two orders are on my desk for signing. We have managed to recruit two experienced technicians, but not all schools are so lucky. Their responsibilities include, amongst other things, stock-taking and ordering. Clear job descriptions help them to do their jobs effectively; they also prevent teaching staff from making unreasonable demands on their time. Weekly meetings of science staff (all teachers, some technicians) help to secure the smooth running of a unit spread over a very wide area of the school.

I sign the orders and note that one is for our slowest supplier, an electronics firm. We now predict our requirements of them and order three months in advance. There is no alternative to using them as we are equipped with several hundred pounds worth of their kit, and can afford only to repair not replace. We really should have looked more closely at this aspect of our microelectronics programme before equipping ourselves through one 'cheap' supplier.

Period 2 Fortnightly meeting with my line manager, the Deputy Head (Curriculum). We discuss the progress of the faculty's review of links with FE colleges. A colleague holds a responsibility allowance for KS4 which includes these links.

I have to meet the Head next Monday to make a short list for a standard scale teaching post: an advertisement saying "suitable for a new entrant to the profession' produced six replies.

I report progress on the implementation of the school's new information technology policy. The move to IBM compatible computers across the school has been welcomed, but we will not give up our older BBC computers, because of the excellent control software and hardware we possess. The faculty will become the repository of the 'Beebs'. I feign disgust, while doing a mental jump for joy at the prospect of a computer in each room. My joy is tempered by the news that, next year, I will be responsible for their upkeep; repairs now take a tenth of my total budget.

Periods 3 and 4: Year 11 – Motion

Or 'Off your trolley' as one of my team calls it. We structure our teaching programme to allow the best possible use of resources. We require over £2500 worth of equipment to teach our 'Motion' topic and therefore have only one class set of apparatus. At present this lives on a trolley which can easily be wheeled from room to room. Increasingly, we are moving children and staff to rooms equipped with resources for particular topics. Close monitoring of costs over the last year suggest that 'things falling off trolleys and breaking' is a major source of wear and tear. My class arrives. As they are working in small groups on their predetermined programme, they collect their apparatus:

group 1 – acceleration;
group 2 – free fall;
group 3 – braking distances;
group 4 – distance/time graphs;
group 5 – "React", a game on the BBC computer designed to teach about braking distances;
group 6; – velocity.

Light gates are set up; trolleys loaded; sand bags dropped. I spend about two minutes with most groups to check that they know what they are attempting to discover, rather longer with two of them. Practical work is reported using a standard format, designed to encourage our pupils to think in terms of Sc1. Tasks tend to be of two kinds. Explorations cover all three strands and are open ended. Pupils meet one of these every five weeks or so. The more traditional 'recipe' experiments also have a place, but these are redesigned to enable pupils to develop skills in one of the three Sc1 strands. We try to organise our practical activities so that pupils can enter and exit them at a range of levels, both for Sc1 and Sc2, 3, 4. Usually we try to keep the number of different activities going on in a room to two or three, with a practical circus being the only exception. This structure has proved useful in maintaining the sanity of both teaching and technical staff. A poster on the wall reveals the 'house style' for reports (Fig 2)

Figure 2

REPORTING EXPERIMENTS

When reporting experiments, use the following headings

Task	an outline of what you have to investigate.
Introduction	notes giving background information.
Variables	list some of the things you can alter, underline the ones you are going to investigate. which ones are you going to measure?
Hypothesis	the idea that your experiment is going to test.
Plan	an outline of your method.
Results	what happened! try to use a simple table or graph.
Conclusions	an explanation of your results. was your hypothesis right? what patterns did you see?
Evaluation	just how good was your experiment? what could you have done to improve it?
Applications	who could use your results?
Teamwork	did you work well in your group?

I check their homework and progress. The group and I agree, or not, that targets have been appropriately set and met. I add several notes to my records, which are a mixture of prose and grades, a more sophisticated form of the 0–3 scale used at KS3. Generally 2 or 3 suggests a good understanding of concepts at a particular level. Too many 3's and I am not pushing my pupils hard enough: too many 0's or 1's and I am going over their heads.

The pupils produce a range of outcomes. Ticker-tape proves useful for studying distance/time graphs, even though our computers can produce graphs more neatly and rather faster. Hands on experience of this material still seems to help a large number of children to grasp the idea of velocity. Data from our invented data base reveals that it is not terribly sensible to be 16, at a party and intending to ride your new motor bike home. This message will be reinforced in our Personal and Social Education (PSE) lessons by our community liaison officer. Good citizenship is more than voting in elections and is coordinated across the school, like other National Curriculum themes. Science is responsible for the teaching of much of the health education theme, as well as a good deal of the environment one, in close cooperation with Humanities. Whole-school planning groups ensure that these are delivered in the most appropriate context.

The PSE programme is superimposed on top of the faculty structure to 'backstop' the gaps and to provide a coherence that might otherwise be missing.

As the end of the double lesson approaches, I receive several pieces of work to mark from each pupil. Typically, every block of about four lesson on this topic produces two or three hours of marking. Sometimes I see rather more pieces than I mark. Some pieces will be marked against strict criteria, shared with the pupils, and carefully annotated; others will simply be marked as 'seen'. Our faculty marking policy suggests an approach to marking that balances the demands on the staff with the expectations of the pupils and their parents. The school's 'Language across the curriculum' policy also guides our marking. Newly qualified teachers find our detailed guidelines especially useful. Quality assurance is provided by different members of the team marking identical pieces of work, and then discussing how individuals applied the policies and our criteria. We require that duplicate copies of marks are kept centrally in the science office. The IT working party is investigating ways of utilising an optical mark reader to reduce the load of marking on colleagues.

The pupils leave the room knowing that they have some preparatory work to complete for the next lesson. There is also an on-going project that they work on at home, and in the lesson if they finish early, on the design of road vehicles. The most able will investigate the theoretical aspects of momentum, but only one or two in a group reach these dizzy heights.

Lunchtime Once a week, lunchtime is used for an informal meeting of the science staff (no agenda) when the team may review some aspect of its activity, or simply respond to a directive from the school or LEA. Once a month, formal meetings occur: these tend to be for planning. Termly, we meet for an extended period to review one or more aspects of our work, a particular topic perhaps, or the programme for a year or longer.

Periods 5 and 6 My Year 9 group this afternoon will be investigating silage! In a rural comprehensive, a rural science approach to science seems entirely consistent with the school's aims for education, expressed through our mission statement, which defines the long term goals for the school. And anyway we can get free materials from the local agricultural merchant, although the instructions on the packets tend to indicate rather larger quantities of grass than my pupils might use. 'For ten tonnes of grass... ' ('Yes Jo, I know your dad will let you borrow his new tractor, but the head would not allow a forty-tonne silage clamp in the corner of the school field!') Increasingly, we make use of local employers, to provide both relevance and financial support.

I have asked the pupils to prepare for the lesson by doing some simple research on silage. We hold photocopies of relevant, copyright-free material that may be taken home by the pupils for planning purposes. Our notion of resource-based learning involves press cuttings in a box, just as much as the CD ROM machine in the library, presently on loan from the LEA. Resource-based learning need not necessarily prove expensive. The pupils' task is to discover the best conditions for silage production. I encourage them to work as a large cooperative group, but with each individual taking responsibility for a specific task. The level of outcome will be determined by what I see, as much as by their reports. Most of the pupils will be given the opportunity to discuss the task with me in some detail. I have to remember to take 'time-outs' to note down my observations: I find it totally unsatisfactory trying to remember who I helped, and to what extent, after the pupils have gone home. Explorations get marked in detail: each piece will be annotated and given a colour grade. (I know, but numbers get boring and all our pupils know their rainbow!)

The technicians will have got out the basic materials for the lesson in advance. (Our schemes of work have detailed technician notes as well). Obviously, the apparatus provides some major hints to the pupils on how they might perform the experiment, but we feel this is fair. Each room is equipped with all the basic glassware and related apparatus, so the disturbance of the technicians during lesson times is kept to a minimum. Some explorations require that the pupils put their lesson requirements to their teacher a week in advance just as the teachers have to do for the technicians. Like some teachers, some pupils find this very difficult!

And after the lesson? As a head of faculty, I have meetings on two or three afternoons a week: my colleagues tend to have one or two. Today, I will change into my sports kit and get beaten at badminton by a fifteen-year-old upstart – well several actually: but it does help to see the pupils in a different context. Tonight? I am drafting an article for the ASE…

In Conclusion

Like most state schools in this country this one has spent the last three years struggling to come to terms with a science curriculum in a constant state of flux. Two major revisions in the programmes of study, and several minor ones as a result of dissatisfaction with a first interpretation of the National Curriculum, have left the school in a position where the science teachers can recognise good practice, but often find it difficult to implement. The progress which has been made has depended on the co-operation of employers, parents, pupils and professional colleagues: the importance of developing positive relationships with partners in the educational process cannot, in our opinion, be understated.

Throughout the changes of the last decade we have been guided primarily by one question, "How will it benefit the pupils?". The case study presented here has tried to identify some of the ways in which secondary schools are trying to ensure that pupils receive the best possible education. Not all of our lessons match the best ones discussed above but schools are increasingly using a range of teaching styles in order to motivate and enthuse their customers; for customers they most certainly are, and schools that fail to appreciate this and offer anything less than a quality product, will not only fail their pupils but may end up out of business.

Secondary schools are becoming increasingly used to the language of the management consultant: 'development plans', 'performance indicators' and 'total quality management' all feature on the agenda of management courses for teachers. These systems offer not a threat to science teachers but rather an opportunity: to develop new skills; and to take part in a revolution in the management of schools in general, and of science departments in particular. It may even be that the next edition of this publication starts with these concepts and then moves on to the classroom. Unlikely? So tell us; how do you know you are doing a good job?

Terry Parkin is a Head of Science in a 12–16 High School having worked in industry and research before entering teaching. He has served on the ASE council and the Assessments and Examinations Committee

Jenny Versey is a senior teacher for curriculum in a High School. She is on the ASE Assessment and Examinations Committee and the Eastern Region Committee and is a past regional officer of the Secondary Science Curriculum Review.

Progression and Continuity in Science
The Norfolk Experience

Brian Betts

7a

A document well worth revisiting in the light of current developments is Science 5–16: a statement of policy (DES 1985). It marks an important turning point, for this made a clear statement that primary science must be a part of the curriculum in all schools.

It also put the issues of continuity and progression firmly on the map, with a clear statement about the need for liaison and continuity between the primary and secondary phases. It points to the need for mutual recognition of the special responsibilities of each phase and to give value to the work undertaken by partner schools.

For many years primary school science was a peripheral activity, often lurking in the guise of 'nature-study', and regarded very much as an add-on activity. This is not to decry the value of the study of natural history but rather to highlight the methodology employed in its teaching which paid little heed to the processes of inquiry and experimentation and generally presented a collection of rather indigestible facts. However a number of enthusiastic primary teachers with an awareness and understanding of the importance and relevance of science in the curriculum, developed process-based work, often stemming from the 'nature-study' activities, which made important contributions to the education of the children in their schools. These cases were, however, in the minority and had little impact in terms of continuity between primary and secondary phases, there being a generally held view that science education did not begin in earnest until children reach the secondary school.

Science 5–16 provided a guide for much of the work done in Norfolk during the period from 1985 to 1990, when a primary science project team worked across the county supporting schools in discovering and understanding the exciting nature of investigative science. Because of the mix of infant, first, junior, primary, middle and high schools, liaison and continuity were vitally important. Local support groups were set up and these were very effective in encouraging liaison activities. Often groups would elect to produce their own local schemes of work and set up centres, in one of the schools, to pool and share teaching resources and equipment. Funding towards this was, when possible, provided by the project team. The idea of the 'science topic box' containing all the necessary items for a particular theme proved to be popular. Team members were very active in schools and with local groups.

Secondary schools were keen to participate but were often concerned about the coverage of science content. To help in this, some set up INSET sessions for primary colleagues within their areas. Secondary schools recognised the value of the work on the processes of science in the primary schools and felt that the heightened levels of science understanding and skills achieved would be a major bonuses to their own work, particularly in the first two secondary years. There was some way to go to reach an overall consensus regarding the content element and it is not unreasonable to say that there was a perception amongst some colleagues that science content should not be seriously tackled until children reached secondary schools. This should not, however detract from the overall effectiveness of this period of development and the excellent work done by so many to build new relationships and share professional expertise in the cause of science education and for the welfare of children.

With the advent of the National Curriculum, these early experiences and efforts proved to have been of enormous benefit. They enabled schools to look at the requirements of the NC and, with liaison structures and networks already in place, to work to the common format which it provides. One of the great benefits of the Science National Curriculum is that it offers a basis for a continuum of science education from 5 to 16 years, both in terms of investigative work and content. It provided an additional impetus to the work of local area groups, removed any sense of 'divide' between phases and gave a greater sense of involvement to all concerned. As schools have continued to work together, an important feature which has developed has been the element of equality of partnership, with colleagues from all types of schools and phases receiving equal, mutual regard.

A particular difficulty which needed to be addressed was the mismatch between the key stage age bands and those of the Norfolk schools: first schools 5–8yrs., middle schools 8–12 yrs., primary schools 5–11 yrs., and high schools either 11 or 12-16yrs. In some cases, high schools receive pupils from more than twenty different middle schools. In other cases, the situation is more manageable with partner schools all being within the same catchment area. A number of high schools receive pupils at age 11 and at age 12.

There was a clear need to provide some advice to help with this situation so, through a working group, in close liaison with a large number of teachers, Norfolk Science produced two documents to meet these needs. Both have since been updated to the new (1992) Science National Curriculum.

In outline the documents work in the following way:-

- For Key Stage two, sections of Sc2, Sc3 and Sc4 programmes of study have been allocated to year 3 in first schools and to years 4, 5 and 6 in middle schools.
- Similarly, for Key Stage three, sections of Sc2, Sc3 and Sc4 programmes of study have been allocated to year 7 in middle schools and to years 8 and 9 in high schools.
- The programme of study for Sc1 has been given equal emphasis for all years in each Key Stage.

To illustrate the principle a sample page of the Key Stage Three document is shown in fig 1.

A further document entitled 'A Guide to Primary Science Development' has been written which covers most aspects and concerns of incorporating science into a school's primary curriculum. This was also produced as a result of close liaison between teachers from the primary and secondary sectors. These documents are widely used in Norfolk schools and have proved to be very effective in support of liaison and in establishing progression and continuity in science education.

Figure 1 Key Stage 3: Programme of Study Relating to Attainment Target 4

Physical processes
Strand: (iii) Forces and their effects

Y7 (Middle School)	Y8-Y9 (High School)
a. Pupils should investigate the effectiveness of simple machines and tools such as pulleys and levers and how they can be used to solve everyday problems.	
b. Pupils should discover that forces can act to change the shape of things, to begin to move or stop them, and should investigate the factors involved in producing and maintaining motion.	
c. This work should make reference to friction and be related to human and vehicular movement with particular reference to road safety.	
	d. Their investigations should include the measurement of speed and use the relationship between distance, speed and time
	e. They should investigate how stopping distance is affected by speed.
	f. Pupils should investigate turning forces and the centre of mass in solid objects, the stability of everyday objects and the action of levers.
	g. They should investigate how the effect of a force applied over different areas results in different pressures, and how forces enable floating and sinking.
h. This work should relate to design and evaluation of structures, for example, *bridges and boats*. [See note in section 3.]	h. This work should relate to design and evaluation of structures, for example, *bridges and boats*. [See note in section 3.]
	i. Pupils should appreciate the relationship between force, work and power.

Letters indicate the order in which sentences appear in the strand.

References

Science National Curriculum: Key Stage Two – A Document for Guidance and Liaison. 1992. Norfolk Education Authority

Science Key Stage Three: Norfolk Science Non-Statutory Guidance. 1992. Norfolk Education Authority

A Guide to Primary Science Policy. Norfolk Education Authority 1992

Science 5-16 a statement of policy 1985 DES/WO.

Brian Betts is General Advisor for Science in Norfolk LEA.

Progression and Continuity in Science

Brenda Keogh and Stuart Naylor

What is Continuity and What is Progression?

Continuity and progression are often regarded as synonymous. This is not surprising, since efforts used to achieve one will often also be effective in achieving the other. But this is not always so. There are times when it would be more helpful to view each of them separately to ensure that they are both being successfully addressed. Just as it cannot be assumed that liaison will guarantee continuity so no assumptions can be made that continuity will necessarily lead to progression. Continuity is primarily about communication between teachers, whereas the emphasis in progression is more concerned with teacher-pupil interaction.

Continuity

Continuity is a continuous process in which all involved share views on aims and objectives, curriculum content and delivery, and methods of assessment and recording. It implies a consistency in expectation of what children can do, and in the use of suitable teaching and learning styles. Without this, problems are likely to arise as pupils move between classes or groups. These problems will be most visible moving across phases (eg infants to juniors). They will also be evident moving from year to year in primary schools and from subject to subject in secondary schools.

Teachers can continue to relate to pupils differently and employ different approaches when working with pupils to achieve common ends. Successful attempts at achieving continuity recognise diversity and build from it to enhance the learning experience of pupils.

Progression

Progression is moving forwards through a defined sequence of learning targets. There is the implication of increasing demand, challenge, complexity and achievement. However, teachers know that learning is a complex process in which consolidation and, at times, apparent regression, play an important part. Progression in learning involves teachers making day to day decisions about selecting experiences in which these concerns are recognised.

Why are Continuity and Progression Important?

Some of the reasons include:

- to prevent duplication in learning
- to promote development in learning
- to maintain motivation, which may be the most important factor determining a pupil's level of success.
- to enable the NC to be implemented effectively by ensuring that there is a balanced coverage of its content and a common understanding of its intentions
- to help provide a clearer sense of whole school purpose and goals which are shared.

Continuity and progression have been a long term concern for teachers and others involved in education. In 1931, the Hadow Report stated:

> '...that the process of education from five to the end of the secondary stage, should be envisaged as a coherent whole. That there should be no sharp edges between infant, junior and post primary stages, and that transition from one stage to the succeeding stage should be as smooth and as gradual as possible.'

A considerable amount of time and effort has gone into the development of schemes of work and individual programmes in science. The value of this can be seen in the improvement in the quality and quantity of science experienced by pupils in the primary phase, and in the movement towards the provision of a balanced science curriculum for all secondary pupils. However, the impact on continuity and progression has been limited.

> 'The introduction of the National Curriculum has highlighted the need for improved curriculum continuity between and within schools' (HMI 1991)

Continuity and progression have tended to be viewed as an issue relating to transition between primary and secondary schools. This is where most successful teacher effort has been directed and where most research and writing has been focussed. It is easy to see why this is so. Primary to secondary transition is probably the most visible and complex situation involving issues related to continuity and progression. HMI (DES 1980) made reference to the particular importance of transfer and other writers have done likewise.

In many situations, however, the transfer between infant and junior schools is no less problematic and from the perspective of most pupils, transition occurs annually. Once we start focussing on the curriculum experienced by the pupils (see, for example, Naylor and Mcmurdo 1990), it is not difficult to see that their concerns will include continuity within as well as between schools and progression from one learning experience to the next.

It is at the class and whole school level that we should be focussing more of our attention. This is not to ignore the importance of transition between schools. In fact, experience of the process of transition and the development of successful strategies are a useful resource to draw on to inform future progress within schools.

Why Hasn't it Happened Already?

A lengthy list of difficulties in establishing curriculum continuity is given in Jarman (1990). It has been suggested that:

> *'the reason that some teachers do not engage in such an enterprise is not because they believe it to be unimportant, but because they believe it to be impossible.'* (Stillman, 1984, quoted in Jarman, 1990. p23).

However, identifying obstacles is simply the first step in finding ways to overcome them! When we begin to look more carefully at the sources of those difficulties, some of them begin to seem a bit more manageable.

LEA priorities

Since LEA's have had, understandably, other priorities for developing science in schools, the schools' own priorities have reflected this.

Developing a shared view

There is still a clear need for the development of a shared view of how learning best takes place and of the teacher's and pupil's role in the learning process. The findings of groups such as CLISP and SPACE have already had a positive impact in this respect.

Idealistic view

An idealistic view of continuity and progression can easily appear to demand a high level of planning, assessment and recording and contact with other colleagues, pupils and parents. A more realistic view would set more manageable short term goals whilst not losing sight of the overall direction.

Autonomy

A move towards continuity and progression can seem a threat to teachers' autonomy. Professional expertise and autonomy are highly valued. However, providing maximum support for pupils' progression in learning must surely be the most important concern.

Contacts between teachers

Within schools there is a limited amount of formal and informal contact in which views on curriculum planning and delivery can be shared. In many situations, it is unlikely that teachers will observe how science is delivered in each other's classrooms. Visiting classrooms and sharing classes are not seen as the norm in many schools. Even where there is a desire to do this, there will be many other demands on the time available. Commitment from the senior management team to the potential value of contacts with colleagues will be essential, so will creative thinking about how this may be achieved.

Another thing to do! Continuity and progression can easily be seen as 'another thing to do'. In fact, continuity and progression will be important outcomes of curriculum development, but only if they are made explicit as part of the process.

Time management Development implies the need for contact with pupils and colleagues. Contact takes time. There is a feeling already that there is not enough time available to achieve all that needs to be done. Few schools have made the evaluation of the use of time a priority, yet most of those who do, find that there are more effective ways of managing their time. However, effective time management has to be a central issue in making continuity and progression an integral part of whole school development.

How much does the National Curriculum Help?

With a centrally controlled curriculum, continuity within and between schools ought, in principle, to be more manageable.

Jarman (1990) felt that the following aspects of the National Curriculum would prove useful in promoting continuity and progression.

- It is a continuous course from Key Stage 1 to Key Stage 4
- It has common Programmes of Study and Attainment Targets
- It uses common assessment procedures relating to common Statements of Attainment
- It uses the same strands throughout the four Key Stages
- The same documents are available for all teachers.

Nevertheless, she goes on to point out that

> *'whilst it may encourage continuity, it will not ensure continuity'.* (p26)

The NC has highlighted the need for discussions on continuity and progression and provided the focus for them. In Bolton, for example, groups of primary and secondary teachers met to come to some common agreement on what the SoAs mean. (Bolton 1991). The need to map out what lies between some of the SoAs has also resulted in some useful developments, see, for example, Peacock (1991) or Fagg et al. (1990).

However, the NC does raise a number of challenging questions which still need to be explored:

- How does the fact that learning in science is not usually linear relate to the ten levels of attainment?
- How can the ATs take context into account? The context for level 3 at age seven is likely to be very different from that of age fourteen.
- How can the question of overload in the NC be addressed?

The Importance of Matching

It is easy to look at a scheme of work and feel that it will naturally lead to continuity and progression. For the individual pupil it may feel rather different. It doesn't matter what the curriculum is like in theory, it is how the curriculum is experienced by pupils that matters.

> *'Providing appropriate learning experiences... requires careful planning and sensitive teaching by teachers with a broad understanding of science and the ability to match the work to their pupils' capabilities. Activities must challenge all pupils and, at the same time, provide them all with success at some meaningful level.'* (NCC 1989 p A9)

Matching involves attempting to get the degree of challenge and success right – for many of the pupils for much of the time, at least. It means seeking to provide opportunities to consolidate and extend existing ideas and skills. Better matching will lead to better progression.

Curriculum plans describe the intended experience for the pupils. However what children learn depends on the interaction between the plans, the teacher and the pupils. Matching, and therefore progression in learning, must take this interaction into account.

Research groups such as the primary SPACE Project or the CLIS Project have highlighted the importance of this interaction. They are currently producing materials to support teachers in anticipating pupils' ideas and responding to them. The 'constructivist' approach which they advocate is increasingly accepted as an effective way of teaching science.

This approach stresses the importance of recognising and building on the learner's existing ideas. Teaching science has to be more than simply providing opportunity for practical activities and explanations to go with them. It also has to include helping pupils to reflect on their existing ideas, to devise investigations to test them out, to review their ideas in the light of evidence and to realise the limitations of their ideas.

These aspects of teaching are difficult to prescribe in advance. Any scheme of work must allow sufficient flexibility to enable the teacher to respond to the pupils' own ideas. Continuity and progression do not simply rely on curriculum planning.

Much science teaching already reflects this constructivist view of learning. Its influence can also be seen in the *Non-Statutory Guidance for Science*. However, this approach does not mean planning separate activities for each pupil, nor is it necessary to assess everything before starting to do any teaching.

How then can effective matching be achieved? A very useful outline is given in Harlen (1985, chapter 6), where matching is described as a dynamic process in which the teacher attempts to adjust the activity according to the pupils' responses.

In this view of matching the teacher's initial plans will identify suitable starting points and will normally provide opportunity for the pupils to share their ideas in one way or another. It will become clear from their responses whether adjustments are needed to make the activity more familiar, more accessible, more wide-ranging or more challenging. The teacher will attempt to reshape the activity or the learning environment where necessary in order to ensure that pupils are given meaningful challenges which lead to development of their ideas. This is shown diagrammatically in figure 1.

The process of teaching in itself allows the teacher to gather some information to use in making judgements about pupils' capabilities, about their responses and about the learning environment provided. These judgements then provide a firmer basis for setting the right level of challenge.

Developing the skills involved in assessment and evaluation will help teachers in matching more effectively. However pupils also have an important role in ensuring matching. Their roles will include sharing their existing ideas; learning to set their own challenges (eg through learning how to ask questions which are open to investigation); and seeing the purpose in keeping the teacher fully informed about their involvement and progress. By promoting these roles for pupils it is possible to help them to take on a greater share of the responsibility for ensuring effective matching.

What about the teacher's role? The responsive approach to matching described above suggests that it will vary according to the pupils' responses, and that it will include:

- Capturing the pupils' interest and making sure that they have the opportunity to express their ideas
- Providing a range of activities and being able to adapt these in a variety of ways
- Monitoring the pupils' responses using a range of informal methods
- Providing a flexible and supportive learning environment

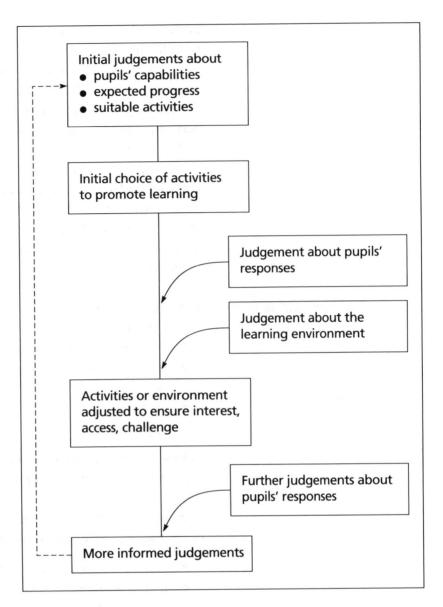

Figure 1 A responsive approach to matching (adapted from Harlen 1985, page 144)

To a large extent these kinds of things go on intuitively. Better matching, and therefore better progression, will come from a more systematic and conscious attempt to take on these roles.

Progression in Scientific Procedures

Descriptions of the expected stages of the development in scientific procedures (such as those in the SoAs) are necessary for making judgements about children's existing capabilities.

However, this is far too demanding to do in a systematic and detailed way for individual pupils, particularly in large classes. A more manageable way forward would be to base decisions on a general intention to raise the pupils' awareness of how to use a scientific approach.

Very young children will often use some aspects of a scientific approach (in discovering that the soap always sinks and the rubber duck always floats, for example), but they will have little understanding of what it means to work scientifically. The long-term intention must be to get pupils to begin to understand what it means to use a scientific approach, until, ultimately it becomes an automatic way of working.

Clearly, getting the pupils 'doing science' must be an essential part of raising their awareness, though doing science will not be sufficient on its own.

The main stages in the constructivist approach can also provide guidance for teachers concerned with the development of scientific skills. Just as clarification, reflection, challenge, application and review will lead to deeper understanding of ideas, so they will also lead to greater awareness of scientific approaches.

Teachers will need to:

- Be explicit about what approach has been used during an activity
- Ask challenging questions about the approach used
- Provide opportunity to modify the approach and to apply new approaches
- Help pupils to evaluate and reflect on alternative approaches

In this way the approach used can also be made the focus for the pupils' attention, through, for example, overt discussion of science skills.

Working in this way suggests a number of additional aspects of the teacher's role. These will include:

- helping pupils to see the need for a scientific approach
- demonstrating or explaining specific techniques when necessary, such as using a microscope or folding a filter paper
- occasionally emphasising different aspects of the procedure
- discussing effective approaches (such as examples of other pupils' work)
- referring back to the pupils' original aims and plans when reviewing
- making judgements about how effectively pupils are using a scientific approach

Many classroom activities provide valuable opportunities to practise using a scientific approach. However, the purpose of the activities must be made clear: if the pupils only reflect on the results of what they did rather than on how they did it then they may end up not extending their skills at all. Doing science does not necessarily lead to learning how to do science.

Progression in Understanding Scientific Ideas

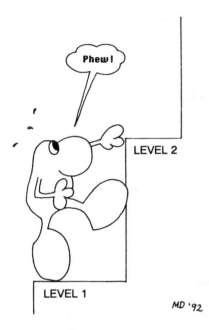

The steps between the SoAs are generally too large to be tackled in one go.

Planning for progression requires a vision of where we are going. A scheme of work represents an attempt to put that vision into practice, so that progression in understanding will result.

In the same way that the National Curriculum attempts to describe the expected stages in the development of scientific skills, it also attempts to do this for scientific ideas. The NC does not really provide the kind of vision that teachers need. The steps between the SoAs are generally too large to be tackled in one go, so that a single step will normally have several activities associated with it.

Some useful recent work describes in much finer detail the possible stages in the development of scientific ideas. Peacock (1991) outlines a detailed sequence of ideas in the area of floating and sinking. CLISP are currently producing a series of guides to describe the progression in scientific ideas at Key Stage 3.

Although these sequences of ideas are invaluable, they also need to be balanced by other perspectives. They need to be assimilated for use on a day-to-day basis in responding to the pupils' own ideas. This raises a serious question: how are teachers to respond when they are unable to assimilate these detailed sequences or when such sequences are not available? Pupils will still have their own ideas and it will still be necessary to make some kind of response to them.

A general framework will help to provide an overall view of how scientific understanding might develop and support decisions about how to respond to the pupils' own ideas. A suggested framework is shown in figure 2.

The section on matching indicated the importance of teachers adapting activities to make them more accessible or more challenging, according to how the pupils initially respond. This general framework provides some guidance on how to adapt activities in this way. It gives a broad indication of the type of activity which is likely to be appropriate for pupils at various stages in their learning, in any conceptual area.

Whatever the age of the learner, exploring will precede investigating which will precede researching . Younger pupils will be encouraged to concentrate on experiencing and exploring phenomena; this is an essential stage in their early development of scientific ideas. Further challenge can be provided by supporting the pupils in attempting to find explanations for their experience and beginning to investigate their ideas more systematically.

Older pupils will normally be encouraged to place a stronger emphasis on systematic investigation and research. However it would be a mistake to ignore the need for exploration. Even teachers will want to 'play' with new materials, equipment or ideas! One important feature of this general framework is the way that it highlights the distinction between observable and

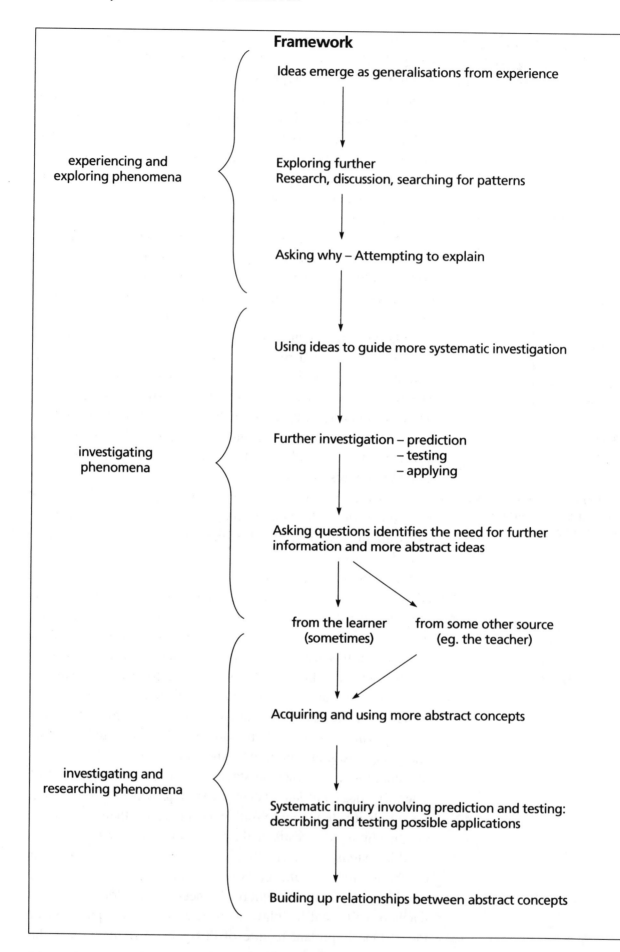

Framework

Ideas emerge as generalisations from experience

experiencing and exploring phenomena

Exploring further
Research, discussion, searching for patterns

Asking why – Attempting to explain

Using ideas to guide more systematic investigation

investigating phenomena

Further investigation – prediction
– testing
– applying

Asking questions identifies the need for further information and more abstract ideas

from the learner (sometimes)   from some other source (eg. the teacher)

investigating and researching phenomena

Acquiring and using more abstract concepts

Systematic inquiry involving prediction and testing: describing and testing possible applications

Buiding up relationships between abstract concepts

Figure 2 Progression in Conceptual Understanding

Some illustrations

Something happens – I see what happens or someone helps me to see I look more closely – Have I seen what is really happening	Ice melts It feels cold, it feels wet... the outside melts first
Does it always happen the same? Can I change what happens or can I see something make it change?	Sometimes it melts faster I can warm it up I can wrap it up
Why does it happen? Can I explain what I think?	When it was near the radiator it melted faster When I wrapped it in the newspaper it did not melt as fast
What do you think makes a difference? Can I change what happens in a systematic way so that I really find out what matters?	It seems to be something to do with being warmer or stopping it getting warm I can measure the temperature, the time, etc. I can try to identify variables
Can I try it in other ways and get the same pattern of results?	I will use bigger blocks of ice/higher temperature/ lower temperature/different insulation, etc
Can I explain what is happening in observable terms?	The higher the temperature – the faster it melts The greater the volume – the slower it melts More insulation – slower melting
Is there more I can find out or is there something you can tell me to help me to understand more about why it happens?	You tell me about particles. I read a book with more information about solids, liquids and gases (I am unlikely to discover atoms on my own)
Can I use what I know to expain what is happening in non-observable terms?	I can now explain melting using what I know about particles and explain why the temperature makes a difference
Can I use the idea to explain other changes?	I realise that condensation, freezing and evaporation all use the same theory
Can I use other ideas to explain a greater range of events?	I can explain ice floating (volume and density) and think about the possible arrangement of particles

non-observable events. Many early scientific concepts will emerge naturally through experience (the idea of solids, liquids and gases for example). Through investigation these ideas can be refined and explanations sought which are consistent with the evidence available.

However there is a limit to what the pupils can discover on their own. Once we enter the realm of more abstract ideas which are not directly observable then investigation becomes insufficient. Abstract ideas, such as electrons or gravitational force, are created not discovered; we cannot simply expect pupils to discover these complex concepts for themselves. The teacher has an important role in providing access to these new ideas in the most appropriate way.

Progression in the development of these ideas will not be achieved simply by providing "the theory". It will rely instead on modelling, predicting, testing, interpreting, reviewing and applying theoretical ideas in a meaningful way. The skills of scientific investigation therefore play a vital role in the development of scientific ideas.

Practical Ways Forward

When making decisions, it is important to be realistic. No one can do everything and certainly not by tomorrow! Like matching, progression is an ideal to aim for rather than something which is completely attainable. We have identified below some of the things that can be done to improve the experience of many pupils.

What can you do with your own class?
Recognise pupils' capabilities

Recognising what pupils are able to do for themselves or for each other is important in enabling you to use your time most productively. Identify something which you feel the pupils may be able to do, think through any implications for your classroom organisation, then let the pupils have a go. Don't expect things to be perfect first time – but it will get better.

Identify the pupils' previous experience

When starting work on a new area, spend time with the class discussing their previous experience in that area. This should help avoid repetition and help to give you some indication of what pupils' ideas are.

Encourage feedback from pupils

At the end of sessions, ensure that there is time for feedback from the pupils. Take this as another opportunity to listen to and challenge their ideas; to get them to justify their ideas; to question each others' ideas, to raise new questions to be explored; and to redirect or refocus if necessary.

Reflect on your learning

Reflect on something you have learnt in science recently. What strategies did you use? How do these strategies compare with the ones you are using with your pupils? Have you asked your pupils what helps them to learn best?

Encourage pupils to reflect on their own learning.
At regular intervals encourage the pupils to look back over work and reflect on what they have achieved. This will help them to understand the purpose of the activity and the criteria for success, so enabling them to take more responsibility for their own learning.

Provide opportunities for demonstrating learning
Give the pupils as many opportunities as possible to show in some tangible way what they understand and can do. A written report, may be the most appropriate way, or asking pupils to think about issues, to answer questions, to provide annotated drawings or posters, to produce a concept map or summarise how their views have changed.

Provide guidance for recording
Making thinking visible is not always easy, particularly in relation to scientific skills. Structuring the pupils' recording may help to clarify what their thinking is. Recording sheets such as those for the 1992 KS 1 SATs for Sc1 may be useful. The intention would be to give the learners the best opportunity to show their current understanding of scientific skills.

Record experience
Achieving continuity in learning relies on knowing something about the kinds of experiences pupils have already had and the point at which they stopped learning. You may find it helpful to have separate sheets of paper for each of the strands in science on which to briefly jot down the main experiences provided for the class. It will be helpful to identify the point at which learning ceased and to make a note of individual pupils who struggled or advanced further than the majority of the class.

Note significant points in the pupils' learning
Speech bubbles stuck into their books or included in folders can be used by you or the pupils to record points of significance to return to at a later stage. This will help the pupils to share the responsibility for follow-up, as well as keeping the comments in the most useful place.

What can you do with the other teachers?
Contribute to discussions
Ensure that your ideas about science are heard. Continuity and progression depend on each teacher's recognition of the approaches of the other teachers in the school and on beginning to work towards common approaches.

Ask questions of other teachers
Ask questions of the previous teacher, eg:

- Which areas of science did you cover?
- Which did the pupils find most difficult /easy/most interesting?

- Which approaches best motivated the pupils?
- Which aspects of skill development need help?
- How independent are the pupils. How much responsibility are they able to take?
- What kinds of records have been kept? Which of these were most useful?

Provide information for other teachers

Have the same kind of conversation with the teacher who will be receiving pupils from you. This time, focus on the type of information which you will be able to pass on. What information will the next teacher find helpful? Are you using a system which gives you what you want and which is able to effectively inform the next teacher?

There are two purposes for these conversations. One is to enable you and the next teacher to have a clear picture of the pupils and their experiences. The other purpose is to enable you to have discussions about, and therefore raise awareness of, issues related to continuity and progression.

Work alongside your colleagues

If you have some non-contact time available, try to negotiate to visit other teacher's classrooms and have colleagues visit you. During these visits you could look at:

- how science is taught in other classes, particularly those before and after yours
- particular approaches or ideas which you would like to try, perhaps with a colleague
- classroom organisation and teaching styles
- the next group of pupils you will be working with.

The important principle is to work with colleagues towards common approaches to science, learning and the roles and expectations of the children.

Progression within a class and continuity within a school are fundamental concerns of education. Problems at transition may happen to be the most visible, and while these are important they should not be seen in isolation. The purpose of liaison is to lead to better continuity; the purpose of achieving continuity is to lead to better progression in learning.

References

Bolton LEA (1991) *My level 3 – your level 3?* Bolton LEA

CLiS Project (1987) *A constructivist view of learning and teaching in science.* University of Leeds

DES (1980) *A View of the Curriculum.* HMSO

DES (1989) *Science Key Stage 1 and 3.* HMSO

Fagg, S., Skelton, S., Aherne, P. and Thorber, A. (1990) *Science for All.* Fulton

Hadow Report. Great Britain Board of Education Consultative Committee (1931) *The Primary School.* HMSO

Harlen, W. (1985) *Teaching and Learning Primary Science.* Chapman.

Harlen, W. (1992) *The Teaching of Science.* Fulton.

Jarman, R. (1990) *Primary science – secondary science continuity : a new ERA?* School Science Review Vol 71 No 257 pp 19-29

Leeds City Council/CLIS (1992) *Leeds National Curriculum Science Support Project* Leeds City Council/University of Leeds

Marshall, P. (1988) *Transition and Continuity in the Educational Process.* Kogan Page

NCC (1989) *Science Non-Statutory Guidance.* National Curriculum Council

Naylor, S. & McMurdo, A. (1990) *Supporting Science in Schools.* Breakthrough Educational Publications

Peacock, G. (1991) *Floating and Sinking.* Sheffield City Polytechnic/NES Arnold

Secondary Science Curriculum Review (1984) *Primary Science, Secondary Science: some issues at the interface.* SSCR

Secondary Science Curriculum Review (1987) *Better Science: Building primary – secondary links.* Heinemann/ASE

SPACE Project (1992) *SPACE Teachers' Handbook.* Collins

Stillman, A. and Maychell, K. (1984) *School to School: LEA and teacher involvement in educational continuity.* NFER Nelson

Tickle, L. (1985) 'From Class Teacher to Specialist Teachers: curricular continuity and school organisation' in Derricott, R. (Ed) *Curriculum Continuity: primary to secondary.* NFER Nelson

Brenda Keogh and Stuart Naylor work in the School of Education at Crewe and Alsager College of Higher Education and Manchester Polytechnic respectively. They both have experience as primary and secondary teachers and as laboratory technicians; and share an interest in in-service teacher education. Currently, they are members of the ASE Working Party on Progression and Continuity.

Section 2: Primary Science in Action

Classroom Strategies

Mike Schilling

Getting Started
Children's learning in science needs to be structured if it is to be coherent – just as in any other area of the curriculum. The National Curriculum Attainment Targets provide a structure for planning and the challenge to teachers in a school is to ensure that the children's experiences are related to the entitlement that the National Curriculum in Science describes.

Timetabling
Planning needs to be shared by teachers to prevent unnecessary repetition and to provide for continuity in learning. Traditionally, planning in primary schools has been based on topic work and from this, opportunities for learning science have been structured.

Since the introduction of the National Curriculum many teachers have found that topics with an overt science theme have served their purpose better – in order that all areas of science can be addressed.

Sometimes specific science sessions are timetabled and the science curriculum is covered in this way.

There can be times – in games sessions or arising out of maths or geography work, for example – where opportunities to explore ideas in science arise spontaneously. One head teacher said that the best science in his school used to happen during class registration before school assembly! The judgment was based on the number and quality of ideas, questions and observations which were shared informally, at that time of the day, in a class discussion between teacher and children. The children would often be recalling out-of-school experiences, from the previous evening.

Whether learning in science is topic based, specifically timetabled or spontaneous, it is essential for the teacher to have taken time to assimilate the requirements of the NC, for the appropriate Key Stage, in order to have a feel for the areas of knowledge and understanding which need to be covered.

Planning
One of the advantages of having a curriculum described for all the years of compulsory schooling is that planning for children's learning in the different areas of the curriculum can have a coherence. This facilitates progression through a school and

ensures equivalence between schools. Children's learning experiences can, indeed must, continue to be varied but the intended learning and the anticipated outcomes are clearly described by the curriculum.

Teachers, familiar with the agreed outcomes, can devise plans for a comprehensive coverage of the curriculum. Consequently, collaborative planning is becoming increasingly common in primary schools (HMI, 1992). The school as a whole needs to allocate aspects of science, from the Programmes of Study, which are to be covered by each year group. When the curriculum has been shared between the year groups, teachers from each year group or KS can work through those parts of the PoS which are their responsibility, to devise learning experiences for their children. The science can be covered by planning topics or science themes. A coherent set of plans, which gives the teachers in each year group a responsibility for covering particular strands in the science curriculum, is essential for the school's scheme of work if it is to provide both progression in learning and continuity of experience.

This is not to suggest that, for example, a topic on Light (Sc4, strand 4) is always taught by the Year 4 teacher nor that it is taught only in Year 4. It is sensible to allocate aspects of the curriculum in this way but it is important to repeat aspects of science work in other contexts, in different years, to reinforce or to develop understanding.

It is important to recognise that this is a description only of planning. Teachers' plans to cover particular areas of work does not imply that the intended learning will always occur. So, the teacher's plans will not necessarily be the same as the children's record sheet.

The plans can usefully be summarised on a topic web which relates aspects of the planned topic to sections of the PoS. The web then needs another 'layer' in order that specific activities, investigations, visits and questions can be identified. Planning this 'layer' must also be the responsibility of the teacher – one cannot rely exclusively on spontaneity if one is to ensure coherence and to avoid unnecessary repetition. See, for example, Figure 1.

Involving Children

When the plans are complete and the learning objectives (in terms of the NC Statements of Attainment, for example) are identified, starting points must be found. In order to generate interest and to provide motivation it is important to start with children's own experiences.

Work on Sc2 (Life and living processes) can, for instance be based on the children themselves, their families, homes, pets and

Figure 1 Part of a Topic Web

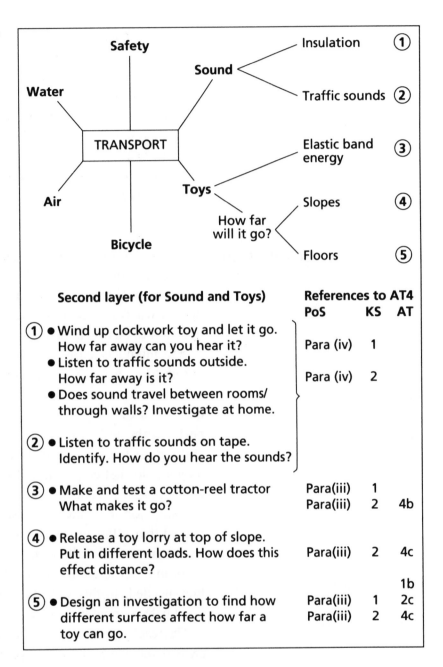

on their home and school outdoor environment. Much of the work in Sc3 (Materials and their properties) requires an investigation of everyday artifacts using the inquisitive approach of an investigative scientist. The work in Sc4 (Physical processes) requires more imagination or 'mental modelling'. Phenomena are observed or investigated (electric current, the effect of forces, light travelling, Sun and Moon moving, for example) and ideas can often be formulated or changed by drawing conclusions from patterns of results.

Many teachers use television programmes and video films as starting points. An excellent opportunity for first-hand experience in which the teacher can participate with the children is to make a visit away from school or to have a speaker visit the school to share some specialist knowledge or expertise. These resources can usually be utilised by the whole class at once and the shared experience can be used as a starting point for work in the classroom.

Having identified a suitable starting point – for example a school nurse talking to the class about hygiene and a healthy diet – the next questions to address are: What will the children actually do?, How should children be involved in science work – and who will decide?

Managing

The teacher must oversee the organisational decisions. For instance, if the children asked the nurse a question which the teacher considered worth pursuing, the teacher will probably decide when it is appropriate for a visit to the library, but the question to be researched remains the child's.

The intended learning will, to some extent, determine what the children actually do. If the teacher wants some children to work at Level 3 in Sc1, they could be encouraged to predict the outcomes of an investigation (strand i) before they actually perform the task. In this case it would be appropriate for the children to follow a set of instructions for the investigation but they would first engage in a discussion of their ideas about what they think will happen. Another child might wish to repeat an investigation to challenge some earlier results because it is suspected that a fair test was not performed (strand iii). He or she might first of all talk with the children who did the previous work in order to clarify the method they used and the equipment they needed. In this way the child will determine what is done practically (strand ii, level 4).

The teacher might decide that it is best to include everyone in a class demonstration or discussion. Demonstrations are appropriate for capturing all the children's attention and safety considerations can dictate that an activity should be performed only by the teacher. If there is a point to be made to the whole class a demonstration is appropriate. For example, in an investigation of pulse rate, all the children might undertake a specific exercise during a PE session, and the teacher could take the opportunity to demonstrate to all the children how to find the pulse on the wrist.

When the teacher structures the learning experiences in the classroom an important consideration is whether children will work as a whole class, in groups (all doing the same work), in groups (engaged in different pursuits) or individually. After the initial session or visit, the teacher might recap with a preliminary discussion involving the whole class. Subsequent organisation might depend on the resources available. For example, if the school nurse is able to stay to work with groups of children in the class, only one of the groups will be able to undertake that work at any one time. It might then be appropriate to organise a circus of activities round which groups rotate. It is not always a good thing for children to be working in groups. A feature attributed to group work is the opportunity it can present for a child within the group to be an 'easy rider' and to contribute nothing to the work of the group. Dominant children can lead the discussion and decisions of the group. It is difficult to attribute outcomes to individuals in the group and it can be important to find opportunities for individuals to show evidence of understanding or capability on their own.

One of the advantages of having children work in groups is that the teacher can closely monitor the performance of some of the children in the class. The inevitable disadvantage is that a lot of the children are relatively unsupervised at any one time. It really is a question of what the children are to learn and how the teacher can best facilitate their learning. DH Lawrence is quoted as saying 'I can instruct a hundred but I doubt whether I could attempt to educate a dozen!'

In one science session, the teacher instructed the whole class in the use of a thermometer. Groups of children subsequently set about their practical work. It was only by closely monitoring the activities of those groups which needed to use the thermometer that the teacher was able to see that the instructions had been misunderstood and that the children overlooked the need to remove the thermometer from its packet before attempting to measure temperatures! Another example of the difference between instructing and educating is the frequent finding from research into children's performance in science process skills (Russell et al, 1988 [chapter 11]; Schilling et al, 1990 [chapter 6]) that although they know (from instructions) how to use a ruler or how to draw a bar chart, for instance, they have little idea about when it is appropriate, in the course of an investigation, to do these things. A teacher checking the plans of a group which is about to undertake an investigation of individual differences or which is setting about recording its results, as part of a topic on 'Ourselves', can intervene by asking 'How are you going to measure the children's head sizes?' or 'What sort of chart do you want to use for the results?'

Sometimes it is useful to provide a circus of activities round which groups of children work. The purpose of the activities might be to apply practical skills in science, to explore ideas or to apply understanding. It can be a useful means of sharing limited resources while still enabling all the children in the class to be involved in science.

After learning something about electric circuits which have bulbs in, children could apply their understanding by including different components in a circuit; they could be directed to try including more bulbs in the circuit and to apply their practical skills of observing, recording and interpreting by considering the relative brightness of the bulbs in the different circuits; ideas can be explored about Earth in Space, for example, by asking questions at each station in the circus to which children make responses by drawing: 'What do you think is the shape of the Earth?'; 'How do you think day and night happen?'; 'How do you think that the different phases of the moon occur?'; 'How do you think the seasons happen?' The 'activities' in this case are thinking activities in which children are invited to record their ideas. The teacher can subsequently lead a discussion based on the children's recorded ideas and encourage questions and ideas for practical investigative work which will test out the initial ideas.

In deciding the composition of the groups in which children will work, the teacher needs to consider whether to use friendship, ability, gender or social and cultural background as a criterion for asking children to work together. In order that activities are suited to individual children's capabilities and attitudes, such criteria might equally well determine that a child works alone.

It might be deemed appropriate by the teacher to organise groups in the class such that only half of the children are engaged in learning in science. Others will be involved in work in another area of the curriculum, particularly if this requires less close monitoring. There have been reports (HMI, 1989 [paras 69, 75]; Alexander et al, 1992 [para 97]) which suggest that integrated work of this sort can be less focused. The justification for such an arrangement has to be related to the quality of the work that the monitored children are engaged in as well as to the value of the work with which the children, with whom the teacher can spend less time, are occupied.

The decision about grouping children for their work in science is likely to be the teacher's. That decision will be determined by the nature of the activity, the resources available, the need to assess learning outcomes and the needs and capabilities of individual children. Flexibility in approach is essential if the ideas and enthusiasms of the children are to be catered for; such sensitivity on the part of the teacher is essential in order to provide for or maintain children's motivation for the work.

Resourcing

If the teacher's plans dictate that there is likely to be a need for some special equipment (for measuring, observing or recording, for example) in the classroom, where will it be put and how will its use be organised?

Some equipment can be made accessible (assuming that it is already available in school) but there will often be occasions (particularly in response to spontaneous questions and ideas) when the teacher or the children will have to search for equipment, or even improvise. Unless each class has its own supply of apparatus and equipment, it is an important part of planning to identify particular needs for specific apparatus.

A class of children was investigating the food preferences of snails. The children worked in groups and each group decided how it was going to carry out the investigation. The teacher's intention was to assess the children's ability to plan. The snails and the selection of food were made available to the children but there were no means of measurement set out. The teacher wanted to see whether the children would choose to time, weigh, or measure distance in their investigations as an indication of their ability to carry out a fair test. In order to be able to make an assessment of the children's observed performance, the teacher offered no hints about the use of measuring apparatus.

At an earlier stage in children's development, it would be appropriate to lead them through an investigation and to explain why the different stages are important. For example the food preferences of two different types of bird might be investigated by setting out the details of a comparative investigation on a work card which a group of children can follow. The teacher's role in this case would be to explain the various stages rather than to ask about them.

Rather as with the decisions about grouping children, decisions about the deployment and use of physical resources will be determined by the intended learning and the need to maintain children's interest and motivation. It is again important to be flexible and to be imaginative, for example in response to spontaneous requests for equipment, but it is also essential to have a regard for the safe use of equipment.

Meeting Children's Needs

Careful planning, with appropriate attention given to learning outcomes, provides the opportunity to make different provision for children with different needs and levels of achievement. Another aspect of differentiating the provision which is made for children in a class is the different interests that the individuals have. Appropriate starting points for work in science can be identified in a preliminary discussion, between children and teacher, when areas of curiosity and interest might begin to emerge. This can provide an opportunity for the teacher to set the work in a context meaningful for the children. For example, work at level 2 in Sc2 (Sc2, 2b) could begin with descriptions of the children's own pets, or of animals seen during a visit to the zoo. This would be a more appropriate context in which to begin to consider observable features than the use of books or posters.

Not only will children in the class have different levels of understanding about the work, they will also exhibit different levels of competence in the process skills. Clearly, the teacher needs to understand the progress which might be charted through a conceptual area in science and within a particular science process skill to be able to provide opportunities for learning which are at the right levels of conceptual understanding and procedural demand.

The appropriateness of experiences to help children make progress in science depends, then, on the contextual, conceptual and procedural complexity of the work.

Having planned the work and made decisions about grouping the children and providing the resources, the teacher's role in the session needs to be considered. The extent to which the teacher is active or passive depends again on the aims of the work. It is important to see the role of teacher as that of enquirer as well as that of deliverer or problem solver.

Being a Teacher:
Teacher as leader, organiser and initiator of ideas

The teacher might take a leading role in the initiation of practical work by providing the questions for investigation or by suggesting measurements which might be made or by designing ways of recording results. The teacher will organise visits and the use of the local environment. It might also be the teacher who organises the groupings of children in the class.

Teacher as learner

Exploration in science (first hand or using secondary sources) is something in which the teacher can be engaged as much as children. Science is an ever-changing body of knowledge and it is unrealistic to expect only to teach facts. Just as a practising scientist has to reconstruct understanding in the light of new evidence so a teacher can help children to explore and extend their understanding by, for example, exploring with them. Teachers have found it to be a useful strategy to pretend not to know or understand (the outcome of an experiment, for example) in order to provide a child with the opportunity not only to formulate a question for investigation but also to be able to devise the actual investigation.

Teacher as guide

The extent and timing of teachers' interventions in children's learning in science need careful consideration. To provide too much direction or too many solutions and answers can destroy children's motivation. So too does the frustration of perceived failure, which children can experience when they are unclear how to begin an investigation, how to improvise a piece of equipment or what to record.

For example, if a child is to carry out an investigation of the eye-sight of his or her classmates, but is not a particularly accomplished writer, it would serve only to frustrate that child to have to spend time making the eye-test chart – particularly if the teacher's intention was to assess the design of the investigation and the reliability of the results (Sc1, 3c) and not the appropriateness of the instrument used. So it would be better to provide the child with the chart or to pair him of her with another child who could competently make the instrument.

One teacher found it valuable to provide a note-taking service to groups of children. The children were then able to discuss their plans, uninhibited by the need to write them down. When they had clarified and agreed their ideas they dictated to the teacher what to record. In this way, planning skills were encouraged, or assessed, by the teacher and not the children's writing skills.

However, at a later stage in the child's development it will be deemed appropriate (or the child might take the initiative) for the method of recording or for the planning details to be devised by the child, without the intervention of the teacher.

Exploring and Developing Ideas

One of the most difficult and yet most important skills for the teacher to develop, in the context of science exploration, is that of questioning. That is, both asking and responding to questions. It is important, in trying to explore children's own ideas, to be able to ask a question that is both open and non-threatening.

MD '92

'Did you notice which was the tallest sunflower?' is a question which invites the response 'Yes' or 'No'. If the teacher's aim is to encourage a discussion about why the sunflower which is tallest grew so well, it would be better to start with a question like 'What did you notice about the way the sunflowers grew?' This provides an opportunity for children to give a fuller, more personal, response.

A further question 'What do flowers need to grow?' does not contain that important word 'You', which can convey a sense that the teacher actually is interested to know what a particular individual has to say. 'Why do you think the sunflowers were not all the same height?' is a different question which is designed to explore the same area of understanding about growing plants (Sc2, 2a). By starting with the question 'What did you notice...' the opportunity is provided for a range of possible answers.

This gives rise to the second aspect of questioning which is important. If a child provides an answer, or raises a question which was not a part of the teacher's planning, it is important to treat the unanticipated idea with respect by deferring discussion until later or by adapting the direction of the discussion or activity to take account of the new idea. If a child reports, for example, that it had been noticed that all the leaves were the same shape, an opportunity is provided for activities which develop observation and classification skills which, although not planned, would be not inappropriate to this activity (Sc1, 2b; Sc2, 2b).

So a response 'That's interesting... I wonder if all leaves are the same shape?' would be better than the blunter, and more closed 'What else did you notice?' The underlying aim is for the questioning to develop the child's confidence in his or her own ideas and to encourage a sharing of all these ideas. 'Is that what you wanted me to say?' is an impression to try to avoid: see, for example, the poem *The Answer* (Ahlberg, 1989).

What happens if... ? Why does... ? How can I... ? When/where will... ? These are all questions which invite a direct answer from the teacher. There are times when this is appropriate and the teacher is able to give the answer. However it will also be the case that at times, although the provision of a direct answer would be appropriate, it is not possible because the teacher does not know the answer. So the teacher has to engage in the consultation of secondary sources, either on his or her own or with the help of the children, if this is practicable. It might not be possible to tell the answer from memory, but there would be nothing wrong in finding the answer in a book and reading it.

It is in this way that exploration in science can begin – by simply talking and sharing ideas. The technique of turning a child's question back to the child in order to explore the ideas behind the question is described more fully by Sheila Jelly (in Harlen, 1985).

As children are encouraged to explore their own understanding they will find that their ideas are challenged. The teacher must judge what level of understanding is appropriate for the child and provide evidence which challenges existing ideas. Discussion and application of ideas together with a consideration of alternative explanations can help to begin to change existing ideas.

A class of children was considering why boats float. They looked at different types of boat and investigated with plasticene shapes in bowls of water. Their ideas included the hypothesis that although heavy things usually sink, they float when they move fast through the water. They had two subsequent experiences which convinced many of the children that it is shape alone which determines whether something floats or sinks: they visited a container ship which was unloading at the nearby docks and noticed that, as the containers were unloaded, the ship 'went up in the water'; they carefully arranged masses in a large ice-cream tub so that it still floated although it contained over thirty times its own weight.

In neither case was the vessel moving and most of the children dismissed this as a criterion which determines the ability to float. The teacher decided, however, that it was appropriate at this point to leave the investigation into the factors affecting floating and sinking because it would be inappropriate for Year 3 children to be introduced to the concept of density.

Developing Science Process Skills

As children's ideas are explored, so ideas for investigation begin to emerge. Children can be encouraged to involve themselves in the design of investigations. Some teachers have encouraged children to use a planning board in order to help to improve their planning skills (Harlen, 1985 [chapter 6]). Children can also be asked to draw up a 'shopping list' of equipment needs which will help to alleviate the problem described earlier of having to improvise or borrow at short notice.

To encourage a critical approach to their work it is valuable to ask children to review each stage of an investigation. When their plans are drawn up, it is interesting to share the ideas so that children might identify areas where, for instance, important variables have not been controlled or that necessary measurements are not, apparently, to be recorded.

When the activities have been completed, the questions and ideas can be reviewed and the results can be analysed. An important skill in science is that of interpreting evidence by looking for patterns in results and observations or by applying existing knowledge to phenomena and results. Teachers have found that children rarely take the opportunity to interpret results unless the teacher makes a specific effort to introduce the skill.

For example, if a class is engaged in a topic on The Weather and different groups are collecting different sets of data (wind speed; wind direction; cloud cover; rainfall; temperature, for example) the results can be displayed after a few days for all the class to see. It is important to ascertain that the results from one group make sense to another group. The teacher can ask questions of the charts and graphs: 'Which was the hottest/wettest/cloudiest day last week?'; 'What links can you see between the amount of cloud and the temperature/rainfall/wind direction?' In this way, the children's skills of identifying patterns and interpreting results can be encouraged or assessed.

Several teachers described the importance of giving children sufficient time: time to design an investigation; time to reflect on its practicability and to refer the design to the original aim of the work; time to review outcomes and even time to repeat the investigation having modified procedures. This sort of approach not only provides for a greater ownership of and involvement in their work, by children, but also develops the process skills which are essential to the pursuit of scientific understanding.

It is useful (both in terms of motivation and in terms of developing language skills) to devise ways in which children's records of their work can be shared with others. Displays and assemblies in the school hall are places where children can communicate their findings. Groups within a class can relate their work one to another; school or class newspapers are a useful and personal means of sharing.

In order to develop in his children a constructively critical approach to their work in science, one teacher used a video camera to record classroom activities. The groups of children (who were not in a leafy suburb but working, as a class of 34, in a school in the middle of a working class town) watched their performance in the different activities after the science session and offered comments and criticisms. They often focused on the way they had worked together, rather than on the science work; it improved the collaborative nature of the group work in the class for that year.

Looking at What Was Achieved

Underlying all the strategies, examples and illustrations outlined in this chapter is the point that the teacher must be clear about the learning objectives. Behind each part of the teacher's planning is a particular intention. In order to evaluate the appropriateness of that planning and to attempt to monitor any progress that children have made, opportunities also need to be found for judging, marking and otherwise assessing their achievements. Furthermore, there needs to be a manageable and meaningful means of recording such judgements.

The assessments that a teacher makes about a child's achievement will be based on the things that the child says or does, or on something that is written or drawn. In order to obtain this evidence, the teacher has to plan carefully the questions to ask and to design activities with particular outcomes in mind.

Teaching and learning in science can require some radical rethinking of classroom practice, if the kinds of discussion, negotiation, sharing and reflection, which have been described in this chapter, are to be achieved.

References

Ahlberg A. 1989. *Heard it in the Playground.* London. Viking Kestrel.

Alexander R., Rose J. and Woodhead C. 1992. *Curriculum Organisation and Classroom Practice in Primary Schools: a discussion paper.* London. DES

HMI. 1989. *Aspects of Primary Education: The Teaching and Learning of Science.* London. DES.

HMI. 1992. *Science at Key Stage 1 and 2.* London. HMSO.

Harlen W. (ed) 1985 *Primary Science: Taking the Plunge.* Oxford. Heinemann.

Harlen W. 1992. *The Teaching of Science.* London. Fulton.

Harlen W., Macro C., Schilling M., Malvern D. and Reed K. 1990. *Progress in Primary Science.* London. Routledge.

Jelly S. 1985 *'Helping children raise questions and answering them'*, in Harlen W, 1985

Russell T. (ed), Black P., Harlen W., Johnson S. and Palacio D. 1988. *Science at Age 11: A Review of APU Survey Findings 1980–84.* London. HMSO.

Schilling M., Hargreaves L., Harlen W. and Russell T. 1990. *Assessing Science in the Primary Classroom: Written Tasks.* London. Chapman.

Other useful reading

Harlen W. and Jelly S. 1989. *Developing Science in the Primary Classroom.* Edinburgh. Oliver and Boyd.

Hodgson B. and Scanlon E. (eds) 1985. *Approaching Primary Science.* Chapman.

Raper G. and Stringer J. 1987. *Encouraging Primary Science.* London. Cassell.

Mike Schilling taught in Leicestershire primary schools, then was appointed as Lecturer in Primary Science at Leicester University. He is currently a research fellow and deputy director at the Centre for Research in Primary Science and Technology (CRIPSAT) at Liverpool University.

9 Integrating Assessment into the Curriculum

Anne Foden

Setting the Scene

Assessment is a word which causes a multitude of different reactions, which tend to be coloured by our own previous experience and very few of which are positive. Many people, particularly in primary schools, feel that it is something very new that has been imposed with the National Curriculum and which is getting in the way of allowing us to get on with the job of educating children. In fact it is not new; it has always been at the heart of good primary teaching. Teachers have constantly made on-going assessments of children's reactions, responses and achievements in order to inform them about what experiences or tasks each child needs to attempt next.

What is new about assessment within the NC is that it is criterion referenced – we are assessing children's work against certain given criteria. Although the changes have been quite major, they are evolutionary rather than revolutionary. We are now required to externalise much of what we intuitively know as a result of our everyday experience of working with the children. This is the information that we are often unaware we have collected until we stand back and reflect on a child's progress.

Our professional instincts about a child's achievement arise from the accumulation of information both on conscious and intuitive levels. In the past we have gathered all this information without necessarily sifting out the useful parts. The skills of assessment we are currently developing should help us in this sifting process, which in turn will help us to be more selective in what we gather. The intuitive knowledge still has a vital part to play, but the process of matching achievement to specific criteria should help us to build a more objective view of a child's achievements.

Assessment informs us about children's learning and helps us to plan the next steps. It also enables us to provide a summary of a child's progress in all areas of learning. Within the NC, it helps us to map progress with reference to statements of attainment and use appropriate parts of the Programmes of Study to plan the next learning experiences. Assessment is a tool to be made use of – it is not something to be done for its own sake. We use the information gained for summative reports, planning learning, diagnosing needs and problems. This does not imply that all the assessment has to be formally carried out and recorded. There is still a vital role for informal, incidental assessment. It is essential to use information from a wide variety of sources in building up a rounded picture of a child's achievements. This will be explored in more detail later in the chapter.

The Integral Nature of Assessment

It is essential that assessment continues to be an integral part of teaching and learning. If this ceases to be the case then assessment ceases to be useful.

> *"The assessment process itself should not determine what is to be taught and learned."* National Curriculum Task Group on Assessment and Testing report, 1987

It is vitally important that we remember this. We teach children far more than can be assessed. Therefore we must assess what we value as part of children's education, not give value only to that part we assess.

It is equally important to ensure that assessment is not a bolt-on addition at the end of a period of time or learning package. It needs to be planned into children's learning experiences and be an integral part of what we, as teachers, do each day with children.

Much assessment in primary schools prior to the introduction of NC was informal and incidental. It was often very difficult to identify all the sources of information or evidence leading to judgments about children's abilities and achievements, but teachers were using these judgments constantly in deciding the next steps for a child. However we were not used to making assessments relating to specific criteria. Internalising the criteria is a long job, particularly when they are regularly revised. However once they are internalised much of the assessment will occur incidentally, without needing the detail of planning it currently requires.

Figure 1. The inter-linking of planning, teaching/learning, assessment and recording.

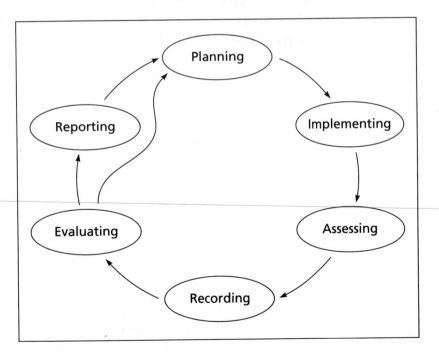

National Curriculum Task Group on Assessment and Testing report (TGAT)

This report provided the framework and laid down the criteria for assessing NC. The report advocated that:

- *The system should be criterion-referenced. This means that the decisions about an individual child's achievement are made with respect to given criteria, irrespective of the performance of other children.*
- *The system should give some continuity to a child's assessment throughout their years of education. In NC, a child will achieve the criteria which define a particular level (in any Attainment Target) and will then be working towards achieving the criteria that define the next level. Thus the lines of progression will be clear.*
- *There should be a common language so that assessments can be discussed, compared and shared. This process of moderation will lead to a common understanding of their meaning, which will in turn lead to common standards.*
- *The outcomes of the assessment process should be used to inform the decisions about the child's next steps of learning. Thus the system needs to be formative.*

Legal requirements

At present we are required to make two types of assessment of children's achievements – on-going Teacher Assessment (TA) and towards the end of a key stage, Standard Assessment Task (SATs).

By September 1994, all children in Key Stages 1 and 2 will be assessed by Teacher Assessment and given SATs during Years 3 and 6.

Teacher Assessment and Standard Assessment Tasks

Both types of assessment have vital contributions to make in building up a picture of the child's achievement. It is necessary not to lose sight of the positive aspects of both despite the teething problems.

Table 1: Aspects of assessment

Teacher Assessment	Standard Assessment Task
On-going, formative	Summative
Contributes to an ever-changing picture built up over time	Snapshot of small parts of the whole picture, taken at one particular time
Integral part of normal work	Externally imposed
Danger of only seeing the expected	Possibility of seeing the unexpected
Assesses more than National Curriculum and Statements of Attainment	Assesses a restricted number of Statements of Attainment only

This is a rather simplified view, but it is important to remember that a SAT, however well-structured, is only telling us about a child's achievement at a particular moment in time. TA, because of its continuous nature, tells us more about the pattern of progress and enables us to decide when a child has fully grasped something and when further consolidation is needed. It is also concerned with greater detail than that given by the SoAs.

TA can also assess some aspects of a child's achievement which it is not possible to assess in any other way. The child's attitudes are one example of this. We build up an impression of these over time. This must be treated cautiously, because children do respond differently with different teachers and in different situations, However they are an important part of the picture of a child's progress.

There is always a danger of seeing what we expect to see. No matter how hard we try, our expectations are influenced, to a greater or lesser extent, by our previous knowledge and experience. An externally written task can give us the opportunity to be surprised by a child – either by the unexpected achievement or by unanticipated problems.

It is also vital that TA contributes to any summative assessment. Clearly the greater knowledge it gives us of a child's achievements must play a part in the End of Key Stage Summary. This summary cannot be adequately made from the results of externally imposed assessment alone.

Having established the background against which assessment is taking place, I now wish to focus on some of the practicalities of carrying out TA.

Planning Assessment

I have already indicated the importance of planning assessment as an integral part of the whole process of teaching and learning. The following may seem obvious but I think it is helpful to keep some basic practicalities at the fore-front. Otherwise it is easy to get overwhelmed by each new initiative as it hits us and lose sight of what we are really about – helping children to develop skills, acquire knowledge and gain concepts.

- Identify learning outcomes
- Identify contexts
- Identify learning activities
- Identify assessment opportunities in the learning activities

    From the learning objectives, identify those activities intended for use for assessment and the children who will be assessed. It is not possible, or appropriate, to assess all the children during every activity – a few children a day and some activities, not all.

- Identify criteria available for assessment.

  This must not preclude any incidental or unexpected assessments. We must leave room in our planning for this. The criteria are not restricted to SoAs. The statements will be a significant part but we must not forget the areas that are not represented by SoAs. Sometimes, only part of SoA will be present in the activity. For example, knowledge of the simple properties of sound and light (Sc4/1c) will not be shown in one activity.

- Select criteria to be used

A wide range of criteria will be available within any learning activity. The selection of a manageable number to use is vital. When selecting these from within the identified ATs there are several important points to bear in mind:

- Choose those that will be obvious and fit comfortably and naturally into the planned activity. It is always possible to find more and more SoAs that might be present in the activity but this results in overload in both content and time.

- Do not repeatedly re-assess the same SoAs with the same children – unless a child has made significant developments since the previous assessment.

- Keep the number of SoAs small. The precise number will depend on their nature and the activity.

- Some only occur occasionally, e.g. electricity, and therefore need to be assessed whenever the opportunity arises.

- Others occur regularly, (e.g. measuring), and allow much more flexibility on deciding who to assess, when to assess and how frequently.

- Others are present constantly, (e.g. observing), and it is likely that assessments of these will occur incidentally when a child shows a significant development.

However assessment of such statements must not be forgotten.

- Plan activities for other children
- Carry out the activity

  Effective classroom management must underpin the assessment process. Therefore, it is very important that our planning takes into account the children's ability to work independently, the organisation of resources within the classroom, the support available within the classroom and the children's respect of each others' needs.

- Share outcomes

  Having carried out the activity, if appropriate, the achievement needs to be shared with the child. This may be quite informal ("You used that magnifier very well" or "I'm pleased you were able to decide to use that size container without anybody else suggesting it"), or it may be more formal as part of the review process involved in the Records of Achievement.

- Evaluate and use to plan next steps

Whether or not the assessment outcomes are shared with the children they will influence plans for future learning activities.

If this does not happen then the assessment has been purely for the sake of assessment – there are too many demands on us for this to be acceptable.

Remember – if the assessment is not useful then it is not worth making.

Evidence

There are many ways of making assessments and various types of evidence are collected in the process. "Evidence" may sound rather legalistic, but I prefer to interpret it as anything that informs our assessment. This includes what the child has done, said, drawn, written, reported verbally, recorded on the computer, produced as an end-product, etc. Clearly, different types of evidence will be produced by different activities and indeed by different children carrying out the same activity. For example, a group of children observing and classifying minibeasts may produce drawings, charts, photographs, descriptive writing or describe their work to another group of children. All these could show achievement of "being able to sort familiar living things into broad groups according to observable features", (Sc2, 2b).

Methods of Assessment

Assessment opportunities will present themselves in many different situations. Consideration needs to be given to the most effective techniques to use in these various situations.

On some occasions it will be necessary to observe the children working, focussing on what they do and the conversations they have during the activity. For example, this would be the most appropriate way to assess children's ability to observe closely or make a simple electrical circuit.

At other times, it will be necessary to ask open-ended questions in order to allow the children to show their understanding and knowledge. For example, to establish whether or not children can link their observations with their predictions, or establish criteria used for sorting living things into broad groups. It is often necessary to question children in order to confirm their understanding and knowledge – for example, when their awareness of the dangers associated with electricity is being assessed.

On other occasions, the assessment can be made from the work produced on paper after an activity, whether it be written, graphical or drawn, or from a verbal account of the processes undertaken by the children. The written evidence does not necessarily need to be a straight account. Often, for example, a creative piece of writing or a comic strip can show the child's understanding very clearly.

Many science activities require a mixture of observing, questioning and looking at the end product in order to make assessments. We must always remember that what children put on paper does not necessarily reflect their level of understanding. Whilst we must not neglect the development of recording skills, we must also credit the more complex understanding shown by children through conversation, questioning and activity. For example, when assessing the grouping of materials it is possible to ask the child to record the outcome of their grouping. It is also desirable to look at the end result of this activity and question the children in order to establish their understanding. Children need to be given the opportunity to demonstrate their achievements and the method of assessment used should reflect this. This highlights the important contribution Teacher Assessment has to make to the summative assessments as it gives a broader picture than can necessarily be shown in a Standard Assessment Task.

I have vivid memories of observing a 6 year old experimenting with balls made of different materials and the effect of putting them in water. He repeatedly tried the sponge ball to see how it would behave – he squashed it and put it in water, placed it on the surface, squashed it under water, held it under the water and so on. He was unable to write or even verbalise what he was doing, but the concentration and the wish to investigate his own personal theory were clearly shown by his behaviour. He was raising questions in his own mind and searching for an answer. This was a significant achievement for a child who was, at that time, unable to show any achievement on paper.

It also contributes to the achievement of two statements of attainment. Sc1, 2b (carry out an investigation in which he makes a series of related observations) as shown by the systematic way he was investigating and Sc1, 2c (uses his observations to support conclusions and compare what he has observed with what he expected). The fact that although the outcome puzzled him he carried on investigating shows that he was comparing observations with expectations.

Asking children the right question is important in the process of making assessments. Too often we narrow our questions in such a way as to prevent children from communicating their knowledge and understanding. It is well worth spending some time developing the skill of open-ended questioning.

How Many Times?

In making assessments the question "how many times" is often asked. There is no clear answer to this. It is a matter of professional judgment. Firstly we are assessing the child at a particular time. An assessment a week, a month or a year later may yield a different outcome. There are no guarantees against this. Children will not always continue to know or be able to do something which they have been assessed as having achieved previously. This is the nature of learning – we cannot remember everything we have learnt, although once given a reminder we may recall it fairly easily. However we, as teachers, cannot be constantly re-assessing the same parts of the curriculum. We need to record what we judge about a child's achievement at that time and accept that is all we are able to do.

By building up a picture of a child's achievements over time, from a variety of evidence, we can develop a more rounded picture of that child's achievements. We need also to make decisions about the way forward for that child. These are decisions that have always been at the heart of teaching and, as such, we must not forget them in the clamour of levels and SoAs.

Our knowledge of the child helps us to make a judgment about the reliability of the assessment. We know whether the child is likely to give a different answer, or perform differently each time or whether they tend to be consistent in the area being assessed. This knowledge informs us about whether or not there is a need to re-assess the child's achievements.

Building a Picture

It is also important to remember the limits of each type of assessment. Writing does not generally reflect the child's full understanding, particularly at the stage where a child is still developing basic skills in writing. Conversations may not always reflect a child's whole understanding either, unless some time is spent probing fairly deeply, some children mimic others' words without understanding what they say. Sometimes it is not possible to disentangle individual's contributions within a group and assessments must be recorded for the whole group. Other children are sometimes unable to show their achievement because of the chemistry of the group. We need to collect several different parts of the picture, over a period of time and build up a rounded view of the child's achievements. This is at the heart of continuous, formative assessment.

Recording Assessments

Having made our assessments, we now must record them. It is impossible to record everything, We only need to record that which will be useful at a later date.

We are required to record progress through the NC and, I suggest, we need to keep records of children's achievement of

SoAs. The most workable way to do this is by using the words as a chart (rather like the NCC poster) and highlighting, or colouring, each SoA or part of it, as it is achieved. If a colour code is used for each year, dating is probably unnecessary.

This system will show areas where children may achieve highly at an early age and will highlight any unevenness in development, or potential areas that need changing in the National Curriculum science document. It enables us to show where a child is in relation to specific criteria, not merely as a number or a level.

I also suggest that we need to keep the science strands separate for recording purposes. The strands of progression are then clearly identified which should make both using and completing the records much more efficient. The NCC poster illustrates the different areas of science very clearly.

Recording of context is also important. It may often be possible to do this for groups of children rather than individuals.

We must not lose sight of the fact that children don't grow more quickly if we measure them more frequently. Assessment is not a mark on a piece of paper. The best evidence is the child itself. We must also remember that NC is a minimum framework, not a constraining straitjacket. If we feel it is important to record more than the NC, e.g. attitudes, skill development, then we are free to do so, in whatever manner we feel is appropriate.

We cannot record all our observations of children. One of the most useful strategies I have heard suggested is to start by recording the unusual or unexpected. We remember the normal, but when a child does not achieve as expected we need to remind ourselves and use this information to adapt our plans. We need to consider carefully what it is useful to record. I think this is best achieved by starting with a minimal record and building it up as it is felt necessary. In other words consider noting the abnormal, rather than the normal. If we record a child's outstanding achievement or unexpected area of difficulty, we may not act on it the first time; but by the second or third recording we will bring it to the top of our priority list and respond as necessary. We will remember the normal developments but we must be careful not to lose sight of the outstanding achievements or unexpected difficulties.

Positive Aspects of Standard Assessment Tasks

Whilst not wishing to give the impression that the tasks are without a variety of teething problems, I do wish to draw attention to the positive benefits of these tasks and their administration. I do feel that they have helped to develop a range of assessment skills for the teachers who have administered (and survived!) them.

They have helped us to interpret statements of attainment and developed our understanding of the range of acceptable evidence. They have helped us consider children's achievements in a slightly different way, given us some insight into children's thought processes and sharpened our questioning skills.

Not all of these are directly attributable to the Standard Assessment Tasks; some are a result of spending extended periods of time working with a small group of children.

The tasks also have a place in informing continuous TA. They can add another part to the picture.

Evaluation

Evaluation links assessment to planning teaching and learning. It has two purposes. One is concerned with evaluating the process summatively in order to inform reports on the child's progress; the other is concerned with evaluating on a more on-going basis in order to inform the planning of the next steps. It is the latter purpose which I am considering here.

Much of evaluation happens in a very informal way as a normal part of the day-to-day interaction between teacher and child. There are occasions when a more formal evaluation may be useful. In assessing a child's progress against specific SoAs, it is likely that in most cases the child will achieve as expected. But, there are also occasions when a child either achieves more than was expected or experiences difficulty when none was anticipated. In these cases the planned work can be adjusted accordingly.

Some teachers use evaluation techniques when planning a new area of work. They give the children a task (practical, written or spoken) in order to establish what they already understand. There is a variety of techniques available to help with this process – for example, concept mapping, work from the Children's Learning in Science Project (CLISP) and the Science Processes and Concept Exploration (SPACE) project. Having established the children's initial understanding, teachers are then able to plan for children to develop their understanding further.

Evaluation should also consider the appropriateness of the task for the child. It is not just a matter of saying "that went well", but is also about trying to identify the successful elements. These can be many and varied – the context caught the children's interest, the level of knowledge required was appropriate, the challenge was within their reach, etc.

Another aspect of evaluation is the process of reviewing which is undertaken as part of the process of Records of Achievement. This ensures that the child is an integral part of the whole process. The end product of the review process is the setting of targets. These targets then themselves become part of the next review with the child. This process also ensures that the child has a clear picture of what is expected and understands what constitutes achievement. All these are different and very important aspects of evaluation.

The essential ingredient for successful teaching and learning is the integrated nature of the whole process of planning, teaching, assessment and recording. None of the parts can exist effectively without the others. This is true no matter what legal requirements we have to fulfil – it is at the heart of successful education.

And finally...

The main points outlined in this chapter are re-stated.

- We know about many of a child's achievements intuitively. We need to formalise part of this knowledge and National Curriculum gives us a framework to start this process.
- Assessment is not something which takes place in isolation. It is part of the cyclical process involving planning, teaching and evaluation.
- The way forward is up to us as professionals. We must use our professional skills in developing the system we have in order to make it manageable and useful.

References

Children's Learning in Science project, University of Leeds

Primary SPACE (Science Processes and Concept Exploration) Project, Centre for Research in Primary Science and Technology, University of Liverpool and Centre for Educational Studies, King's College London

HMSO (1992), *Assessment Recording and Reporting,* A report by H M Inspectorate on the second year, 1990–1

Department of Education and Science and the Welsh Office (1987), *Task Group on Assessment and Testing,* A Report

Cheshire Unit of Pupil Assessment, *Primary Records of Achievement STAIR project*

SEAC (1991), *Teacher Assessment Packs A, B, C*

HMSO (1991,1992), *Standard Assessment Tasks*

Elstgees, Jos , *The right question at the right time* (from *Taking the plunge,* edited by Wynne Harlen)

National Primary Centre, Westminster College, Oxford

Science in the National Curriculum (1991) DES

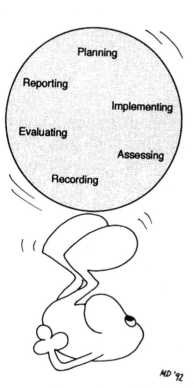

Planning
Reporting
Implementing
Evaluating
Assessing
Recording

MD '92

The assessment cycle

Anne Foden was a primary teacher for ten years and then an ESG advisory teacher for primary science and technology. She is currently a district assessment co-ordinator in Cheshire. She is a member of ASE's Assessment and Examinations Committee and a member of the SEAC science committee.

Providing Resources for Primary Science

Kevin Hunn

Being Resourceful
An Introduction

The terms 'scientific approach' and 'common sense' share a great deal. They both require observations, consideration of ideas and needs, questions to be asked and focussed , considered actions, interpretations and evaluations. Managing resources is largely common sense, so in theory, a firm grasp of the scientific approach should equip us to be good managers. However, a difficulty arises because many of the variables are outside our control. There is usually insufficient time and support for preparing and developing materials, limited space for storage and use, limited money to maintain and develop, and insufficient adult support to enable each child to develop in the way we would wish.

You may be pleased to know that the intention of this chapter is not to reinforce negative thoughts and add to the depression. On the contrary it should help to explore possibilities, extend the range of the variables and give some useful ideas along the way. I hope you have time to read it!

When we talk of resources we often think of the equipment and materials for investigations. However this chapter examines resources in the broader sense: the amount of time we have, the space for activities and storage, the people who can help, the places we might visit, the choice of printed materials and the money available for improved use of resources. Most important of all it examines our role as the main resource and ways in which we can be resourceful. The Collins dictionary definition of resourceful is: 'Ingenious, capable, full of initiative especially in dealing with difficult situations'. The questions we ask ourselves and the decisions we make have a large effect, however limited our parameters.

Three questions which may help are:

- What do we have already?
- How do we use the resources?
- What needs to be done?

Whole School Policy Decisions

The principles adopted by a teacher and the school will greatly influence decisions, therefore in any review of resource use, it is probably as well to begin with examination of first principles and to reach agreement at the whole school level. The following questions, largely common sense, may help in policy discussions:

- Who should decide what resources are needed?
- What priority is to be given to science resources ?
- A whole school review of science resources will inform policy decisions.

School Resource Review

Before any large scale development of Science resources can be made, it is a good idea to review what resources are in the school and how they are used.

Resources available for science

Time will be saved if a resources sheet is given to staff. It might look like this:

resource	no. in stock	location	cost	quantity	no. needed	date	checked

Resources held centrally can be entered on a similar list. There are several advantages to this system. It can

- help to pinpoint needs
- be used as a basis for updating as new resources arrive .
- be very useful when planning activities – you know what is available.

If placed on a spreadsheet (e.g. Works) this list can be used to print out in a number of formats, identify needs rapidly, calculate costs, produce lists for ordering and has the bonus of being very easy to update.

Other questions to ask of all teachers are:

- How do we meet other needs which arise during science based activities? (e.g. – for measuring equipment, communication materials, construction materials and tools, structured play equipment, IT software and hardware, audio-visual materials)
- Who comes in to work with the children? How much are visitors used in the school at present?
- Where do we take the children? (habitats, workplaces, etc.)
- What printed materials do we use? (for ideas, for background understanding, for methods, for organisation, for assessment and recording)
- What printed materials are used by the children?
- Are we aware of the safety aspects and dangers connected with science activities?

How are the resources used?

- How well are they used?
- Which of the available resources are used at present? Which are not used? Why?

- How much responsibility do the children have? How much time is 'wasted' collecting resources for the children? Can the children identify what they need themselves, where it is and how to find it? Do they return resources effectively? How much do they help in developing resources?
- Who helps us in the classroom? How effective is the adult help?
- Which resources do we have available in our classrooms? Are they sufficient?
- What resources do we share? What is easy to share? What causes difficulties? What do we borrow/loan?
- Where are the shared science resources kept? What is the storage system? Are they easy to access? How well are they maintained?
- Is anyone in charge of maintaining resources?

Use of teacher time

Frequently we end up using up our own resources in time, energy and sometimes money to find, collect, make, modify, develop, prepare and buy resources. What must be kept in mind is that teacher time is valuable and when developing resources we need to manage our time carefully. We need to seek support in time, money and expertise and be willing to delegate tasks and not do everything ourselves.

A clear view of the existing situation should be revealed through this review. Agreement can be reached on priorities and targets can be set. Notes can also be kept during a review to list obvious needs and items to be repaired or replaced.

Developing Resources
Pupil involvement

Learning in science involves the children in much first hand experience of resources and, if encouraged, the children will express their own ideas and needs. If these needs and ideas match the objectives of their teacher children can help a great deal. They can evaluate the resources they use (which are appropriate, hard to use, fun, in short supply, difficult to find). They can help to evaluate and identify new resources (good places to go to, people who are interesting, interesting books and materials, try out borrowed materials to find the best, etc.). They can add to collections. It is often useful to start a topic with a collection of materials. It could start with what was left from the last time and be added to by the children and by the teacher. This involves the children right from the start in observation, sorting and exploration at home. It has the added advantage of making parents more aware of what is being done at school. An initial collection can also provide the resource for investigations and materials to test.

Children taking responsibility for particular resources or a resource area can also help with maintenance e.g. check the electrical equipment, keep the interest table tidy, weed the vegetables, water the plants, make drawings for the equipment trays, etc. A coherent school policy can greatly assist in developing and teaching children responsibility so they are willing to help in their school.

Adult involvement and contexts

Resource development should not just be the responsibility of one member of staff, the task is made easier if all teachers are involved. Many schools have found it worthwhile putting effort into encouraging others to help rather than just providing for themselves.

Governors and parents may be able to help, and gain knowledge of the resource needs of a modern school curriculum. A display of science materials and their use on a parent's evening is good for the school's image. Spread the word in newsletters and have collection boxes in the entrance.

Organisations and industry – many organisations produce free or inexpensive resources. Addresses can be found in the ASE conference handbook , books, schemes and TV/radio pamphlets. The local science centre or ASE helpline can give advice.

Curriculum and classroom organisation

It is necessary to consider carefully how resources will be used and how you use them.. There is a proliferation of material now that there is an agreed area of content within the National Curriculum. Lack of consideration and unnecessary haste could lead to under-use or inappropriate materials being purchased. How will the resources be used – for group work, whole classes, half classes or in a demonstration? This will tell you many of each item is required. The resources, or lack of them, should not dictate teaching style.

Consider also the suitability of the equipment. What is the:

- manipulative demand – fit together, hold, use, who will cope with it?
- interpretive demand e.g. reading scales, instructions for use, etc.
- safety demand – obviously safe to more risky
- concept demand to understand what it does (e.g. compare a magnet with a barometer.)
- dependency demand e.g. adult time needed to help use it, explain, etc.

How can resources be developed economically?

Should you:

- develop one aspect of resources, e.g. one topic at a time?
- mend equipment and replace consumables;
- have a general upgrade;
- initially target a year group, particular topics, etc. with a rolling programme;

- concentrate on general purpose equipment e.g. measures, magnifiers, containers, supports;
- improve the schools' collections;
- develop class based resources;
- make fuller use and develop the resources available in the school and school grounds;
- examine parental support;
- improve the storage, access and maintenance systems;
- meet children's special needs and enable differentiation
- consider a combination of the above, etc.?

There is not always the need for specific scientific items, in fact the National Curriculum frequently refers to materials which are from contexts familiar to the children. It is quite surprising how involved children can become with quite simple materials. Activities like exploring a tub of water and its properties, asking questions about a brick, comparing four types of paper to find the best for a particular task, can highly motivate children. What is familiar to us is often the opposite for children. Develop a few good collections containing a wide range of examples. Then buy a few scientific items such as magnifiers, measuring instruments, etc.

Knowledge of resources available

Most manufacturers now produce primary catalogues and circulate all schools which are on their mailing list. If you are unsure that you have all the catalogues contact your local teacher's centre or examine the ASE conference handbook for up to date names and addresses. Other very useful sources of information can be: The ASE publications department, The School Science Service (CLEAPSS), magazines and colleagues. The catalogues are generally well illustrated but sometimes it is worth handling items before buying. There are exhibitions of resources at conferences, or the local Teachers' Centre or business unit could be contacted to arrange displays, etc. When looking at resources consider durability, quality, ease of use and safety.

The appendix contains a comprehensive list of resources which may be useful in a primary school. They are arranged under headings which have evolved in many primary schools and been reflected in the National Curriculum.

Drawing up Lists

Lists of requirements need to be made by each teacher or year group. Essentials can be asterisked. The resource coordinator can decide which items to collect, buy, loan or share. Then final decisions can be made. It is worth keeping a copy of the order so that items can easily be checked off and added to the science stock list when they arrive.

Inspecting and Delivery

Suppliers are not always able to send everything at once but list 'items to follow'. This can be a nuisance but keeping the original list helps to keep a check when items arrive. It helps to add new items to the stock list immediately and note any to follow.

It is worth displaying the new items in the staff room for a day or two, discuss their use and then store the items where everyone can find them.

Resources in Use
Sharing resources between schools

Some schools share their resources with others. In some cases, particularly small schools, this may be the only realistic way of giving access to certain equipment. It also has the advantage that staffs can combine and not only share the load of resource development but also the expertise and ideas to go with the resources.

Loaning resources

Loaning can also be very useful for trials and evaluating materials with the children before purchase. Many LEAs and museum services have these facilities. However you can't always have items when you need them, it takes time to arrange, collect and return items in good condition and it requires very careful administration to make it work effectively.

Resource Organisation, Access and Storage

Resources are better used when people:

- know of their existence and know how much or many there are
- know how and when to use them
- know where to find them
- have agreed to and abide by a system for their use, so
- are confident they will be there, in a usable condition, or
- can easily find out where they have gone
- use, check, return items
- Some schools have improved the use of existing resources through the agreed expectation that all children should be trained to collect and return items.
- have a number of resources based in each classroom

In the hurly-burly of a busy school day, our own class resources tend to be better used and maintained. Most of us like to have space and our own resources at hand in the classroom. Many classes do have their own minimal stock of equipment particularly magnifiers and measuring instruments. These can be extremely useful to add to displays, to answer questions, etc – the main advantage being that they are there on hand.

Storage

It is not always easy to find a central place to store equipment, but space must be found. It may help to walk round the school together to reassess storage space. Some schools have resources which are mobile in trolleys or have developed a science area (though this may not always be accessible when needed), some schools have cleared a 'little-used' cupboard or set of drawers. Others, with no existing spare space use cardboard or plastic boxes from supermarkets, shoe shops, etc. Using these free boxes to organise the resources, helps to work out what size boxes you will eventually need and how many. Throwaway boxes leave money for buying other resources but can mean the collections soon become tattered and disorganised. It is worth getting sturdy plastic, corriflute or stiff card boxes and then labelling them with a list of contents. Boxing up greatly helps in the borrowing and distribution of resources.

Organising resources

Resources can be categorised:

- by topics, projects or themes;
- by use e.g. observation aids, containers etc;
- alphabetically but used with teacher lists to show relevant items for topics with their locations;
- for particular activities / published schemes
- by teaching year
- by National Curriculum Strands
- by a combination e.g. general materials and topic headings

Resources are better used when these procedures are followed:

- somebody has a clearly defined responsibility for overseeing resources.
- teachers are responsible for the resources in their own classroom
- teachers are jointly responsible for shared resources in their year group
- regular checks are kept on tidiness
- items are well boxed up – the whole box being borrowed, not single items which can easily be misplaced.
- boxes are labelled showing contents so they can easily be checked.
- a record is kept near the storage area (with attached pencil) to record initials when borrowing and returning, breakages or items needed.
- some helpers (children, parents, etc.) are trained to regularly check and keep the resources in order especially if the school days are very hectic.

Pupil printed materials

These might be stored with the topic boxes with references to other materials which will not go in the box – posters, speakers, locations, etc. Loose-leaf folders for the collection of work cards, photocopied sheets, ideas, illustrations, magazine articles, etc can be very useful if accumulated over time.

Teacher materials   These materials might be stored in the staff room or an easily accessible place and cross referenced to the topics.

Printed Materials

Many of the questions asked about equipment apply to choosing printed materials. In addition, we need to ask the following:

1. How is it to be used? For example, when choosing a scheme of work – is it to be the only one the school uses, or are there to be several to pick and choose from?

2. What do we need it for? Will it:
   - give us ideas for activities and starting points? (ideas which work e.g. for single activities, topics – broad, focussed or specific.)
   - help with our understanding of the science process and question raising?
   - help with our classroom organisation and ways of working?
   - develop our background science knowledge in a particular area?
   - reduce the time it takes to produce recording sheets?
   - help identify assessment opportunities?
   - structure our school based Inset
   - ensure we cover the National Curriculum in a progressive manner?
   - enable more differentiation in science activities?

3. How will it be useful for the children? Will it:
   - stimulate and raise children's questions and lead to 'open' investigations e.g. through stories, illustrations, problem setting, etc.
   - develop particular Sc1 skills e.g. enabling comparisons, interpreting, etc.
   - provide a useful secondary source of background/factual information
   - structure their activities sometimes e.g. work cards for illustrative work
   - help them communicate/record their findings
   - encourage them to share and discuss, read aloud, browse
   - focus their research,
   - increase awareness of safety aspects
   - develop attitudes such as enjoyment, confidence, persistence, etc.?

No published scheme fulfils every criterion, and compromises must be made.

What do the children find most helpful, useful, interesting, understandable. Which layout do they prefer, (It might be a useful DT project to evaluate the science printed materials in school.)

4. When choosing printed materials, consider these aspects:

- Who is it for?
- What do you get for the money?
- What does it consist of?
- How is it arranged – it is easy to access?
- The approach to science – Are the aims clearly stated?
- How open is the material? Does it allow scope for children to develop their own questions and understandings?
- Does it take account of progression, including stepping stones for concept development?
- Does it develop the skills and procedures of science and does it increase the children's own awareness of their progress?
- What kind of assessment does it develop?
- Does the material allow for differentiation?
- Is it related to the children's (or teachers) interests and set in appropriate contexts?
- Which parts will fit with our organisation?
- Presentation – Is it straightforward to read with clear layout, well spaced, appropriate text size?
- What level of reading skills does it require?
- Is there gender or race bias?
- Are the Illustrations well integrated and complimentary to the text?
- Does it contain a range of of well matched recording techniques (charts, tables, graphs, Venn diagrams, flow charts, etc.
- What is the production quality? Is it durable? Is it wasteful of paper?
- What context does it need to be set in? What level of adult help does it require? What are the resource demands?
- What does it not do?
- Finally and most important – Does it enthuse and capture the imagination? Is it thought provoking, inspirational?

Safety The ASE publication *Be Safe* is an extremely useful safety guide. Besides being an essential read in itself it contains a comprehensive bibliography.

Teachers and children need an awareness of dangers, risks and how to prevent avoidable injury. It is part of every teacher's role to draw attention to the risks without scare-mongering. Ideas in printed materials cannot all be assumed to be safe. Decisions also need to made concerning the children within the group – are they responsible, aware or capable of doing silly things? The numbers of children or weather conditions could make a seemingly safe activity much more risky. Risks are greatly reduced when children have developed an awareness of dangers combined with a responsible attitude towards themselves and the immediate, local and global environment.

Accidents can happen, so a First Aid kit should be easily accessible to deal with damage, burns, eyes, avoiding infection, swallowing. Teachers should be familiar with the schools accident policy and procedures which in turn should reflect the LEA and National guidance.

Some of the risk areas are highlighted below in the form of questions teachers can help their children to internalise, so that whatever they are doing safety becomes one of their natural considerations.

1. Am I aware of what keeps me healthy? – hygiene, diet, rest, exercise, safe actions.

2. Can these materials or this situation damage my body?
   - on a large scale – fall onto me from a height (secure fixing, keep heavy loads low down), drown me (ponds, rivers etc.), suffocate me, could I fall off/out/onto, be run over, slip. Am I aware that materials may be more dangerous the bigger they are, the faster they go, the harder they are?
   - burn me? heat, chemical, electrical, sun in the eyes, cooking, scalding
   - cut me? Do I know how to use tools safely? Work with more resistant materials requires larger forces to change them and as a result there is more risk. Glass objects should be used carefully and if broken, do I know what to do?
   - stick to my body? Glue guns should be used under close supervision and super glues not used at all.
   - enter my eyes? Do I avoid objects flicking or splashing into my eyes? Do I avoid touching my eyes when working with materials (particularly plant materials). Do I avoid strong light particularly from the sun and magnifiers. Do I wear goggles when there are risks?
   - enter my ears? Do I know the dangers of loud sounds or objects being put in my ear?
   - enter my nose? Do I know the risks and dangers of smelling certain solids, liquids (particularly solvents) and gases (fumes from burning, exhaust, gas etc.? If a material is used in smell tests do I avoid small particles entering my nose (e.g. using muslin)
   - enter my mouth? Do I know which materials can be safely tasted and when I can do so? Am I aware of the dangers of eating/tasting certain materials (medicines, plants/animal/ waste material, infected material, alcohol and other drugs, living things) Do I suck my thumb when working with materials?

- infect me? – Am I aware of the need to cover materials, to reduce germs by washing hands/keeping hands covered, keeping hair tied back and the basic need for hygiene? Are shared materials disinfected? (e.g. with Milton)
- aggravate my complaint? Am I able to take part in fitness investigations? Do I know which materials and circumstances to avoid? (e.g. for asthma, allergy, eczema, epilepsy, pace-maker, etc.)
- cause emotional stress? beg work on differences, genetics etc.

3. Do I know the risks and how to avoid them?
   - HIV, household materials, visits, BSE, pollutants, germs, Weil's disease, tetanus, fertilisers and pesticides, hepatitis, etc.

4. Do I know the conventional warning signs on packaging? (See *Be Safe* pp.15, 21).

References

CLEAPSS School Science Service, Brunel University, Uxbridge UB8 3PH

Various LEA reference materials

Choosing published science materials (revised Oct. 89)

ASE *Be Safe* (2nd edition revised 1990) ASE

Advice/Reviews of resources and safety in the ASE journals *'Primary Science Review'* and *'Education in Science'*

Questions magazine Birmingham

Your own square mile 1991 Welsh Curriculum Council

Health for Life 1989 Nelson

D of E leaflets and guides, such as:
HIV and AIDS Guide for the Education Service 1992

Kevin Hunn taught in various primary schools before being appointed to his current post as an advisory teacher for primary science and technology.

11 Information Technology and Primary Science

Maddy Campbell and Dave Murray

Information Technology capability, as specified in the National Curriculum Technology, emphasises the cross-curricular use of open-ended software tools, word processors and information handling software. This article is intended to illustrate the extent to which IT can be used in primary science and, more importantly, how it can support and facilitate learning in this area. The chapter will focus largely on IT applications which support the science process and can be used in a wide range of contexts.

Word Processing

Word processing, with unsophisticated packages such as Folio, Caxton and Phases, is now a common activity in primary classrooms. This is probably because of all the potential uses of IT, word processing has the most obvious educational benefits, while at the same time, being one of the more accessible aspects of IT. The fluidity of text encourages children to evaluate and re-draft their ideas, and a computer provides a useful environment for collaborative writing activities. Children can see the product developing on screen, it is easily read and typing can be shared without a messy mix of different writing styles. The large, clear print facilities also aid the presentation and sharing of findings, while small print can be used for individual copies.

These characteristics of writing on a computer are of considerable potential for the planning and reporting stages of science activities. Collaborative recording allows children to share understanding of phenomena and processes, and the text can easily be changed as they check each others' views and challenge the ideas being presented. In this, way, all the children in a group can come to a richer collective understanding of the events being recorded. Similarly, if plans for an investigation are drafted collaboratively, using a word processing package, aspects of the process, such as fair testing, could be emphasised, and initial ideas would be open to discussion and revision.

More advanced word processing software, such as Pendown or Flexiwrite, have a cut and paste facility which allows chunks of text to be moved around and re-sequenced. This facility can help where children are having difficulty with more structured recording of activities. If a child has written a report which is poorly sequenced, they can experiment with the ordering of the text without the tedious labour of paper and pencil re-copying.

The concept keyboard Used in association with a word processing program, the concept keyboard offers enormous potential for supporting writing in science. Programs such a s Stylus can accept inputs from a concept keyboard. Other word processing packages need overlay design software such as Concept or Conform. Overylay can be used to insert a word, phrase or sentence to the screen text. It is easy to 'program' in the messages, designing an effective overlay on paper is the most challenging part of the process!

Stylus can be used to provide writers with building blocks of words or phrases to use in the construction of their texts. Several writing skills, including spelling and transcription, can be circumvented with this facility, and thus, children can focus on communication and composition. Attractive overlay designs can also act as a stimulus and motivate the reluctant writer.

Teachers can design overlays to support recording for particular topics. (Fig 1) Here, specialist 'scientific' vocabulary and linking words are provided in a stimulating format to encourage children to record information about pond creatures. Not only will the overlay support the writing, but the user will become familiar with the vocabulary. Overlays designed for older children might include more demanding vocabulary, and the children would write much of the text themselves.

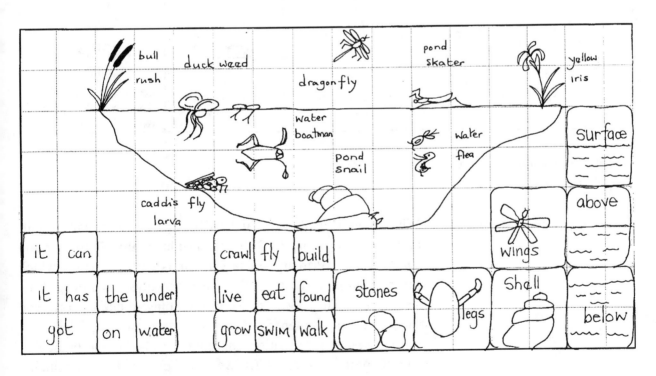

Figure 1 Concept keyboard overlay to encourage use of 'scientific' vocabulary.

Overlays can also be designed to enable quick assessment, again, by removing the need to write manually. For example:

- Sequence what you did when you made the cakes with the nursery nurse.
- There is no evidence of what happened because you ate the results!
- Choose from the jumbled set of pictures (Fig 2) to record what you did.
- Pressing each picture in the order required, will provide an appropriate sentence and enable the child to succeed with recording skills.

Heat up the oven.	mix sugar and margarine	Add the egg to the mixture	Collect everything together before you begin	Take cakes out of oven and leave to cool
wash your hands.	seive the flour into the mixture	put on your apron.	Add the currants and mix well	Put a spoonful of mixture in each cake case. Put in the oven.

Figure 2 Sequencing concept keyboard overlay

Information Handling

Which type of ball is the highest bouncer? Are the tallest children the best jumpers? Do different plants grow in sunny and shaded areas? Primary science abounds with questions which can be answered by the collection and analysis of information. This data is likely to be suited to recording in tabular form and can provide the content for a computer database.

One type of information handling software is the branching datafile program such as *The Sorting Game or Routes*. Initially, two examples from the data are entered and a question to differentiate between them. For example, a red and a blue flower. From this point, many more items with associated questions can be added to build up a tree structure. These programs can be used as an alternative to paper and pencil activities on making keys. The main advantage of using the computer here, as well as high motivation, is that there is little danger of the key running off the paper!

However, typing information into a database is a time-consuming affair – so why bother? Information handling software can very quickly list, sort, order and graphically represent relatively large amounts of data. For instance, if eating information on eating habits is stored, children can sort the data (into order by weight, e.g.) and print a list of favourite foods to see if there are any relationships between the two. A pie chart of the snack foods children bring to school can be generated quickly from the data to provide a general picture. Information on a datafile can be compared with data obtained in previous years, or with other groups in the school. Facilities such as these release children from the mechanics of sorting and graphing , thus enabling them to focus on the higher order skills of interpretation and analysis.

Planning the file   The initial structure of the datafile is important. It is more likely to be a task for the teacher than the child. (Designing datafiles is a level 5 activity in the NC Technology). Planning the file is often critical if children are to be able to obtain the maximum amount of information from the raw data. Consider, for instance, a survey of plants found in two or more different habitat. The children might use a PE hoop to sample and record the species in flower. Several samples would be taken in each area. One way to structure the datafile would be to create a record for each sample, perhaps like this:

> Location: shaded
> In flower: bluebell, primrose.
> Leaf only: wood anemone, dog's mercury
> Soil depth: 7 cm.

But unfortunately, most database software used at primary level does not separate out items under each fieldname. Thus, in a graph of plants in flower obtained from this data, the above fieldname would be counted as one 'bluebell, primrose'. The program is unable to graph the occurrence of bluebells as distinct from primroses. A more useful strategy would be to produce a record for each occurrence of each species:

> Plant: bluebell
> Location: shaded
> In flower: yes
> Soil depth: 7 cm.

Whilst this would involve more typing of information, the resulting data would be far more accessible and readily analysed. The time taken to create a substantial datafile could be frustratingly slow, especially when computer access is still limited. A second frustration is caused by children's mistyping, which can lead to the creation of 'new' species such as the 'promrose', which produces strange results. It is very important for children to check the entered data for errors and inconsistencies. One solution to these problems is software such as Concept, Concept Designer or Conform, which can be used to create concept keyboard overlays incorporating many of the key words. These can then be used in conjunction with the database program to make data entry both quick and accurate.

One program particularly worth mentioning here is GraphIt. This is a simple program which lets users create a basic data table. The data can be sorted and presented in a range of types (Fig 3) and can be edited and saved later. GraphIt can only deal with one category of information at a time, so it is not truly a database program. However, it is easy to use, provides a useful range of facilities for interpreting simple scientific findings and introduces many of the features of information handling programs.

Figure 3 GraphIt bar graph display

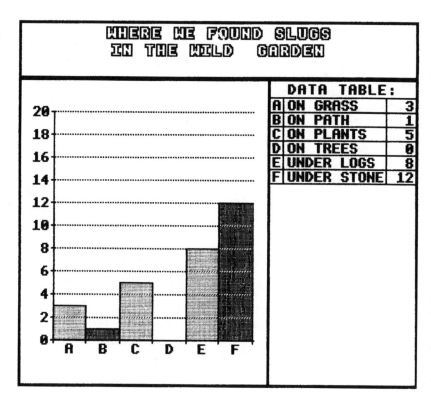

Spreadsheets Data from recording observations of weather or a traffic census, would seem to cry out for the use of a database. However, teachers trying to make use of IT in this context have been frustrated by finding graphing to be unintelligible. What is wanted is a simple line graph, but typically, information handling software is designed to identify similarities and groupings. So, for example, when a simple daily rainfall graph is requested, the program's usual response is to count days of similar rainfall and present totals for various categories.

The biggest weakness of commonly used information handling programs, is their lack of a facility to display graphically change over time. But, there are alternatives, simple spreadsheet software such as Grasshopper, can display a line graph of temperature over a period of time.

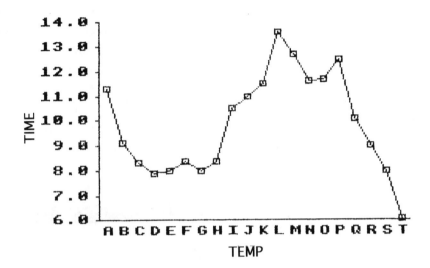

Figure 4 Grasshopper line graph of temperature

Other spreadsheet characteristics make them particularly useful for dealing with information in science. They can perform calculations, a useful facility when investigations are repeated and an average is wanted. Whilst spreadsheets are primarily designed to deal with numerical information, Grasshopper can perform many of the functions of a database in words as well. Spreadsheets present the data on a grid. One group of children, familiar with databases and spreadsheets, said they preferred working with the spreadsheet because much more of the information was visible on the screen at any time, and it could be edited easily if a mistake was noticed. Most common database software has an editing facility.

As with datafile, the structure of a spreadsheet can also be made by the teacher, e.g. embed a formula for speed so that children can enter a time, and the speed for their model car is displayed. Despite some less than user-friendly manuals, simple spreadsheets, such as Grasshopper, are very straightforward to use and provide an ideal tool to help children make sense of the results of their activities, investigations and surveys.

Data Logging

Few schools, as yet, have access to data logging sensors and software, so a brief explanation may be useful. Data on temperature, light, sound and movement, for example, can be collected using various counters and sensors. These are linked to a computer via a small box of electronics called an interface. The data logging software records and presents the information.

Interfaces of various levels of sophistication can be purchased, some of which enable several sensors or counters to be used at once. The most sophisticated interfaces have internal batteries and can log information continuously for up to twenty-four hours, without being connected to either the computer or mains power.

Typically, the software available will provide line graphs off the data being recorded and will allow data to be saved so that graphs can be studied later. Other software, in particular, Intro Prism, has been designed to make data logging easily accessible across the primary age range. Intro Prism consists of several programs. *4Show* (Fig 5) provides a continually up-dated display from a single sensor. The four styles allow young children to focus on which one is meaningful and appropriate.

Figure 5 4Show screen display

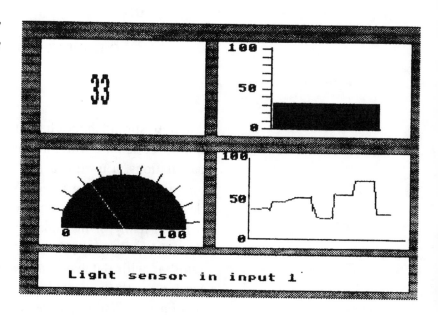

Light sensor in input 1

NCET's Primary Data Logging Project has produced a wealth of case study material which illustrates the wide range of uses for this type of resource. Reception children used temperature probes to compare the insulating properties of materials. The clear display of Intro Prism offered considerable advantages over the normal thermometer scale, and temperature probes are safe for young children to use.

Junior children used light intensity sensors to compare the outputs of bulbs and different strength batteries. Others, working on safety, measured the light reflected from different materials.

The data logging system enabled accurate measurement and recording of a phenomenon normally difficult to quantify.

Accurate, regular, readings, over long periods, and with several sensors, becomes possible without the need for constant attention from the children. Children can, for example, use the remote recording facility and a touch sensitive switch to monitor and record visits to a bird table over a full day. Another important feature of data logging is the possibility of direct comparisons being made; either by collecting data from a number of sensors simultaneously, or by displaying a number of values from one sensor on the same graph.

Advanced data logging equipment is capable of taking several readings a second. Opportunities are thus opened up for investigating events or stages of events with very short time scales. A group investigating the heat retention properties of different cups were able to note an immediate drop in temperature of water poured into a ceramic cup (Fig 6) which did not occur with plastic or polystyrene beakers. They discussed the graphical display with the teacher and became aware that the properties of the materials used in the cups impacted on the temperature of the water, but it was difficult to get a clear message from the data.

Figure 6 Line graph of heat retention investigation

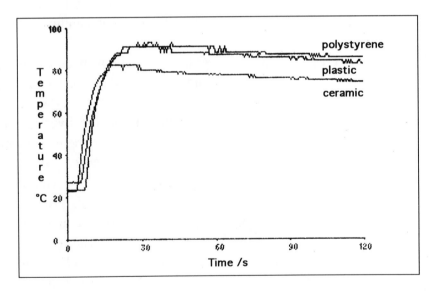

Simulations There is some general concern over the use of simulations in science, a discipline in which first-hand experience is so important. Why use a pond dipping program when children can fall in for themselves? However, using such a program before going to a pond could familiarise children with the type of creatures likely to be found there and raise their awareness of the different pond environs. A more powerful argument for using simulations is that they allow children to experience things otherwise impossible in the classroom.

The *Suburban Fox* immerses children in the struggle for survival. Computer simulations offer active participation which generates personal involvement. When you have tried to escape from the pack of hounds, you will understand this point completely.

In some simulation, children can alter the conditions in the model and see the outcomes of the changes they have implemented. Again, where the simulation offers something which can't be achieved in the classroom, this can usefully stimulate science skills and knowledge.

In the *Pond Life* package, creatures can be identified and ponds created which can be stocked with specified numbers of various animals and plants. The interactions of these can be monitored, as, for example, species feed on each other, and an equilibrium is achieved. What is of particular interest at upper primary level, is that various pollutants can be introduced and their impact observed and investigated.

Many schools now have wild areas. *Making a Wild Life Garden* is a program where different layouts and plant configurations can be designed. A year's growth can be simulated in minutes. The program indicates the success, or otherwise, of plantings and the range and quantity of animal species attracted by the particular design. This program could be usefully used before building a real garden to raise awareness of the interaction between microclimate, plants and animals.

Touch Explorer Plus

This is a unique program which supports the presentation of information. Imagine a concept keyboard with several layers of information. The overlay could contain a plan of the school grounds. Press the overlay and each location is described; a damp, dark corner here and a bright, dry, airy playground there. The exciting facet of *Touch Explorer Plus* is that an option is available to switch to various other levels of information. The range of uses of this program merit a chapter in themselves, it can be used, for example, by children with a range of language capabilities; they can record and display change over time in different depths of detail. Possibly the most attractive use of *Touch Explorer Plus* is as a framework for children's own observation, research and recording. Whilst the basic structure of an overlay system needs to be provided by the teacher, it provides a novel and stimulating recording format, and the end result, presented on the computer, can create a great sense of achievement.

The Not Too Distant Future

Whilst some of the applications of IT may be new to some readers, there are still more exciting developments which will have a significant impact on primary science. Already some schools are collaborating in projects using electronic mail which is a computer telephone line used to send files from one school to another. One school sampled local river water and shared the information with schools across the country.

The use of 'compact disc read only memory' CDROM, is beginning to make an impact in education. The ROM drives allow very quick access to the enormous amounts of information stored on CDs. The CDs can hold software, hi-fi sound, text and colour images. Television quality video is becoming available. These will have a dramatic effect on all aspects of education. As yet, the cost is high and the range of materials not extensive, but what is available is of high quality.

A more immediate development in classrooms is the move towards mass market personal computer systems which are becoming increasingly inexpensive. Classrooms will have one or two powerful desk-top computers linked to good quality colour printers. They will be supplemented by 'laptop' computers which will be able to undertake most of the everyday tasks such as word processing and information handling. Each child could have the use of a laptop, and one day they may be seen roaming the school armed with a laptop and an array of sensors!

Increased access to hardware will result in children developing good keyboard skills from an early age, they will be familiar with a range of basic software tools and be able to choose to use computers whenever they are appropriate. Children will use computers to support many of their science investigations and the potential gains offered by IT will become an everyday reality.

Resources

The following information is not intended to provide a comprehensive guide. Items have been selected because they are of good quality and often available inexpensively through LEA IT centres. Much can be done quite easily with a few pieces of hardware and software, for example, word processing, spreadsheets, databases and datalogging equipment.

Word processing

Allwrite powerful easy to use word processor. Publisher: ILECC, Machine RM Nimbus PC 186.

Caxton simple word processor. Publisher: Newman College, Machine: RM480Z, RM Nimbus PC 186.

Pendown powerful word processor. Publisher: Longman Logotron, Machine: Acorn A3000

Phases easy to use word processor. Publisher: NW SEMERC, Machine: Acorn A3000

Stylus simple word processor with built-in overlay designer. Publisher: MAPE/Newman College, Machine: RM Nimbus PC 186.

Stylus Plus as Stylus plus cut and paste facility. Publisher: MAPE/Newman College, Machine: BBC B/Master.

Concept Keyboard	*Concept* a general purpose overlay design program. Publisher: ILECC, Machine: RM Nimbus PC 186. Publisher: NCET, Machine: BBC B/Master
	Concept Designer a versatile overlay design program. Publisher: Longman Logotron, Machine: Acorn A3000
	Conform a simple general purpose overlay design program. Publisher: NW SEMERC, Machine: Acorn A3000
	Support Science through IT includes overlay materials for Prompt/Writer and Touch Explorer Plus. Publisher: NCET, Machine: BBC B/Master, RM Nimbus PC 186. (Note: Whilst the INSET activities are very useful several primary practitioners introduced to the material recently were less impressed with the overlay materials.)
	Touch Explorer Plus information presentation with overlays. Publisher: NCET, Machine: BBC B/Master. Publisher: NSNSU, Machine: RM Nimbus PC 186, Acorn A3000. (Note A3000 version needs Concept Designer if producing your own material.)
Information Handling/ *Spreadsheet*	*Clipboard* excellent information handling package. Publisher: Black Cat Software. Machine: RM Nimbus PC 186.
	Data Handling in Primary Science INSET pack. Publisher: NCET, Machine: BBC B/Master (Note: Includes Information Handling Pack software.)
	GraphIt simple data table and graphing facilities. Publisher: MAPE/Newman College, Machine: BBC B/Master, RM Nimbus PC 186, Acorn A3000.
	Grass information handling program. Publisher: MAPE/Newman College, Machine: BBC B/Master, RM 408Z, RM Nimbus PC 186, Acorn A3000.
	Grasshopper easy to use spreadsheet program. Publisher: Newman College, Machine: BBC B/Master, RM Nimbus PC 186, Acorn A3000.
	Information Handling Pack includes Ourfacts and Sorting Game. Publisher: NCET, Machine BBC B/Master.
	Junior Pinpoint versatile, easy to use package. Publisher: Longman Logotron, Machine: Acorn A3000.
	Routes simple branching database. Publisher: Newman College, machine: Acorn A3000.
	Sorting Game simple branching database. Publisher: NCET, Machine: BBC B/Master. (Note: Available as part of the Information Handling Pack.)
	Using Spreadsheets in the Primary Classroom an INSET pack with examples aimed at Primary level. Publisher: NW SEMERC, machine: BBC B/Master, RM Nimbus PC 186. (Note: Example files provided but you need your own copy of *Grasshopper*.)

Data logging   *Prism/Intro Prism* simple data logging package. Publisher: NCET, Machine: BBC B/Master. (Note: works with *Sense* (Educational Electronics), *Sense IT* (Deltronics and *Measure IT* (RESOURCE) interfaces.)

Sensing Science Resource Pack Sense interface, excellent INSET pack plus software. Publisher: Educational Electronics, Machine: BBC B/Master, RM Nimbus PC 186, Acorn A3000.

Touch and Go easy to use control and data logging package. Publisher: NCET, Machine: Acorn A3000 (Note: based on BBC programs Contact and Prism (see above)). Needs a micro with an analogue/user port module fitted.

Science Measurement Toolkit. Sense IT Deltronics.

Simulations   *Making a Wildlife Garden* design a habitat and see the wildlife attracted. Publisher: Longman Logotron, Machine: BBC B/Master.

Pondlife simulates pond ecology and effects of pollution. Publisher: Mercury, Machine: BBC B/Master, RM Nimbus PC 186, Acorn A3000

Suburban Fox daily life of a fox, good support material. Publisher: Ginn, Machine: BBC B/Master, RM 480Z. (Note: No longer available.)

Publishers   Black Cat Software, 3 Beacons View, Mount Street, Brecon, Powys, LD3 7LY.

Deltronics, 91 Heol-y-Parc, Cefneithin, Llanelli, Dyfed, SA14 7DL.

Educational Electronics, Woburn Lodge, Waterloo Road, Leighton Buzzard, LU7 7NR.

ILECC, John Ruskin Street, London, SE5 0PQ.

Longman Logotron, 124 Cambridge Science Park, Milton Road, Cambridge, CB4 4ZS.

Mercury Educational products, 8–10 Lower James Streeet, London, W1R 3PL.

NCET, Unit 6, Sir William Lyons Road, Coventry, CV4 7AL.

Newman College, Genners Lane, Bartley Green, Birmingham, B32 3NT.

NSNSU, c/o RESOURCE, Exeter Road, Wheatley, Doncaster, DN2 4PY.

NW SEMERC, Fitton Hill CDC, Rosary Road, Oldham OL8 2QE

RESOURCE, Exeter Road, Wheatley, Doncaster, DN2 4PY.

Madeline Campbell is an ex-primary teacher, having taught in Coventry, Lancashire and Cumbria across the 5-11 age-range. She became an ESG Science and Technology Advisory Teacher in 1988, then a National Curriculum Support Teacher for Key Stage 1. She now teaches at St. Martin's College of H.E., Lancaster, where she is a member of the primary science team. She is a member of the ASE Primary Committee.

David Murray taught in primary schools for nine years, for much of the time as a science and IT co-ordinator. He was an advisory teacher for two years before taking up his present primary IT post at St Martin's College.

Science in the Whole Curriculum

Rosemary Sherrington

12

Of Candles and the Curriculum

Imagine a candle burning on the table in front of you.
Think, for a moment, about what you see.
What does it bring to mind?
What do you know about candles?
What questions are raised in your mind?

Here are some from a class of children:
What are candles made of?
How long do they last?
What is the flame made of?
Are all candle flames the same?
Will a red candle make a red flame?
…or a blue candle a blue flame?
Can we draw and paint the candle flames?
How much light is coming from the candle?
What is light?
Do you remember the story about the three sons whose father asked them all to fill his barn, and one of them filled it with the light of a candle?
How did people manage in history?

What is interesting about these questions is their variety. They come both from the whole of a child's experience and from their imaginations, without heed to our adult understanding of subject compartments. Children do not necessarily see the boundaries between one form of knowledge and another.

Adults compartmentalise their knowledge. A scientist would observe and enquire about the nature of light and attempt to quantify the phenomenon. An artist might ask what effect the candle and its light are having on things around and consider how and in what medium to represent them. A writer would ponder on the symbolism of light. All of us will have several perspectives, which together form our understanding of candles. Indeed, one definition of an educated person is that s/he has just such a collection of perspectives which constitute understanding. The question to ask is how then are we to develop children's understanding – of candles or of anything else – so that they acquire just such a collection of perspectives?

Andrew, 9, was late. He came in, looked around, and saw one group of children designing weather symbols to put on a map, another drawing a strip cartoon, and a third tape-recording an interview. His own group was in the middle of an animated discussion. The class was compiling a newspaper.

"What lesson's this?, he asked his teacher.

"English".

"Oh, right", he said and sat down with his group.

Andrew knew where he was, the term "English" raised expectations in his mind and helped him to orientate himself. He knew what to do.

Primary children do, then, know something about differences between the subjects, they do have ideas about what English and Science are, they are expressed as expectations about what they do in those 'lessons'. It is not that the boundaries do not exist at all for them, but that they have yet to be teased out. They are, as Jeff Thompson says, "intertwined".

As children progress through the education system, they find that their lessons become increasingly separate from each other and compartmentalised into different subject areas. Children begin to understand the more significant differences between the disciplines, they become aware of contrasting lines of enquiry which engage the creativity of scientists, mathematicians, artists and others. But the separate disciplines represent the worked out, polished up, mature structures of knowledge and methods of enquiry, in their most complete form. They do not represent the primary child's level of understanding and mode of thinking.

The questions which the children asked about the candle could open up interesting activities. The scientific questions could be answered by investigations and measurement, some others by the search for factual information, and yet others by artistic interpretation or literary response.

At primary level, we have the opportunity to begin with children's natural curiosity and develop their interests and learning through intertwined methods of enquiry. The ways in which children are encouraged to pose questions and pursue enquiries are one of the major characteristics of primary education. By pursuing their own enquiries, guided by the teachers, children will develop both conceptual and procedural understanding of the world around them. A cross-curricular or integrated approach has relevance for primary children. There is, then, a lot to lose if the integrated approach to primary education is under attack.

But is Topic Work to be Snuffed Out?

The National Curriculum is a subject based curriculum. It has been developed subject by subject. It is only now, with the arrival of the last of the curriculum orders, that we are able to see it as a whole, something that many of the developers may not have done.

Topic work has been judged by HMI (1989) as lacking in depth, that is, having very little knowledge content, and being poorly planned for progression and differentiation. Further, in *The Teaching and Learning of Science* (1989), they find that the more subjects touched on within a topic, the more the problems. We should remember, however, the great differences between children when they enter school and when they leave the primary sector for secondary education.

At infant level, PoS and SoAs are simpler and more general. A topic at infant level can be a useful basic framework on which to hang most of your work with the children. As the children progress, the content becomes more complex, so topics need a narrower focus.

More light has been shed on these problems by Alexander, Rose and Woodhead (1992), who question whether the new subject requirements of the National Curriculum can be reconciled with the established commitment in primary education to cross-curriculum planning:

> "*A substantive amount of separate subject teaching will be necessary if every aspect of each programme of study is to be covered effectively*".

Some people have taken this to be the kiss of death for topic and thematic work and the start of full scale subject teaching in the primary school. But this may not necessarily be so. There are two important issues here, one concerns the manageability of the primary curriculum, the other, the role of specialists in primary schools. I would like to address the issue of manageability first, then come to that of specialist teaching.

Common sense tells us that combining areas of the curriculum makes it more manageable. Also, there are many teachers who accept that an integrated curriculum is "good practice". But there is no denying that there are problems with topic work. It is easy to lose sight of the aims of each separate subject within an integrated approach, which can lead to shallow and narrow work. Planning for topics has often omitted planning for progression and differentiation. It is difficult to track the knowledge and skills attained by each of the children. Planning can be time-consuming and classroom organisation, a nightmare.

The Core of the Curriculum

If, however, we look at the curriculum from a different angle, at the shared and discrete aspects of the various curriculum subjects, I believe we may re-establish depth and rigour to our planning and teaching. The key issues are then, what do the individual subjects have in common at primary level, and what is it that makes them separate?

Science has joined English and mathematics as a core subject. *Policy to Practice* states why:

> "*The three core subjects encompass essential concepts, knowledge and skills without which other learning cannot take place effectively*". (DES 1989)

This is about the shared aspects of the curriculum.

Concepts and Knowledge

The water cycle

There are knowledge areas of the curriculum which overlap. These are relatively easily discerned from the NC Orders. For example, geography and science each include weather and earth studies.

The concept of number is a fundamental of measurement. Children count things in maths and science. Many teachers would say that pupils who cannot do maths fail because they do not understand the English of the maths books. For example, there are many ways of writing the requirement for subtraction. Thus, there is a need to convey number qualitatively in writing, using such words as many, few, host, crowd, lots, several, etc. I would argue that if children are to learn to use key concepts, they need both to be taught in the context of individual subjects and flexibly in topic work. Life is one very large topic, after all.

Procedures and skills

Many of the procedures and skills of maths, science and English are, also, shared. Here are some of them:

- Children observe, sort, compare, contrast and classify in all three subjects;
- they pose questions, make predictions and imaginative leaps;
- they draw on previous experience and make links between various learning experiences;
- they must learn to make appropriate choices as to line of action and to use alternative strategies when their first choices prove unworkable;
- they interpret and explain their findings and represent their learning in a variety of ways;
- they communicate and interact continuously.

These skills and procedures are common to all areas of the curriculum, not just the core subjects.

Attitudes

A third area of extreme importance to learning, which runs through all the subjects, is the development of attitudes. These are not easily assessed, are only implied in the National Curriculum, and must not be forgotten. They are vital to a child's ability to learn. They are independent of subject boundaries, but success in each subject area contributes to the development of positive learning attitudes; they include curios, co-oper-ation, responsibility, critical and open-mindedness, creativity and inventiveness, confidence and enjoyment.

Figure 1 Diagrammatic representation of the discrete and common areas of the curriculum

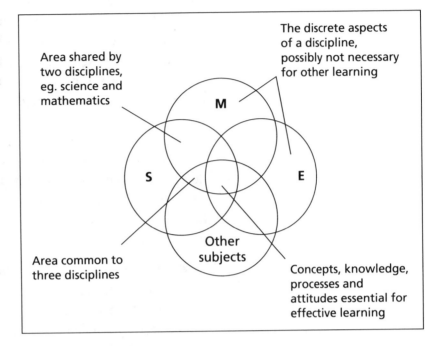

Genuine interlinking of the subjects becomes possible when we clarify the common concepts, knowledge, processes and attitudes. These are the new 'basics' of education. It makes a nonsense of the 'back to basics' argument now that science has become a core subject with its contribution as an essential part of education.

A further reason for linking the subjects is that work in one subject can provide a context for learning in another. Science, as we know, involves children in doing active, independent, excit-ing things. Their responses to the experiences of science should be expressed in a variety of ways. Most children love to draw and paint; scientific activities can be expressed and represented through an artistic response. Children's art can tell us a great deal about their understanding of science. Science can improve children's drawing skills and artistic interpretation of events by making them look and think very carefully. Art thus provides a context for learning in science, and science for art. Because of this reciprocity, one subject can support another. We must not ignore the chance we have at primary level to exploit this to the full. (See also Chapter 13 Language and Science.)

The Heart of Science: Variables

Whilst there are essential shared areas of knowledge, concepts and skills, there are also discrete aspects of each subject. What distinguishes science from all other disciplines is not absolutely clear-cut. One of the differences which children perceive is the knowledge base of the different disciplines. Certainly, there do seem to be distinct areas of subject matter which 'belong' to the scientists, for example, they would investigate the nature of the light, and the temperature of the candle flame. What 'belongs' to the study of science is expressed in the National Curriculum. But who do the stars 'belong' to?

One of the strongest characteristics of modern science is the tight interrelation between experimental procedure and the theory or knowledge of science. As we have seen, many of the procedures of science – questioning, predicting, recording, inferring and so on, are useful to and can be easily understood in terms of other subjects. However, the procedures involved with designing and carrying out investigations, which lie at the heart of science, are easily forgotten, under developed and unrehearsed, especially in a topic approach to learning. These procedures are progressive:

- Knowing what makes a fair test – that for a fair comparison to be made, all things must be kept the same except what you are looking at. You can only decide which seeds germinate the fastest if the soil, temperature, moisture and other conditions are kept the same for all the seeds;

- Identifying variables – knowing, for example, which qualities may affect the speed of a buggy: the material, shape or size of the sail: its weight; the surface it travels on...

- Manipulating variables, if you think (hypothesise) that the size of the sail affects the speed, then you design your investigation to measure the effect on the speed of the buggy of different sizes of sail, and control the other variables.

- Choosing the range of the variables involved, you have to decide which sizes of sail to make which would have a measurable effect on the speed of the buggy. This may necessitate some preliminary investigation before you perform the experiment proper.

If we look a little further into this, we can see how we are trying to give children some idea of one aspect of the open-endedness of science, of the fascination of trying to disentangle from nature how it works. The scientist investigating how the buggy's speed depends on sail size might also try square sails, round sails, or triangular sails. S/he might 'accidentally' find that an important factor is how taut the sail was – a scientific accident of the kind where, because the mind is tuned to looking carefully in controlled situations, something is seen and noticed in a new way. And so a whole new area for investigation opens up.

These procedures are a very important part of what separates science from other disciplines. If children are not engaged on these activities during their science work, at appropriate levels, then they are not doing science.

Integrating the Primary Curriculum

Integrating the subjects into a topic is a much more complex approach to learning than we often realise. Planning topics with rigour and depth means taking account of the commonalities and the individuality of each curriculum area. The arguments developed here would lead to this sort of approach to developing topic work:

- Brainstorm around the central theme. For younger children, keep the ideas coming from as broad an area as practicable. For older juniors, use one subject as a starting point, and restrict other subject areas to two or three. Each may be given equal billing or – and this might be easier – one subject should be the starting point. Some topics could, for example, be science based. Ideas which are to be integrated into such a topic would follow easily and not have to be dragged in, which can happen if a topic is based on a large number of subjects.
- Activities are sometimes easier to plan if your Topic Web takes the form of questions.
- Look at the areas of shared concepts, processes and attitudes such as those described earlier. To make best use of a cross discipline topic it is important to consider these early on and adjust the topic web accordingly.
- Think how you can develop the science and the other curriculum areas:
  - match activities to the NC (in science, art, history, maths and English).
  - keeping one subject at the centre of the topic makes planning more manageable for older primary children.

Figure 2 shows an example.

The topic begins with children watching and observing a candle burning. The questions which the children ask about candles could be the starting point for the development of the topic. Science is the base subject. You could choose from and group the children's questions into those which link strongly to the science and those which support other subjects, as here, with art and history. Inevitably, the investigations will suggest maths and language-related activities.

When planning the activities for any teaching, we must ask whether we are giving children the chance to rehearse the common skills and develop positive attitudes at every possible

193

Figure 2 Planning a topic about candles

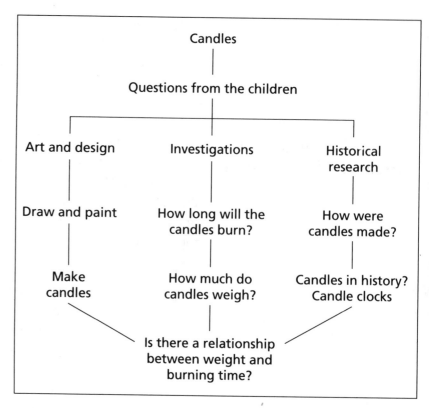

opportunity. We must ask what they mean in terms of the core subjects and the other foundation subjects. What kinds of questions will we encourage children to ask in the various disciplines? What problems in science, art and history can we devise for the children to solve? In what different ways can children communicate an experience?

Children's work should be broad, balanced, differentiated and allow for progression and assessment. It should be challenging and framed within relevant contexts. It should be set within topics to which the children relate and in which they may learn in ways which suit them. It should develop positive attitudes to learning.

For a more detailed example, see Chapter 14a: Science and Environmental Education.

The Danger of Disintegration

A second issue raised by the Alexander et al. report is the place of specialist teaching in the primary school. This applies in particular to the teaching of science, for the issue of teacher confidence remains. It is very tempting to leave the teaching to a specialist. However, too much specialist teaching in primary education will almost certainly impoverish the curriculum. We will lose the vitality and richness which good integrated work offers and we may lose sight of the development of the whole child in what could be a fragmented curriculum.

The National Curriculum is not a syllabus, it is a curriculum of assessable targets, which we must make accessible. We must do so in ways which are relevant to children. Some specialist teaching may be necessary in the later years of Key Stage 2, but it may be better if schools have a specialist coordinator who acts as a consultant, and share curriculum planning in ways which use the strengths of each member of the team, and which, at the same time, maintain a view of the whole.

It will be important to ask what being a science specialist in a primary school is. Certainly, some specialist knowledge of science and its methods of enquiry are needed. But, to be a specialist in a primary school is not only to have expertise at the subject level; in addition, there is a need for a clear understanding of the place of the subject in the whole curriculum and a thorough knowledge of the development of children's thinking.

This chapter has attempted to show that by looking at the shared and discrete areas of the curriculum, work may be integrated at a more rigorous level. There are good educational reasons for combining the subjects and, as we know, there is nothing to hold a candle to the interest and enthusiasm children show for good topic work.

We have only to listen to a general knowledge quiz to know that, as a nation, we are far more likely to be familiar with the details of a Van Gogh painting than with the chemicals in the food we eat or with Newton's Laws. Can we put that right, so that our children gain a more balanced perspective than the person in the street has now?

References

HMI. *The Teaching and Learning of History and Geography.* (1989) HMSO

HMI. *The Teaching and Learning of Science* (1989) HMSO

DES (1989) *From Policy to Practice*

DESWO (1988) *Science for ages 5 to 16*

Alexander. R., Rose. J., and Woodhead. C. (1992). *Curriculum Organisation and Classroom Practice in Primary Schools.* DESWO

Faraday. M. *Chemical History of a Candle*

The author would like to acknowledge the contribution made to this chapter by Felicity Titley.

Rosemary Sherrington taught science in a Comprehensive school, then taught in First and Middle schools before becoming an Advisory Teacher under the ESG Science Project. At present, she is a lecturer in Primary Science at the University of East Anglia.

Science and Language

Rosemary Sherrington

13

Language is the vehicle through which we communicate. We express our thoughts through language, indeed thoughts may not exist until they are spoken or written. We respond to the world around us through language. Understanding is developed through interaction with phenomena and objects and honed and expressed through the use of language. It is the means by which we demonstrate our learning.

Language has a crucial role to play in children's learning of science. In turn, science offers a context for children to develop and improve their skills in using language. The value of language in education is well documented. The aim of this chapter is to explore some of the opportunities there are in science to use language in profitable ways.

Communication

If we want to improve children's use of language in science, we can find valuable help in the research carried out by the team members and teachers under the SPACE project (1990, 1991). Much of it was based on careful listening to what children had to say about science, about the words they used and thus about their ideas and their understanding of science. It is very important to listen to children's ideas in order to understand how and what to teach them, for children often have strong ideas which are at variance with scientific theory. Their ideas are not easily developed and changed, but by understanding what they are, they argue, we are in a better position to give children relevant experiences, encourage them to talk about their thoughts and develop new thinking.

The team's recommendations are all about communication:

- *Get the children to work from their own ideas. First, they should express their ideas, then be encouraged to test them and to generalise from their experiences.*

- *Provide a wide range of evidence and get the children to talk about and discuss their activities and read around the subjects of their enquiry.*

- *Encourage children generally to communicate their ideas to each other – in all sorts of ways, including informal talk, presentations, writing, drawing, interpreting data .... etc.*

● *Have clear policies on vocabulary, for example, encourage everyday words unless a precise meaning is needed for understanding, clarify meanings and collect children's alternative meanings and use of words.*

Listening to the Words Children Use

It is a challenge for us to know when to encourage children to use conventional scientific labels, such as evaporation, condensation or vibration. The SPACE research shows that children use technical words in idiosyncratic ways, their vocabulary includes words used by scientists, but the children do not understand them. (McGuigan. 1990). Merely supplying children with a scientific label in itself does not facilitate understanding. They suggest three strategies for developing children's scientific vocabulary.

● First, clarify the meaning of the word or words.
Last year, at a local Middle School, Daniel told me that gravity

'pushes things downwards'.

We thought that, as part of the strategy for developing his thinking, he needed to have experience of pushes and pulls, and so begin to understand the similarities and differences between the words. We involved Daniel and other children in physical activities which focused on pushing and pulling – along the floor, up and down, to and fro, 'push me pull you', in order to demonstrate the differences in push and pull with regard to themselves. Daniel got direct experience, expressed and confirmed through language. Next, of course, he has to learn about the origin of the force in Earth to give a reason for gravity being a pull and not a push.

● Second, the SPACE researchers suggest collecting alternative words children use to mean the same thing. For example, when dealing with 'stretchy' materials, children use the words 'grow' and stretch' as synonymous. Although the children give different meanings to these words, they are confused. In order to clarify children's understanding about these words in context, , the teacher of a group of 7 year olds selected some materials which would elicit ideas about these words, a spring, a balloon filled with water, treacle toffee and knitting. The children became increasingly confused as their understanding was challenged, eventually, they decided that grow was a permanent state, unlike stretch, which goes back again.

At 7, that will do, as they have grasped an important distinction. Later, we can ask: Does a wall grow when you add bricks? In what ways is that different from animal and plant growth? Do stretchy things always go back – exactly? Later still, we must consider what kind of understanding children can develop at 11, or at 15.

- Third, encourage the children to use everyday words unless they need a precise label to define a process or a phenomenon. Maskill (in conversation) found that children often have everyday meanings for words which are, at first glance, very different from their scientific meaning. For example, the word 'reaction' produced a large variety of meanings, for example, happy, quick, scream, shock and shout. These are everyday meanings, shared by all of us, but not the more precise, scientific meaning. The words do, however, convey movement, activity and excitement – all of which can be picked up in chemistry as the children get older. And in some, there is the sense of something happening as a result of something else, an association which will be needed in physics.

Learning through Talking

What do we mean when we say, 'There's too much talking in here! Quieten down!' What kinds of talk will we accept in a classroom? How do we encourage useful interaction? What is useful about interaction?

'French teachers give Britain a lesson', exclaimed The Sunday Times on 19th January, 1992. 'In two-thirds of English classrooms children talk almost all the time, while three-quarters of French classrooms are virtually silent.'

This was cited as an example of 'trendy teaching'. So just what is useful and productive about children talking?

Both physical and mental activity are vital for learning. Physical activity is essential since we learn by manipulating objects of the world around us. Children enjoy scientific enquiry because it offers them this sort of learning activity – doing things, trying it to see what happens. But physical activity without mental activity does not result in learning. Language is part of the context which brings mental and physical activity together. Douglas Barnes (1976 p. 29) argues that talking is essential to learning, but does not mean formal reporting or answering teachers' closed questions. He means that, in less formal groups, individuals contribute to an understanding of an event, a process or a situation. Recordings of children in such groups where they are freely encouraged to talk, reveal that the children take up each others' ideas, challenge them, elaborate them and test them.

In my experience of listening to tapes of children talking in groups, I have found that they certainly move the learning on together, but they do not always stay on task, they talk about all sorts of things, what's on television, sport, relationships, but then come back to the task in hand, in the end. They also spend time on the group's dynamics, on their roles within it and eventually settle into a satisfactory learning situation. In a friendly group, where the children feel comfortable, they are probably able to express their new and half-formed ideas more freely than with the teacher present. They can reflect, think aloud, as well as communicate ideas which are more fully formed. Listening to children talking often shows that they have an understanding of science beyond what is evident from their written work. At its best, the talk within a group of children shows them listening to each other, with their discussion centred on making comparisons, observing patterns and making generalisations about their experiences.

Children also have to learn to listen to each other in small, informal groups. That is, they have to to learn to use their sense of hearing and skill of interpreting what they hear. We tend to underestimate the importance of encouraging children to listen to each other. When they are working together, sharing ideas, planning activities, giving presentations, they will be able to improve their own thinking and learning by listening to what their friends have to say. Listening is a skill children should be encouraged to value and one which needs practice and frequent reinforcement.

Practical work in groups is strongly endorsed by Barnes, but it should be followed by discussion of the implications of what has been done:

> "*Much learning may be done while children manipulate science apparatus.... or while they are struggling to persuade someone else to do what they want. But learning of this kind may never progress beyond manual skills accompanied by slippery intuitions, unless the learners themselves have an opportunity to go back over such experience and represent it to themselves.*" (Barnes 1976 pp. 30–31)

Children's use of language

I would like to develop the idea of encouraging children to use everyday language further, by looking at the linguistic tools children use to help them understand the world.

Anthropomorphism

Richard, 9, was talking about his science at school. He said he'd been doing evaporation. I asked him why water goes up when it evaporates. His reply was

> "*Evaporation goes up because it wants to be a cloud*".

MD '92

His answer intrigued me because so much of the process seems to have been understood. I started to think about how Richard was using language: In using the words 'evaporation', 'it', he is expressing the process of evaporation as a thing; he's objectifying evaporation, so much so that it has feelings and 'wants' to be a cloud. So he has the process of evaporation expressed as an object, even a living object, with desires and needs. In a sense, the phenomena of evaporation and condensation do have an inevitability about them, they are part of the water cycle; it is possible to hypothesise from Richard's language that perhaps water does recognise that its true place is up there with the clouds!

Richard is using the linguistic tools he has at his disposal, in this case, anthropomorphism.

Metaphor

As part of some recent work in classrooms, I have been listening for children using figures of speech such as metaphor, simile, analogy and anthropomorphism. Children often use metaphor to explain and describe what they experience in science.

> In describing a candle, one of Daniel's pals says,
> 'If I blew on it (the wick), it would curve like a letter "c".'
> 'The flame is like an "r".'
> (of the flame and colours): 'It's like a tulip, it's got a stem.'
> 'The wax is like water, then it goes like ice.'
> The other children knew exactly what she meant.

Sometimes the children will take on a metaphor offered by the teacher. It is Christmas and the children are looking forward to decorating the tree.

> 'It's got spikes' said Kelly.
> 'We call them needles' said the teacher
> 'Why … needles!!!'

Then later when they were discussing what will happen to the tree indoors:

> Kelly says, 'All the needles will drop off.'

Peter and David, aged 10, are trying to describe air, their contributions alternate:

> P: 'Air is invisible.'
> D: 'It feels cold or hot, moves.'
> P: 'You can feel it when you flap your hand.'
> D: 'It's sort of liquid… not wet, not like water, dry liquid.'
> P: 'It isn't heavy, air.'

The boys ideas express their ideas through simile, and as each thinks about what the other has to say, they seem to reach quite a high level of understanding.

Children use metaphor to venture into unknown areas. I heard metaphors used by children in every science lesson I observed. Metaphor is a very powerful linguistic tool for understanding something new in terms of something we know already. Considering how illuminating a metaphor can be, it is surprising how little use is made of metaphor in teaching materials. A lone example is to be found in *Micro-electronics For All*, where the writers talk of logic gates, and describe a further example , using the metaphor – 'like a garden gate with two bolts'.

Scientists will use metaphor to explain a new idea, the metaphor often being taken as the in its own right, often retaining the metaphorical association. It was Michael Faraday who first talked about a magnetic field, and we still use the metaphor. Incidentally, has your computer had a virus?

Children start from everyday meanings and we should not see these familiar connotations as a problem, but should build on them. Gradually, they will move towards more adult notions. We can introduce scientific words when the need arises, often after the child has experienced the phenomenon or process, as long as this does not produce too great a step for their understanding to cope with.

Work Cards

At their best, work cards are attractive, inviting and challenging. They allow children to work independently of the teacher and provide opportunities to explore concepts, skills and processes in a variety of ways. The best work cards are progressive, with step by step instructions and are carefully designed to match children's reading development. Commercial cards are a good source of ideas for activities.When written by the teacher, work cards are tailored for individual children or groups of children, and matched to their interests and levels of scientific and language development.

There are, however, some problems. We miss many learning opportunities which work cards could offer. They could be an invaluable source of communication, but often they do not encourage working together. They could, for example, have built-in objectives which demand that children work together, and which suggest opportunities to talk, write together and make presentations.

Most work cards do quite well when it comes to the knowledge of science, although often there could be more background information on the cards, or at least, references which might be useful. Very few work cards tackle the procedures of science – scientific investigation.

Work cards have limitations which need to be recognised. Work cards ought to allow for progression in scientific investigation, but this presents problems. As the children get 'better' at science, that is, at posing questions, hypothesising, predicting, planning and carrying out experiments and so on, the teacher's role becomes a more and more 'open' one, in that we give the children more opportunities for choice. A work card will, perhaps inevitably, say, 'Look this way,' and imply 'but not this' thereby closing potentially fruitful lines of investigation. It is very difficult to write a work card with an open role which invites the children to choose their own path and then helps them to follow it. How can work cards become progressively more open? Might the truly successful work card only consist of a question mark?

There is a similar challenge when it comes to attempting to differentiate tasks on a single work card. To differentiate by task, it is probably better to have a range of cards based on one problem or topic, from which a child may make a choice. To write cards which differentiate by outcome may mean 'opening up' the card, with the problems outlined above.

Work cards are not independent of the teacher, of his or her hold on the learning, for the objectives of learning science cannot be met through the use of one learning medium alone. Work cards are part of a teaching process which includes discussion, practical work, teacher intervention, feedback and assessment.

With these points in mind, the potential for work cards could be developed. For example, work cards could be written to stress a particular stage in the experimental cycle; they could be designed to raise questions or suggest ways of answering questions, for example. They could take the form of 'How to' cards – how to evaporate, filter, control variables, measure and so on, to develop skills. They could clarify ways to identify and manipulate variables. They could encourage the use of tables, graphs and other ways to collect and analyse data. Or they could give ideas as to how to respond to the activity, by suggesting ways in which to discuss, explain, illustrate, write or make presentations.

Criteria for work cards: Are they:

- Attractive, inviting, challenging?
- Matched to the children's scientific and language levels?
- Clearly written?

Do they:

- Offer 'hands-on' experience?
- Explore a concept *and* a skill or procedure of science?
- How open are they? How do they avoid saying 'Look this way, but don't look this'.
- How do they encourage decision-making, e.g. how do they provide a choice of ways through?
- How do they encourage a variety of responses to the scientific experience?
- What do they not do?
- What must the teacher do ?

Writing to Learn

Writing can be invaluable in helping children to construct meaning from the slippery nature of their experience. Writing helps children make some sense of the flood of observations that occur during an investigation. It requires the writer to order events, to sort through ideas, disregarding some and retaining others. This sifting is part of making sense. Writing helps a child to control and reflect on what they planned, saw, felt and found and provides a structure for their thinking. Writing gives children the opportunity to step back, consider and reconsider their thoughts. A concept of audience develops through reading one's own writing, which prompts further reflection.

Writing also gives children the chance to try out new words, to see them in context, to see how they change, improve or detract from what they are saying. Children not only control their own world by their writing, but, with their developing acknowledgement of audience, are likely to learn that their writing is valued by others as well as themselves.

Research carried out into children's writing for the Exploration of Science Project (Foulds et al. 1992), shows that the majority of children at KS 1 record their science with pictures and simple sentences and in KS2 in the form of a written account. Most of these pieces of writing were descriptive and included what equipment they used and what the children had done. Very few accounts contained analysis or a critique, the children did not write about the conclusions they drew neither did they attempt to explain their findings. (See also Chapter 5 Scientific Investigation). From my own experience, children are rarely encouraged to refer back to work done previously, the page is turned and the work not returned to. It would seem that many valuable and enjoyable learning opportunities offered by writing in science are underdeveloped.

Writing can reinforce learning by involving children in thinking about what they have done more deeply. Science experiences are often intrinsically interesting and children love to write about them. They can be encouraged to express their feelings about their work in many ways. A variety of ways to write not only provides the vehicle for thinking it improves that vehicle, too. Writing can come at any point in the science enquiry cycle. Children may record their ideas and questions, make notes at the planning stage, chart their results as they happen, and record inferences, patterns seen, explanations and further ideas which come from their results.

How children write

Listening to recordings of children working together on pieces of science writing shows how children write. On most occasions, writing is a personal activity where a child may be 'alone in a crowd'. When writing about science, however, the experience which formed the basis of the writing was a shared one. So children may collaborate over their writing. Good collaboration can help learning, 'two heads are better than one'.

Julia and Sally (Y7), were writing about an investigation into floating and shape. They wrote separately, but generated the writing cooperatively. Sally wrote the heading whilst Julia planned the first string of words, then wrote them down, Sally generated the next string and so on. But, even though they worked together on the organisation of the writing and discussed their ideas, their sentences remained individual.

> Sally: *'Various shapes made of aluminium foil, were placed into a tank of water to see what shapes floated and what shapes sunk. The results are quite interesting, they are shown in the table below.'*
> Julia: *'A small, square sheet of Aluminium foil was divided up into various shapes. Each one was placed into a tub of water, to see if they would float or sink. The results are rather puzzling. Some shapes which I thought would sink didn't and vice versa. The results are below.'*

Sandra and Sharon worked differently. Their method involved a system of joint sentence construction, but, as with the others, when it came to complex concepts they came to terms with them individually, by using their own words:

> Sandra: *'Materials which float are made so they have a larger volume to trap the air.'*
> Sharon: *'Materials are made in a shape in a bigger volume to trap the air.'*

Clearly, their ideas need further development. This collaborative situation encouraged the children to discuss difficulties over their understanding of the concepts involved, their role as writers,

> Sandra: *'...better not put that...'*

and, incidentally, over the use of the passive tense. But It seems that writing is still a personal activity, it is a child's own response to an experience. (Sherrington, 1978)

There are two important things to consider when deciding what might be a suitable form in which to to respond to the science experience. First, the writing should match the children's level of language attainment and encourage them to develop their skills further, this means that a variety of written work will come from any one lesson. Secondly, the act of writing should take the science learning further. We need, then, a clear idea of what the objectives of the activity are; the writing should reflect and enhance that learning.

As well as helping children with their learning of science, writing can provide evidence for assessment. It can help us to plan learning experiences according to the children's needs and interests. It tells us what the children have thought about, how they have thought about it, and what they are interested in. It helps us to recognise where children are in their understanding of science. Writing is a good support for the evidence gained from classroom observation and talking to children; it can be read over a longer time span and be used to make more considered judgements.

In general, what kind of writing to do will be suggested by the activity itself. If we know the potential of different ways of writing, we can make appropriate choices which match our objectives.

Writing in primary science is more likely to be a valuable , enjoyable activity when:

- There is a good reason for doing it which the children can understand
- There is a good reason for it in terms of learning science
- It is about something the children have done themselves
- It is in their own language
- There is an opportunity to share the writing task
- When the writing picks up aspects to focus on. Providing headings or starting points can help, such as:

    what are we trying to do?

    how will we do it?

    what will we need?

    what do we think will happen?

    what happened?

    was our prediction right?

    was our experiment right?

    what would we like to try now?

- The children see that their work is valued by being put on display, or read aloud, etc.
- The work takes a variety of forms:

    expressive and personal

    transactional with a concept of audience

    poetic

- The work takes a variety of formats:

    notes, descriptions, diaries, lists

    questions, plans, instructions, explanations

    imaginative and creative work, a story, cartoon, poem or play

    incorporating drawings, graphs, charts and diagrams

- The children can use up-to-date-information technology
  - word processing
  - data bases
  - spread sheets
  - concept keyboards
- The children see writing as a process which can involve note making, conferring, redrafting and presenting
- Children and teachers see the writing as a part of, and not just evidence of, learning

Can Every Science Lesson also be a Language Lesson?

At every stage in the science process, language skills can be developed to assist the learning of science and vice versa. Language is integral to the science cycle, and having a context in which to use language is essential to improving language skills.

References

Barnes D., *From Communication to Curriculum*, 1976 London Penguin

McGuigan Linda *Words, Words, Words* in PSR No 14 Oct. 90 ASE

Foulds K., Gott R., Feasey R. (1992) *Investigative Work in Science*. Exploration of Science Project. A report commissioned by the National Curriculum Council. (Referred to by R.Feasey in Chapter 5 Scientific Investigation.)

Russell and Watt *Evaporation and Condensation*, and *Growth* SPACE Project Research Reports Liverpool University Press 1990

Science for ages 5 to 16 DES 1988

Hymes, Charles. *French Teachers give Britain a lesson.* The Sunday Times 19 January 1992

Sherrington R. (1978) *The Social and cognitive processes of writing*. MA dissertation (unpublished)

Martin Dr D. J. (Ed.) *Microelectronics For All*, 1984 Cambridge, Hobsons Ltd

Cross-curricular Elements:
Science and Environmental Education

Di Bentley

14a

Environmental Education

If opinion polls are to be believed, the next generation of young people will be much more concerned with aspects of the environment than the current one. There is no doubt that education outside school can be very rich in helping children to understand the environment. Television programmes raise issues of 'holes in the ozone layer', 'global warming' etc. However, like many aspects of the world at large, such programmes and features of every day life are only understandable in the light of good teaching. After all, how can we understand the implications of holes in the ozone layer if we have no idea where it is or what it is for? What price global warming if we have a confusion between heat and temperature? If the next generation of young people is to be as concerned as pollsters predict, they need some good teaching in the first place! This chapter looks at the basis for planning an environmental theme through a particular example so that environmental issues are taught thoroughly within the busy classroom. What it does not do is try to persuade individuals that to teach children about the environment is a good thing. I take it for granted that if you are reading this you are already persuaded as to why it should be done and are looking for pragmatic approaches on how to do it.

Topic, Theme or Subject?

It is a difficult decision to decide, in the light of the National Curriculum, whether aspects are best taught through a topic, a theme or as a subject base. Environmental education is much more clear cut than this. As one of the cross curricular themes, it lends itself to a thematic approach and draws upon many aspects of the NC in the construction of a plan for teaching it.

In *Curriculum Guidance 7*, the National Curriculum Council provided a framework for environmental education. This gives 11 objectives. At least 7 of these form an important checklist which matches aspects of the programmes of study in science.

- The natural processes which take place within the environment
- The impact of human activities on the environment
- Environmental issues such as acid rain
- Local, national and international legislative controls to protect the environment

- The environmental interdependence of individuals, groups, communities and nations
- Conflicts which can arise about environmental issues
- The importance of effective action to protect and manage the environment.
(Curriculum Guidance 7: Environmental Education p4, National Curriculum Council)

By far the most difficult part of teaching is that of attitude teaching. Long debates have taken place on whether they are taught or picked up. Skills and attitudes must be taught – explicitly, and planned for – explicitly.

Environmental education then, would seem to be an excellent vehicle for a thematic/topic based approach to teaching. However, there are some other considerations. So much teaching these days seems, quite rightly, to begin with the school policy for that particular curriculum aspect. But do we really need a policy about environmental education. In an ideal world, yes. But the world of education is far from ideal. *Curriculum Guidance 7* has all the aspects of a policy that would ever be needed. The framework on pages 4-12 of *Curriculum Guidance 7* would serve well.

With all this guidance around, how can teachers know what to teach? There are some useful and simple categories provided by the Association for Science Education (ASE) which cut across the advice outlined earlier and make it more manageable when planning schemes of work.

'Opening Doors for Science' (ASE/NCC 1990) states that:

> *"Environmental education through science aims to help pupils to develop and apply science knowledge and skills to make decisions in order to prevent or solve problems concerned with caring for the whole environment. This should be based on their own or other people's scientific evidence."*

Both the NCC and the ASE concur in the view that one of the most important features of environmental education are the 3 aspects 'About', 'In', 'For'. Teaching *about* the environment is the easiest. Teaching *in* the environment can often mean ensuring that the school has a good visits or journey's policy. Teaching *for* the environment is by far the most complex.

*Education **about** the environment.* Concerned with developing knowledge about the content and processes of the environment.

*Education **in** the environment.* Learning science (and geography and history and technology) outside the classroom, in the real context for scientific understanding.

*Education **for** the environment.* Concerned with enabling pupils to form opinions and make decisions about the links between human activity and the environment. This is a challenging part of science education and the most vital context for environmental education. (Adapted from *Opening Doors for Science* pp.5–6 ASE/NCC 1990)

Science and Environmental Education

Recent revisions to the NC for science have made the connections with environmental education less obvious at the level of statements of attainment. The programmes of study for each of the key stages outline aspects of the environment which need to be taught. For example:

Key stage 1

"... (pupils) should be given the opportunity to study how science is applied in a variety of contexts.....They should consider the advantages and drawbacks of applying scientific and technological ideas to themselves, industry, the environment and the community. They should begin to make personal decisions and judgements based upon their scientific knowledge of issues concerning personal health and well being, safety and the care of the environment"

Key stage 2

"(pupils) should use their science knowledge and skills to make decisions and judgements and consider the effect of scientific and technological developments on individuals, communities and environments. Through this study, they should begin to understand the power and limitations of science in solving, industrial, social, and environmental problems and recognise the competing priorities and risks involved".

Although these are obvious features mainly concerned with knowledge and understanding there are less obvious aspects of the programmes which also have a bearing on environmental education. There are also attitudinal aspects of teaching which need to be taken into account. I have adapted work from the NCC working party to create an 'Environmental Charter' for pupils. This forms a useful reference point when teaching about these areas.

An Environmental Charter

By the age of 16, all pupils should have had educational experience, related to local and global contexts which enables them to:

- Understand the natural processes which take place in the environment, including ecological principles and relationships
- Understand that human lives and livelihoods are dependent upon the processes, inter-relationships and resources that exist in the environment

- Be aware of the impact of human activities on the environment, including planning and design
- Understand the processes by which communities organise themselves, initiate and cope with change; appreciate that these processes are affected by a range of considerations (personal, economic, technological, technological, social, aesthetic, political, cultural, ethical and spiritual).
- Be competent in a range of skills which help them to appreciate and enjoy the environment, communicate ideas, and participate in the decision making processes which shape the environment
- View, evaluate, interpret and experience their surroundings critically
- Have insights into a range of environments and cultures, both past and present and appreciate the ways in which different cultural groups perceive and interact with their environment
- Understand the conflicts that may arise over environmental issues, particularly in relation to the use of resources and consider a variety of ways in which to resolve such conflicts.
- Be aware that the current state of the environment has resulted from past decisions and actions and that the future of the environment depends on contemporary decisions and actions to which pupils can and will make a contribution
- Form reasoned opinions on the basis of scientific evidence and develop informed balanced judgements regarding environment issues and identify their own level of commitment towards the care of the environment.
- Be given the opportunity to explore their own and others attitudes to the environment and foster those of
  - Curiosity
  - Respect for evidence
  - Willingness to tolerate uncertainty
  - Critical reflection
  - Perseverance
  - Creativity and Inventiveness
  - Open-mindedness
  - Sensitivity to the living and non-living environment
  - Cooperation with others.

It may be helpful, when planning, to have this charter drawn up as a list so that activities can be placed alongside.

Teaching Approaches

The three aspects of environmental education, about, in and for the environment indicate that in this area more than many others, the use of the right teaching approach is vital. If pupils are to develop and foster attitudes, understand the approaches taken by other cultures to their environment and their needs and interactions with it, a restricted range will not be sufficient. The aims and objectives of environmental education make it clear that particular teaching approaches which foster particular aspects of work need to be used and matched to the needs of individual children. They would include the approaches which focus on:

- learning through direct experience
- exploring opinions, beliefs and values
- decision making
- practical activities and skill development
- linking with home and the community

Many of these would be used in teaching geography, history and science anyway, so there is nothing 'extra' that needs to be done.

Putting it all into Action:
Planning an environmental education theme

Like most good planning, the aims of the theme need to be the first step. The objectives and skills outlined above would be good starting places. In thinking about planning, there are the usual 4 stages:

1. Whole school: where does the topic fit into the overall curriculum in the school in terms of continuity and progression?
2. Key stage: what skills, processes, knowledge, attitudes from the National Curriculum are being developed and in which subjects?
3. Class: what issue is being used as the focus for the skills, how will assessment take place?
4. Individual pupil: what differentiation is needed? by task? by questioning? by outcome? How will this be managed in the classroom?

The thematic approach, an exemplar

One of the joys of environmental education is that it can and indeed, should be delivered with a thematic approach. Step 1 and 2 can be fixed and not be re-visited every year. Steps 3 and 4 above need different decisions on a yearly basis. The exemplar below shows briefly how the planning in stages 1–3 might look. Stage 4 is shown in more detail, as a way of indicating the exciting possibilities of environmental education in the classroom. This is a composite example drawn from the work of several schools.

1. Whole school

The overall curriculum plan of the school indicated a mixture of approaches to delivery of the whole National Curriculum. The curriculum plan was balanced across a key stage, showed where teaching would take place in a thematic way and where it would be topics, within a subject framework. A plan was drawn up for the whole school.

Key Stages 1 and 2: 4 themes across each of the key stages. Themes to be biased towards:

- a historical blend
- an environmental blend
- a scientific blend
- a geographical blend

2. Key Stage: Schemes of work were developed for each subject, showing the progression of skills and knowledge through the key stage.

3. Class: Theme titles and topics were chosen to match the skills to be developed in the key stage. The environmental theme was developed at this stage.

4. Individual: Differentiated work planned week by week for pupils.

Environmental Theme for KS 2: Litter

The objectives were chosen from the objectives for environmental education. In KS1, quite a lot of work had been done on these objectives, so for this theme, teachers chose the following:

- the impact of human activities on the environment
- environmental issues such as pollution
- local and national legislative controls to protect the environment
- the environmental interdependence of individuals, groups, and communities.

Within the theme they particularly wanted to develop;

- problem solving skills,
- personal and social skills
- IT skills

They also felt that this theme lent itself particularly to the development of the attitudes of:

- an appreciation and concern for the environment
- a respect for the opinions of others.

They then targeted relevant knowledge and skills in their scheme of work for each subject, and discussed appropriate approaches. The resulting framework for the unit is in figure 1.

For those seeking more detail the case studies in *Opening Doors for Science* (ASE/NCC 1990) provide a rich source of ideas.

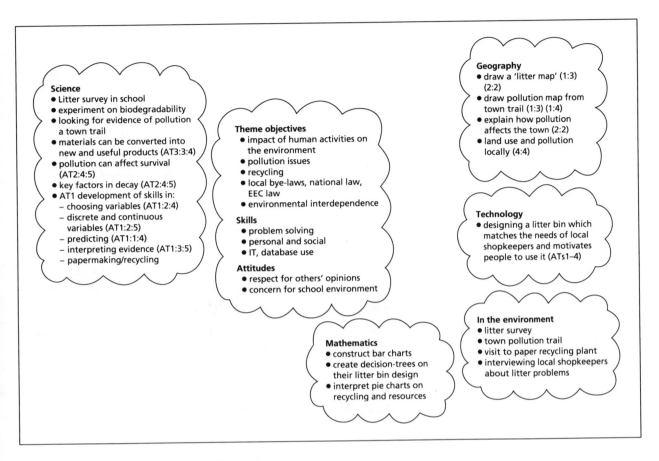

Figure 1 Theme on Litter. Key Stage 2

What Else Needs to be Done if Environmental Education is to be Fully Successful?

There are several things that could be done at a whole school level. Some suggestions are given below. These are the `value added' bits that help the teaching to run more smoothly and cut down on the costs by using resources as effectively as possible. They are not essential.

Auditing the curriculum

Use the checklists to gain a view of how and where the skills, attitudes and information was being taught, where the gaps were and how these might best be rectified. One interesting approach is to use the criteria of education *about, in* and *for* the environment.

Auditing Resources

An essential feature in the days of tightening budgets, ever expanding National Curriculum and the demands of Education in the environment. There are several aspects to consider: materials, equipment, expertise, finance, and working with other schools and the community. (More detail is in Chapter 10: Providing resources for primary science.)

The days of isolation are over. The National Curriculum is placing a requirement for cooperation and planning on teachers that is far in excess of anything that has taken place before. Individual teacher planning is no longer sufficient. Whole school is the way of the future and collaboration is its password.

References Association for Science Education/Nature Conservancy Council
1990. *Opening doors for Science.* Hatfield.

Bentley D. and Watts D.M. 1988 *Learning and Teaching in
School Science: Practical Alternatives.* Open University Press.
Milton Keynes.

Department of Education and Science and the Welsh Office. June
1990 *Geography for ages 5 to 16.* Proposals of the Secretary of
State For Education and Science and the Secretary of State for
Wales.

Department of Education and Science and the Welsh Office.
1990. *Technology in the National Curriculum.* HMSO London

Department of Education and Science and the Welsh Office.
1989. *Science in the National Curriculum.* HMSO London

National Curriculum Council. 1990 *Curriculum Guidance Seven:
Environmental Education.* NCC. York

National Curriculum Council. 1989. *Science in the National
Curriculum: Non Statutory Guidance.* NCC. York

Secondary Science Curriculum Review 1987: *Better Science:
Approaches to Teaching and Learning.* Association for Science
Education/Heinemann. London

Di Bentley is Assistant Dean at the Roehampton Institute.

Cross-curricular Elements:
Science and Health Education

Di Bentley

What is health education? In essence, educating children about health related matters is teaching them to make informed decisions about their own health career. Most definitions include reference to the consideration of physical, social and emotional aspects of life. The NCC for example states that:

> *Essential features of health education are the promotion of quality of life and the physical, social and mental well being of the individual. It covers the provision of information about what is good and what is harmful and involves the development of skills which will help individuals to use their knowledge effectively.*
> (Circular No 5 1989)

Such work involves a variety of skills and knowledge. Primary teachers are no strangers to teaching in such a way that the physical, social and emotional aspects of health are all related in an interdependent way to the subject knowledge. I regard this as being crucial. If we are to assist children to make decisions about their own health related behaviour, in full knowledge of the associated risks, we need to help them learn to take into account the social aspects of such behaviour.

However, health education is far wider than just skills and knowledge. Few would deny that a large number of adults have the skills to make decisions. Yet many of those self-same adults take the view 'it'll never happen to me'. Research has shown that providing accurate information and the opportunity to practise skills of decision making is not enough. Respect for one's body and a feeling of high self esteem are inextricably tied up with health related decisions. The longer people are exposed to such attitudes, the more likely they are to make positive decisions about their health. It is this relationship between the attitudes and the social influences of people's self esteem, that makes health education such a difficult area to achieve in schools.

Implementing Health Education

What can teachers do in primary schools to ensure that good health education takes place? Curriculum Guidance 5 has some suggestions:

First they suggest a policy statement is helpful to assist in developing the consistency so important in aspects of health education. There is also the legal requirement to have a governor's policy on sex education.

Second, they outline 9 aspects of knowledge about health . They are:

1. substance use and misuse
2. sex education
3. family life education
4. safety
5. health related exercise
6. food and nutrition
7. personal hygiene
8. environmental aspects of health education
9. psychological aspects of health education

Third, the curriculum guidance provides a partial scheme of work in each of the 9 components which draws out the level of knowledge children might attain by the end of each key stage. This is a helpful document, and the attempts to match the components against the programmes of study are also helpful.

What is the role of science in health education?

The bulk of the knowledge base for health education comes from science. The understanding of scientific concepts allows children to make informed decisions about health related behaviour. Science has 3 major contributions to make to health education:

1. *...helping young people develop competence in the use of scientific ideas.....(so that) they become an effective basis for positive action and*
2. *...helping youngsters develop competence in the skills of relationships, analysing, inferring and decision making.*
3. *....enabling young people to explore the limitations of scientific knowledge as an exemplification of the human condition.*
(Better science: Health and Science Education 1987 p12)

Understanding the concepts

Much of the best recent research work in science education has been in the area of children's concepts. The theory demonstrates that people make sense of phenomena and experiences by comparing them with their own, internal, 'model of the world'. This model – or conceptual framework – has been built up over time based upon experiences which the individual has had. When new experiences take place, the individual compares them with their conceptual framework. If they are not in conflict, or not too much in conflict, then the new experiences are taken on. If they are in conflict, either the conceptual framework has to change, or the new experience is rejected. Because children have had a variety of different experiences, their concepts of scientific phenomena, and their explanation for why things work as they do, can be an alternative one to the orthodoxy held by scientists or the teacher. In the area of health, children also have alternative concepts. If the teacher is aware of the child's alternative conceptions they can target their teaching of health education to match more effectively with the child's understanding and help the child to question its conceptual framework and bring about change.

Teaching approaches

One of the most important aspects of teaching about health is not the consideration of what to teach but *how* to teach it. The NCC suggests a range of opportunities which include assessing evidence, solving problems, making decisions holding discussions. These opportunities have implications for the teaching approaches and management of the classroom environment. More detail on this area of teaching approaches can be found in *Better Science: Approaches to teaching and learning* (Heinemann/ASE 1987), *Teaching and learning in science: Practical Alternatives* (OU Press 1988), and a variety of TACADE publications.

However, there is no doubt that some teaching approaches lend themselves best to particular types of skill development and others to conceptual development. In planning work that is matched to the needs of individual children, the following checksheets may be helpful.

Checksheet 1 *Learning Opportunities*	*Checksheet 2* *Teaching and Learning Approaches*
Work independently	Project work
Work confidently	Discussion
Assess evidence	Small group work
Make decisions	Audio visual work
Negotiate	Visits
Listen	Case studies
Make relationships	Problem solving
Deal with relationships	Decision making
Solve problems	Self-directed learning
	Role playing
	Simulation
	Games
	Questionnaires
	Surveys
	Value clarification

Figure 1 Myself – Key Stage 1

Science: Investigation
- design a fair test for linking exercise to heart rate
- measure sizes of hands/feet and link to body size
- suggest links between life styles, mass and exercise
- observe different microbes growing
- observe differences in ages of people and animals

Mathematics
- select criteria for a family and safe/unsafe situations
- extract information from tables about exercise and energy use
- extract information from tables about size and growth rate
- measure themselves and parts of their body, draw histograms to compare with others

Teaching/Learning Approach
- role play safe/unsafe situations
- collect data about hand/foot size and enter on data base
- collect data about height against age
- investigate different exercises against heart rate
- discuss case studies of death rituals over the last 100 years
- talk with an old person about their life and health
- design and make a good, safe environment for a hamster
- read about male/females in stereo/non-stereotyped roles

Components

Sex Education
- begin to know about humans developing at different rates
- name parts of the body, understand male and female
- know about personal safety
- appreciate how people work together

Family Life
- know there are different types of family and roles within a family
- know about rituals of birth, death, etc, and talk about emotions
- understand growing from young to old
- acquire skills of caring for young animals

Safety
- know dangers in different environments

Exercise
- know people feel better when they excercise
- know that excercise uses energy which comes from pool

Hygiene
- understand need for personal routines
- understand why some diseases are infectious

Science: Knowledge
- know that humans are different to each other and other living things (2:1:1)
- know that humans and animals need food, warmth, water, shelter, love to grow healthily (2:1:2)
- be able to name and locate their major organs, including sex organs (2:1:4)
- understand how animals and humans make a new individual (2:1:3)
- Know that humans are different to plants and animals
- be able to sort males and females into groups (2:2:2)
- know that food and energy are linked to exercise (2:1:3)
- understand about common childhood diseases and their transmission (2:1:2)
- know that misuse of electricity is dangerous (4:1:1)

Figure 2 Food – Key Stage 2

Science: Investigations
- observe different additives in different foods
- design an experiment to test for decay factors
- classify foods by nutrients
- predict, design and make appropriate diets for different age groups
- log dietary intake
- predict dietary needs against energy use, daily

Mathematics
- interpret charts: frequency diagrams of dental caries
- construct pie-charts/graphs on energy intake and exercise
- understand dentistry (parts/million of flouride in water)
- justify elements of probability in dental caries, food hygiene, death from malnutrition, etc

Teacher Assessment
- use decay factor experiment to assess science (AT1:4 strands 1, 2, 3), maths
- use diets design to test (technology ATs1–4, science AT15 strand 1)

Components

Substance use/misuse
- know the important and beneficial part which drugs have played in society

Family Life
- know about the needs of the old/ill and understand what happens with death
- know about helping agencies

Safety
- be able to use safe procedures with regard to food

Health Related Exercise
- know that exercise strengthens bones and muscles, etc
- know that excess energy is stored as fat
- know that diet is a combination of foods
- know that different nutrients have different effects on the body
- recognise the importance of additives in food

Hygiene
- accept responsibility for personal cleanliness
- know about different cultural practices in relation to food handling
- know about dental decay factors

Science: Knowledge
- understand digestion (2:1:3/5)
- know parts of the digestive system (2:1:3/4)
- know food categories (2:3:4)
- understand E numbers
- understand role of bacteria in food decay/food making (2:3:4)
- understand food chains (2:4:4)
- understand that energy transfer is needed to make things work (4:2:4)

Teaching/Learning Approaches
- write a radio play focusing on food safety
- role play designing a series of diets for old people's home through a simulated company
- read about Pasteur's life
- design and draw posters on the need for exercise or dental health
- survey attitudes to dental health – visits to dentists, number of fillings
- have visit from dentist/nutritionist
- visit a 'health club'
- visit the Science Museum

Putting it all together in the classroom

So, if we have the content, and the skills and attitudes which are important in a health education context, what does the final product look like? What would a plan for a health education theme be at the different key stages?

In developing the themes below, I have started from a familiar place. The theme is 'Myself', for KS1 and 'Food' for KS 2. I have exemplified them by drawing on the NC in different subjects and some of the 9 components suggested by the NCC. (See figs 1 and 2).

Aspects outside the themes

Some of the nine components will not fit easily into the two themes. However, most aspects of the components will fit neatly with other work in the NC. Probably the only component that will require specific teaching in KS 2 will be sex education.

There is also the problem of age-fit. In the NCC's scheme of things, for example, the component 'Substance use and abuse' has the same statement of attainment for children at both KS1 and 2 – "know that all medicines are drugs but not all drugs are medicines". What depth should teachers explore when both these statements are the same? Research shows that the earlier children are exposed to attitudes and understandings about health related matters such as smoking, exercise, etc, the more likely it is that they will make decisions for their own health in the longer term that are beneficial, rather than harmful. Teaching children smoking and health for the first time at 11 is bolting the stable door after the horse has disappeared from sight!

What about the controversial aspects?

Governors, by law (1986 Education Act) need to have a sex education policy. In a very few schools governors say that no sex education should be taught at all. This is not a wise course of action and governors should be persuaded by the professionals to ensure that aspects of sex education are taught from an early age.

The guidance leaves it to teachers to decide at what age the most controversial aspects might be taught. Then they must search elsewhere for how it might be taught. There are some interesting double standards to be found throughout health education. It is permissible, for example, to specify teaching goals for an aspect of health from which many people suffer – dental caries, but not for one which costs the National Health service many millions of pounds each year – smoking related diseases.

And what of AIDS?

One of the major problems in the controversial aspects of health education is that of teaching about attitudes to disease. The guidance implies that AIDS becomes important only in KS3. But children are beginning to form their alternative conceptions about AIDS long before the age of 11. AIDS is something that needs to be tackled much earlier if we are to have a reasonable understanding by the time children reach an age where they need to make decisions about this aspect. Below is a teaching scheme for AIDS in KS1 and 2, which attempts to address some of the issues before age 11. Clearly teachers would not necessarily want to teach it as it stands here, but they may wish to include these areas in other themes or topics, so that a consistent and coherent message was being portrayed on the 'little and often' principle.

Teaching about AIDS in Key Stages 1 and 2

- *Substance use and misuse*
  Why do people associate AIDs with those who take drugs? Do all drug addicts suffer from AIDs? (KS2)
- *Sex education*
  What is safe sex, that adverts keep stressing? (KS2) What do people need to be responsible about? What is the role of sex in AIDs? What is AIDs?
- *Family life education*
  How can we help those who are unfortunate enough to have contracted AIDs? Attitudes to AIDs. (KS1 and 2)
- *Safety*
  How is AIDs transmitted? Why do doctors, paramedics etc take some special precautions? What do we have to do? (KS1 and 2)
- *Food and nutrition*
  Needs of those suffering from the disease. Why it can be fatal. Simple understanding of the terms associated with HIV. What is different between HIV and AIDs. Is there a cure? Can diet make a difference? (KS1 and 2)
- *Personal hygeine*
  Personal hygiene needs and myths about AIDs (KS1 and 2)
- *Psychological aspects of health education*
  Understanding the needs of those with the disease, in contact with the disease, dealing with prejudice and mis-understanding.
- *The holistic approach*
  Many of the aspects of health education are those which are not always taught directly. Several of the psychological aspects for example are frequently part of the everyday expectations created by most teachers in their classroom organisation and management.

A great deal of the success of health education relies on raising a child's self esteem. This features the link between social, physical and emotional aspects of health. However it is not easily or quickly done. The whole school approach to behaviour, to personal responsibility to respect for others and their values and opinions is paramount in helping a child to establish a positive self image. Statements of attainment in the NCC guidance such as 'understand that actions have consequences for oneself and others' are very much the substance of everyday relationships between teacher and child and between children and children in a classroom. They are influenced by the teachers' expectations and attitudes, and by those of the school.

Conclusion   Health education is inextricably linked to attitudes, self esteem, skills and knowledge. It provides a context for teaching science in which scientific knowledge can be put to use to make decisions which will be crucial to children at some point in their lives. This inter-relation of scientific understanding and personal decision making is vital. One cannot be successful without the other. Knowledge is not sufficient alone. children need to make inferences and judgements. Thus, contextualising scientific concepts within a health example is essential if children are to have the opportunity to practise decision making. So too is providing the learning experiences and an environment where decision making can prosper.

References.   Bentley D. and Watts D.M. 1988 *Learning and Teaching in School Science: Practical Alternatives.* Open University Press. Milton Keynes.

Department of Education and Science and the Welsh Office. 1989. *Science in the National Curriculum.* HMSO London

National Curriculum Council. 1990 Circular Number 5: *Curriculum Guidance. Health Education.* NCC. York

National Curriculum Council. 1989. *Science in the National Curriculum: Non Statutory Guidance.* NCC. York

Secondary Science Curriculum Review 1987: *Better Science: Approaches to Teaching and Learning.* Association for Science Education/Heinemann. London

Secondary Science Curriculum Review 1987: *Better Science: Health and Science Education. Association for Science* Education/Heinemann. London

TACADE various publications: e.g.:

Free to Choose: an approach to Drug Education 1985 TACADE. Manchester

14c

Cross-curricular Elements:
Economic and Industrial Understanding (EIU) in Science Education

David Sang

EIU is one of the cross-curricular themes of the National Curriculum. This section looks at the meaning of EIU and how we can set about extending its influence in our teaching. Industry in this context is taken in its broadest sense to include large and small scale industry, business, commerce, national and local government, public and private sectors; anything which contributes to the economic activity of our society.

Science, Industry and our Pupils

Science and industry are intimately linked. We all live in an advanced industrial society and consume industrial products: many of our pupils will go on to work in industry. Science forms the basis of many technological products and processes and can help us interpret and understand the impact of industry on our lives and on the environment.

We can often help pupils to see science as more attractive by setting it in an economic and industrial context. Instead of discussing the deformation of a rectangular beam under stress, we can model crumple zones in cars: instead of discussing the importance of conserving water resources, we can visit a sewage works.

Knowledge, skills and attitudes

The NCC has produced several publications outlining the skills which might be developed within EIU:

Knowledge and Understanding of:

- *key economic concepts, such as production, distribution, and supply and demand*
- *how business enterprise creates wealth for individuals and the community*
- *the organisation of industry and industrial relations*
- *what it means to be a consumer, how consumer decisions are made and the implications of these decisions*
- *the relationship between economy and society in different economic systems*
- *technological developments and their impact on life styles and work places*
- *the role of government and international organisations (for example, the European Community) in regulating the economy and providing services.*

Analytical, personal, and social skills, including the ability to:

- *collect, analyze and interpret economic and industrial data*
- *think carefully about different ways of solving economic problems and making economic decisions*
- *distinguish between statements of fact and value in economic situations*
- *communicate economic ideas accurately and clearly establish working relationships with adults outside school*
- *cooperate as part of a team in enterprise activities*
- *lead and take the initiative*
- *handle differences of economic interest and opinion in a group*
- *communicate effectively and listen to the views of others on economic and industrial issues*

Attitudes, including:

- *an interest in economic and industrial affairs*
- *respect for evidence and rational argument in economic contexts*
- *concern for the use of scarce resources*
- *a sense of responsibility for the consequences of their own economic actions, as individuals and members of groups*
- *sensitivity to the effects of economic choices on the environment*
- *concern for human rights, as these are affected by economic decisions.*
(NCC 1992)

Putting it into Practice – Asking EIU Questions

A list of EIU skills can look intimidating. How can we set about developing these skills in our pupils? One way to start is by posing appropriate simple questions. It is in the nature of EIU questions that pupils can tackle them at a level appropriate to their own understanding (differentiation by outcome). It is the teacher's role to extend the pupils' understanding, and help to draw out the EIU lessons. Here are some EIU questions:

- How much does this cost? Is it worth it? Who paid for it?
- Where do the materials come from?
- What did we do before we had this?
- What is the environmental impact of making, using and throwing away?
- How else could we do this?
- What are the rules for this?
- Who benefits from this? Who loses out?

Example 1: Key Stage 2 pupils might investigate the cleaning of their school. They could interview the cleaners and caretaker to find out about the cleaning materials and implements. Who uses them? How much do they cost; which is best value for money; where does the money come from? Why have plastic buckets replaced metal ones? Who chooses new cleaners? What hours do they work? How much rubbish is produced, and where does it go? These questions are not scientific, but they open up possibilities of many scientific activities: e.g. testing different materials, looking at the environmental impact of waste, the design of different implements. Has scientific advance made cleaning easier?

Example 2: Key Stage 4 pupils might find out about the organisation of the electricity supply. How does demand vary during the day, from summer to winter? Why is this a problem for supply companies and how do they cope? How can consumers be persuaded by varying charges to alter their pattern of usage? How has the organisation of the industry been affected by privatisation?The scientific points raised here might include the operation and efficiency of different power stations; the efficient transmission of electrical power; the development of new generating techniques by new suppliers.

EIU in National Curriculum Science

The Programmes of Study (PoS), together with the examples of activities, give some ideas of where EIU might be developed within science teaching; teachers will also wish to develop their own local examples. Some illustrative examples are given below, each consisting of an extract from the relevant PoS, followed by questions to investigate.

Key Stage 1

"Human activity produces local changes in their environment"

What creatures appear in the school grounds when we go home? What plants grow if we leave part of the field un-mown?

"Road safety activities"

What protects us from cars? Who controls traffic? Could we have more protection? (A visit from a road safety officer?)

"Plants are the ultimate source of all food"

Where do the farmer's crops go? What do the animals eat and where does it come from. How does the cows' milk get to our homes?

Key Stage 2

"The significant features of waste disposal systems"

Who makes compost? Who throws food away? Where do farmers' fertilisers come from? Why are few farms "organic"?

"Properties such as strength, hardness, flexibility...related to everyday uses of materials"

Why does this old car have metal bumpers, this one plastic? How much would you be prepared to pay for a safer car?

"Construct simple circuits"

How can we make a torch for a disabled person? What specialist electrical equipment is already available for disabled people?

Key Stage 3 *"The uses of enzymes and microbes"*

How are microbes used to make yoghurt? How can we design a new flavour of yoghurt? How could we market this product?

"Everyday processes such as corrosion"

How much does rusting cost us? How much does rust prevention cost?

"The use of electronic sound technology... in medical applications"

Who benefits from ultrasonic scanning? Who raised the money for the scanner? Who operates it?

Key Stage 4 *"The social, economic and ethical aspects of cloning and selective breeding"*

Who makes use of the technology? Who owns it? Who regulates it?

"Ionising radiation and its effects"

Who works with radioactive materials? How do they measure and limit their personal exposure?

"How society makes decisions about energy resources"

What types of power station might be constructed locally? What would be their environmental impact? What is the impact of our existing electricity supply system?

Building Confidence – Where to Start?

How can teachers of science, who may have no experience of industry, help to bring school and industry closer together? How can we develop our own experience, so that our teaching of science leads pupils to a greater critical awareness of the nature of industry and the economic system?

We might start by reviewing our current practice:

- Identify EIU content of current schemes of work.
- Identify further opportunities from PoS.
- Compare with EIU skills checklist.
- Plan to fill the gaps.

We must gradually build up our links with industry. Start in a small way, by identifying people with whom we might work:

- Husbands, wives, friends
- Parents, governors
- Careers staff and other colleagues
- Organisations such as SATRO
- Neighbourhood Engineers, professional institutions

We need to collect and learn to use new resources:

- From industry
- Other published materials
- Videos, software
- Articles in the local and national press

We need to develop new activities:

- Modify existing activities
- Plan visits, and invite visitors to school
- Devise new practical work
- Encourage work placements
- Set up case studies, projects, mini-enterprises

The work can be gradually built up, and shared amongst all teachers of science. There is a great stimulus to be derived from working with other colleagues, and with outsiders.

Teacher placements in industry, from a few days to a term, can help teachers to build their awareness and understanding. They can be organised independently, or through the Teacher Placement Service or your local TEC.

In a similar way, people from industry learn a great deal about schools, teachers and pupils when they are invited to participate in school science activities.

The Outcome

Science and EIU can enjoy a symbiotic relationship. EIU can benefit science by providing interesting contexts which show the importance of science; showing pupils how the science they study is linked to other subjects, such as technology, maths and geography; encouraging a greater range of activities and teaching and learning styles; and by helping to forge valuable links with industry.

Science can be of benefit to EIU by bringing EIU into the curriculum in a natural way; providing practical activities related to real-life industrial problems; and by encouraging pupils to tackle industrial, social and economic questions in a critical way within the rigorous framework of science. If, after several years of hard work, you can point to success in these areas, you are doing well!

EIU: Some Awkward Questions

Q: But I don't know anything about industry, do I?

A: This is true for many, and learning can only be a gradual process (see the section "Building confidence" above). Often, the teacher's role is simply to ask questions, and to help pupils to set off in search of answers. There are not always "right answers", but helping pupils to think clearly and critically about the issues raised will help us to develop our own awareness.

Q: This is all about projects, isn't it? Where is the time to come from?

A: Yes, developing EIU puts demands on teachers' time, and on lesson time. However, EIU does not necessarily imply extended project work. You can inject aspects of EIU into your everyday teaching simply by tagging on questions such as, "How much does this cost?" and "Is it worth it?"

Q: Aren't we in danger of indoctrinating our pupils with an "industry is beautiful" ideology?

A: A quick look at the EIU skills checklist will show that an attempt has been made to make it balanced. We can invite trades unionists into our schools as well as managers and ask our pupils to identify differences of economic interest. As in science teaching we expect pupils to use rational argument, to think up different interpretations of available evidence and to evaluate them critically.

References   NCC, 1992, *Science and Economic and Industrial Understanding in Key Stages 3 & 4* 1992, NCC

Sources and Resources   Other NCC publications:
Curriculum Guidance 4:
Education for Economic and Industrial Understanding 1990
Teacher Placements and the National Curriculum 1991
Work Experience and the School Curriculum 1991

The ASE publishes SATIS materials and their Annual Meeting Handbook is a good source of organisations producing suitable material.

The Department of Trade and Industry (DTI) has sponsored the production of two series of 8 videos, *"Electronics Now!"* and *"Innovation-Wealth from Science & Engineering"*, covering science and technology at KS3 & 4, and post-16, They come free with support materials. Contact: Software Production Enterprise Ltd, 4–7 Great Pulteney St, London WIR 3DF

Neighbourhood Engineers groups link schools with engineers who can help with project work, careers events, visits, etc. Contact: Neighbourhood Engineers, The Engineering Council, 10 Maltravers St, London WC2R 3ER.

The Teacher Placement Service aims to give all teachers the opportunity to experience life in industry at least once in every 10 years. Contact: Teacher Placement Service, Understanding British Industry, Sun Alliance House, New Inn Hall St, Oxford OX1 2QE.

David Sang teaches at a High School in Chichester. He has been a member of the editorial teams of SATIS 16–19 and the Nuffield Modular Science Project and has written for the Bath Science 5–16 and 16–19 Projects

The Science Co-ordinator
The Role of the Science Co-ordinator

Derek Bell

15a

The extent to which the role of curriculum co-ordinators has developed in recent years is the result not only of general trends and changes in primary education but also the status of the curriculum area under consideration. Science is perhaps the most outstanding example since its status has been changed so dramatically through the introduction of the National Curriculum.

In addition to changes in the primary school curriculum, the role of curriculum co-ordinator itself has developed from one of looking after some equipment and making a few suggestions about topics and activities to one with greater managerial demands. In the past the Headteacher shouldered the responsibility for the curriculum in a school. Today this is no longer possible and the responsibility for curriculum leadership is being delegated to curriculum co-ordinators. As NCC (1989) state,

> *Where possible, teachers should share responsibility for curriculum leadership to include:*
>
> - *detailing schemes of work in the light of the Programmes of Study;*
> - *working alongside colleagues;*
> - *arranging school-based INSET;*
> - *evaluating curriculum development;*
> - *liaising with other schools;*
> - *keeping 'up-to-date' in the particular subject;*
> - *managing resources.*

This outline of the role of a co-ordinator emphasises the diversity and complexity of the role. It also hints at some of the issues that will face all co-ordinators. This chapter considers some of these issues both in general terms and by reference to specific examples from work carried out by the author.

Policies for Science: The Appointment of Science Co-ordinators

At the time of the HMI survey (DES 1978) only 17 per cent of the schools had a co-ordinator for science and 43 per cent had written guidelines for a scheme of work for science. Since then, there has been a steady increase in the number of schools with a policy and a co-ordinator. However it is worthy of note that variation from LEA to LEA can be quite marked. The main reason for this seems to be that in some LEAs the establishment of science co-ordinators within each school to work with the LEA advisory teachers was seen as an important part of the overall strategy.

The number of schools with a policy for science has shown a similar increase. However the nature and quality of the documents vary enormously. Some schools have invested a great amount of time in agreeing an overall policy and developing an appropriate scheme of work while others appear to follow out dated lists of activities. This would suggest that an examination of the school document should be an important task for the science co-ordinator in many schools.

Now that science has been designated a core subject in the curriculum and each teacher is required to be involved in curriculum leadership from now on all schools will have one member of staff designated as the science co-ordinator and an agreed policy on how the requirements of the National Curriculum in Science will be met.

Relationship Between the Science Co-ordinator and the Headteacher

Support from the headteacher is an essential requirement for the successful development of science within a school. Where the relationship between co-ordinator and headteacher is good then science can be developed successfully as indicated by the following comment from a headteacher about his co-ordinator:

> *"We are fortunate in having a science co-ordinator who is enthusiastic and well qualified in the latest approaches and developments in science. A science 'whole school' policy has evolved from her work in consultation with the staff."*

In this particular school the headteacher had recognised the potential of the co-ordinator and provided the necessary support for her to carry out her role to the benefit of the whole school.

However the type of support from the headteacher is not always appropriate. In one school, for example, the headteacher and the science co-ordinator had a very good working relationship. He supported the co-ordinator by provision of a science room, additional funding and the offer of 'free time' to carry out her role. However he insisted that science had to compete with the other areas of the curriculum in the timetable as well as at staff meetings. This resulted in decisions by the headteacher which hindered the development of science by preventing the co-ordinator from getting the staff as a group to discuss science. Thus there is a need for the science co-ordinator to establish the priorities for science with the headteacher in relation to the rest of the curriculum.

When support from the headteacher is lacking it is often recognised by other teachers who have some sympathy with the co-ordinator. As one teacher observed the greatest difficulty faced by the co-ordinator was:

> *"Lack of real support from headmaster, who does not seem to understand the importance of science in the curriculum and the new approach to it. Pays lip-service but not much else. Gives the impression of wanting science policy and science equipment to show to prospective parents and visiting dignitaries."*

The frustrations are not always on the side of the co-ordinator, as headteachers may also find their co-ordinator lacking and feel limited in what they can do. One headteacher wrote:

> *"In fairness to my co-ordinator she was asked to take on the Science responsibility even though she had no science background. However, despite a great deal of input the person concerned (who incidentally is a senior member of staff) does the bare minimum and the science which was once a vibrant curriculum area is slowly but surely dying. My main criticism is, she does not try to do anything about it which is a poor example to others. Other members of staff are reluctant to help because they end up doing it."*

It is important to develop good working relationships if a particular role is to be effective. It is almost certain that no single factor will make good relationships. However it does seem that the following factors contribute to a good relationship between the science co-ordinator and the headteacher:

- agreed perceptions of what the role involves;
- agreed job description;
- agreed views of science and its place in the curriculum;
- the reasons and manner in which selection of a person for the post can promote confidence and make for a good working relationship;
- expressing the need for overall support and this is not just providing extra resources but involves making time for staff discussions. As one co-ordinator said:

> *"The head is great and will take the whole school so that the staff can spend some time discussing our science topic for next half term. He can't do it very often but every little helps."*

Relationship between Science Co-ordinator and Other Staff

The relationship which the co-ordinator develops with other members of staff is also central to their effectiveness. Many co-ordinators regard communication with staff as the most important part of their job. Co-ordinators assist their colleagues in many ways and respond to a wide range of requests.

The most common request appears to be for resources, although in some cases this is be done reluctantly:

> *"I have never gone to the teacher responsible (for science) for help, and if I did so it would only be to ask about books and equipment available. I like to plan my own science work."*

Another major request is for ideas and suggestions for activities.

But, discussions between class teachers and co-ordinators are often limited to immediate and practical issues as one class teacher explained:

> *"Discussion is only at the level of (a) what I am doing this term and (b) what resources I need. No discussion on suitability of content, practice etc."*

The attitudes of staff to science and the co-ordinator vary enormously but there are three main difficulties that the science co-ordinator might have to overcome.

1. Resistance to the inclusion of science in the curriculum. However, the introduction of the National Curriculum does not guarantee that all teachers accept the need for science, so co-ordinators are still likely to face some resistance as some teachers include science only because 'they have to'.

2. Resistance to change. This seems to produce reactions which refer to a reluctance to change either classroom practice or the approach to curriculum organisation and development.

A second aspect of this resistance to change refers to the wider debate of a 'whole school approach' as opposed to teacher autonomy. One co-ordinator highlights this as being the key to success saying:

> *It is most important that any teacher attempting to be a curriculum leader in science, or any other subject for that matter, develops a 'whole school' attitude so that his/her experience and effectiveness as a leader is not confined to his/her own classroom.*

It would seem equally important for all teachers to develop more of a whole school approach towards curriculum development. However, as the following comments indicate, co-ordinators face some resistance to it:

> *"There are too many long established staff with ideas and methods of their own."*

> *"Certain staff on higher grades (than the co-ordinator) insist on going their own way."*

> *"Convincing other members of staff of a need for a structured, but flexible, policy and scheme to allow for continuity through out the school."*

Perhaps the major problem which faces the co-ordinator here is the feeling of other teachers that they are being criticised as an individual and the work they have done in the past is being devalued. This therefore is a particularly sensitive aspect of the relationship between the science co-ordinator and other members of staff.

3. The lack of confidence shown by class teachers in their ability to teach science, is perhaps the most frequently mentioned difficulty. The following sentiment was expressed in a variety of ways:

> *"The biggest difficulty that a co-ordinator faces is giving confidence to others lacking expertise, who would prefer not to teach science at all."*

However, being more positive, another class teacher felt that a co-ordinator could overcome this difficulty saying:

> *"A good science co-ordinator can bring the subject to life and bring it into the realms of a class teacher terrified of science by past experiences with physics chemistry etc."*

This fear is understandable when the background of primary teachers is taken into consideration.

The relationship between class teachers and co-ordinators is made more delicate by the fact that many co-ordinators feel inadequate because they are not themselves 'scientists'. This means there is a great need for in-service training for both co-ordinators and other class teachers. The size of this problem is immense. Whilst training for co-ordinators will need to be done largely by external agencies, much of the in-service for other teachers will have to be done within the school. This puts further emphasis on the relationship between the co-ordinator and the other teachers. In carrying out this aspect of their role the co-ordinators have to make decisions about the best ways of approaching their colleagues and presenting new ideas. Each situation has to be taken on its merits but what is essential is that the co-ordinator is sensitive to the feelings of the other members of staff.

Perceptions of the Role of the Science Co-ordinator

An important aspect of the role of science co-ordinator is the definition of the role itself and how it is seen by the co-ordinator, headteachers and other teachers in the school. There does seem to be general agreement as to the duties of the co-ordinator.

Table 1 Comparison of ranking groups (A, B, C, D) for Importance and Effectiveness ratings for tasks considered part of the co-ordinator's role.

Ranking group	Importance rating	Effective rating
A	Communication with staff	Communication with headteacher
	Develop a school policy for science	Organisation or resources
	Organisation of resources	
B	Keep up-to-date	Communication with staff
	Provision of resource	Develop a school policy for science
	Communication with headteacher	Provision of resources
	Suggest approaches and starting points	Suggest approaches and starting points
		Keep up-to-date
C	Evaluation of science in curriculum	Evaluation of science in curriculum
	Provide opportunities to improve staff expertise and knowledge in science	Provide opportunities to improve staff expertise and knowledge in science
	Monitoring of pupils' progress in science	Liaison with LEA
	Liaison with LEA	Liaison with outside bodies
D	Work alongside colleagues in their own classroom	Monitoring of pupils' progress in science
	Liaison with other schools	Liaison with other schools
	Liaison with outside bodies	Work alongside colleagues in their own classroom

In general, the chart shows that tasks related to communication and the management of resources are given a high priority. Development of 'whole school' approaches tend to follow while working with colleagues and carrying out in-service work tend to be towards the bottom of the priority list. Similarly, liaison activities with other schools and outside agencies, including LEAs, are not considered to be top priorities.

The role of the co-ordinator is changing and a wider perception is needed. Figure 1 shows a proposed model, discussed in detail in Bell (1992), for the role of the co-ordinator.

Much of the co-ordinator's work at present is that of:

(a) *a facilitator* – providing and organising resources, supplying information and being available for consultation and discussion;

(b) *an initiator* – introducing ideas, developing school policy and suggesting starting points and ideas for topics.

However the demands of the NC require that these two dimensions are strengthened and the co-ordinator expands his /her role into the that of:

(a) *educator* – helping colleagues with their knowledge and understanding of science, running workshops, working alongside colleagues in classrooms and disseminating useful information to keep staff up to date with developments in primary science nationally and locally.

(b) *evaluator* – reviewing and evaluating existing practice, schemes of work, resources and the school policy and programme moderating and monitoring pupils' performance in science across the whole school; evaluating the place of science within the overall curriculum.

(c) *co-ordinator* – compilation of information on all aspects of science teaching and learning in the school; ensuring progression and continuity for pupils within the school and beyond; liaison with other schools, governors, and outside bodies, arranging for staff development in science.

Essential to all of these functions is the ability of the co-ordinator to communicate effectively with headteacher, colleagues and, when appropriate, governors and parents, LEA inspectors and advisory teachers. The model is dynamic and proactive rather than static and reactive. One crucial element in bringing about the changes is the need to train co-ordinators to help them see their role in this wider context. They need to develop their own expertise not only in terms of their scientific understanding but also in terms of their ability to carry out the managerial demands of the role. However the changes cannot take place at once because of the variety of factors influencing the performance of the co-ordinator.

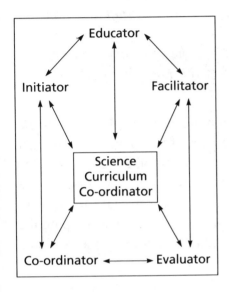

Figure 1 A model for the science curriculum co-ordinator in primary schools

Influences on the Role and Performance of the Co-ordinator

Both the attitudes of other members of staff and support from the headteacher can be crucial to the success or failure of any attempts by the co-ordinator to develop science within the curriculum. Even if the co-ordinator overcomes initial resistance from teachers they have to maintain the momentum. As one headteacher commented:

> *"When the science scheme was being formulated there was a good deal of enthusiasm from all members of staff, even those lacking confidence in their ability to develop scientific skills in the children, yet it has been difficult to sustain this enthusiasm when staff attention was being concentrated on other areas of the curriculum. The most successful teachers in this area are those who have developed the habit of including science in their teaching pattern."*

This comment also emphasises the need for teachers to be encouraged to include science as part of their regular teaching at an early stage in the development process, otherwise there is the danger that it will never become fully established. Indeed, one might argue that the problem is increased because the quality and nature of learning in science is so crucial in developing the skills, knowledge and understanding required by the National Curriculum.

Time

Time is frequently mentioned as the most influential factor on how well a co-ordinator performs his or her role. In some cases this is given as a 'blanket' reason why very little progress has been made. More specific reasons are given in the following comments show:

> *"Time is needed to talk to other members of staff."*

> *"The teacher is a full time class teacher with very little non-contact time freeing her for liaison, contact, evaluation etc."*

> *"In the primary school there is very little spare time for a classteacher, who is also a co-ordinator to liaise, advise and work alongside other staff."*

> *"The major difficulty is time to meet with staff and draw up a policy document."*

Often it is not only the amount of time that is the problem but the frequency of it. There is a limit to how effective a co-ordinator can be if the opportunities for talking to staff are sporadic and irregular. As one co-ordinator said:

"The major difficulty is the lack of fixed and regular opportunities to liaise with other members of staff concerning the development of school science policy and evaluation of pupils' progress. I would recommend to any co-ordinator that regular consultation times should be agreed upon and opportunities be created to facilitate this aspect of the science co-ordinator's role."

Many co-ordinators were prepared to find time during lunch breaks and after school in order to carry out various aspects of their role but this is not always easy.

Conflict of responsibilities

These are usually seen as distinctly negative influences. The conflict may result from:

- the fact that many science co-ordinators had other curricular responsibilities. This situation is particularly true in small schools with inevitable consequences, as indicated by the following comments:

  "Small staff – so each member of staff is responsible for more than one area of the curriculum. No member of staff really wished to be responsible for science. The teacher who has been, is now engaged on revising the English policy."

  Many of the co-ordinators were in fact deputy headteachers who:

  "... have many responsibilities and thus must be continually assessing 'priorities'. It is successfully formulating these priorities which will present the major difficulty."

- an individual's role as both class teacher and co-ordinator. One teacher's comment seemed to encapsulate the dilemma:

  Deciding which is my priority – teaching my class or carrying out duties of science co-ordinator. This is of course linked to the time factor mentioned above. I believe my prime concern must be the general teaching of my class – but this does lead to a conflict as I must also be an effective co-ordinator. This, I find, leads to stress if one is at all conscientious.

  The only solution is more time but this can only be given to science at the expense of time with my own class. This is detrimental to the well-being and progress of the class, especially if they are very young. I find I don't know the answer to this.

Thus there would appear to be a need to improve the personal management skills of the co-ordinators in order to increase their effectiveness and overcome some of the problems caused by the conflicts.

Resources

Availability of resources has a significant influence on the effectiveness of the co-ordinator. However it can be a problem of storage and space as often as a lack of materials. Money, or rather the lack of it, is frequently linked to this issue of resources. Making resources available is seen to be a crucial part of the co-ordinator's role which, despite the difficulties that do exist, is generally done effectively. Many co-ordinators appear to make the organisation of resources a top priority. This can be turned to advantage for by getting the resources for science together it is possible to make an immediate impact and overcome one of the major objections staff have against doing science. Thus with the resources available it is more difficult for the other class teachers to avoid 'having a go at science'.

Opportunities for in-service training

Opportunities for in-service training of both co-ordinators and other class teachers are often seen not only as a significant influence on the effectiveness of the co-ordinator but also as the major solution to many of the problems faced by co-ordinators. Three issues can be identified:

1. Improvement of scientific expertise of both the co-ordinator and the class teachers.
2. The need to tailor courses more specifically to the requirements of the teachers involved.
3. The need for courses designed to improve the co-ordinator's management skills and their awareness of the range of demands of the post. For example:

> *"I now feel that I need further management training in order to effectively chair meetings and develop a soundly structured science policy within the school."*

This need for the development of personal management skills is being more and more widely recognised. Possession of such skills will help to increase the effectiveness of the co-ordinator.

The need for in-service training is indisputable but is only part of the problem. If the in-service is to be effective it must have a lasting influence on the quality of the science work in the school. In addition, the coordinator should encourage the use of expertise brought back by other teachers when attending external courses.

Personal expertise and attitude of the co-ordinator

Last but not least, the personal expertise of the co-ordinator needs to be considered not only in relation to scientific understanding but also to their management abilities. It would seem that the effectiveness of the co-ordinators could be increased through an improvement in their management skills.

Whilst a scientific background is beneficial and can improve effectiveness, enthusiasm and commitment to the job are vital. Indeed being a 'scientist' could be a disadvantage for some co-ordinators, as this class teacher put it:

> "Enthusiasm and commitment to primary philosophy overcomes any lack of science knowledge and encourages non-scientific teachers who can be over-awed by the 'expert' scientist."

This discussion of the factors influencing the effectiveness of the science co-ordinator has reflected the many problems faced by them and some the suggested solutions. Although increases in factors such as time, money, resources and staffing levels can improve a situation, it would seem that the effectiveness of the co-ordinator is influenced most significantly by the attitudes and interaction of the people involved.

The role of the science co-ordinator is a complex one and, at times not an easy one, but there are some things that can make life more bearable:

- *Don't panic* – talk to the headteacher and try to establish what is needed and expected.
- *Don't try to do everything at once* – identify the priorities and set achievable targets.
- *Do something* – make a start on the tasks set and work at these.
- *Talk to other staff* – build up the working relationships.
- *Remember* – the role of the co-ordinator is not trivial and casual but subtle and effective.

References:

Bell, D. (1992) *Co-ordinating science in the primary school: a role model.* In press. EriE Special issue on Primary Science.
A Framework for the primary curriculum. (1989) NCC, York.

Dr Derek Bell is Senior Lecturer in Education at the Liverpool Institute of Higher Education. His particular interests include children's ideas in science, he was a member of the SPACE Project; and curriculum co-ordination in primary schools.

15b The Science Co-ordinator
Not Trivial and Casual, but Subtle and Effective – a Case Study

Anthony Cudworth

"Some are born scientists, others have science thrust upon them." (Questions, March 1989)

This is the reaction of one teacher when her headteacher suggested that she take on a post of responsibility for science.

I can personally identify with that sentiment for having come to my present school to be maths co-ordinator, I was asked to take on the science, and then expected to produce a new document to meet the requirements of the National Curriculum as quickly as possible.

For me the opportunity provided a real challenge, that is, to develop science throughout the school in a way that had not existed before, but the manner in which I was being asked to "develop" that science has been a source of much personal concern.

A co-ordinator's job I believe, is to offer practical support and guidance to colleagues and to relieve them of as much organisational burden as possible – not to "thrust" attitudes and practices upon them. Success relies as much on establishing and maintaining relationships as on the quality of the idea.

As if to endorse this belief, the ASE pamphlet *"A Post of Responsibility in Science"* sees the role as that of a consultant. The person who holds the post requires *"qualities of leadership, tact and enthusiasm for science learning"* as well as *"a good background of scientific knowledge and understanding of science as a way of working"*.

The document goes on:

> *"However, the attitude of the holder of the scale post is of far more importance than traditional knowledge and qualifications. Teaching methods and subject matter constantly change. Somebody willing to admit, at times, to not knowing, but alert to the need for finding out and for keeping up to date, is likely to be active in seeking the help that science advisors and advisory teachers can provide. Such a person will also use in-service training, meetings at Teachers' Centres and relevant books and articles, and encourage other members of staff to take advantage of the same opportunities."*

I also believe that initiating change with an established staff can be difficult in that familiarity breeds contempt. They see what they are doing as successful and don't see any reason for altering it, especially if the new face appears to be advocating alternative practices with little evidence to support them. If they are then pressurised into accepting these changes without the opportunity of coming to terms with the underlying philosophy for their inclusion they are even more likely to resist rather than support them.

Consequently, the model I really wanted to initiate was one which truly involved all of the staff in rethinking what they do and in identifying areas of concern. I wanted the time and opportunity to initiate this with my colleagues without undue pressure and without jeopardising continuity in other areas of the curriculum.

At the same time I hoped that any changes to attitudes and practices could be made within the context of the whole organisation of the school.

There were, however, two further factors which were influencing the development of Inset within the school generally. The first concerned the arrangement of classes. Until the present academic year, classes were a combination of single age, mixed age and mixed ability. As a result there seemed no fully co-ordinated approach to curriculum planning. Where classes overlapped, some teachers worked together, but generally there was very little awareness between the staff of what was going on in each others' classrooms.

The second concerned the pattern of school-based Inset. The main input was the regular Monday meetings involving all the staff. Invariably these were led by the headteacher who had decided the content in consultation with the deputy headteacher and the senior post holder, but with little reference to the other members of staff. The matters for "discussion" would be wide-ranging and often with little or no continuity from one week to another. The result was a lot of muddled thinking, frustration and resentment, particularly from the more established members of staff.

Given then, that this was the context in which I was to set up school-based staff development programmes in science, how was I to start?

Unfortunately my colleagues did not, as yet, see science as a priority. The advent of the National Curriculum may have removed the option of ignoring science in the primary school but I was ready to use alternative ways of raising awareness. My chosen strategy was one which I considered offered some support whilst gradually heightening the awareness of science.

The first thing I decided, was to produce some topic sheets that provided starting points for scientific investigation, example activities, accessible parts of the Programmes of Study, and a list of sources and resources. I offered these to colleagues as a resource, not as a definitive method of carrying out science.

At the same time, I started putting together a resources base of readily accessible books and equipment, circularising a list of its contents to the staff, and encouraging them to come and try out the equipment for themselves.

Next, I wrote a brief policy statement for science in the school making it clear to the staff that it was no more than a discussion document. Needless to say, this document contained many of the practices that I hoped would be adopted eventually.

Lastly, for my own credibility. I endeavoured to set up investigative science in my own classroom. Again, not with the intention of putting myself forward as someone with great ability, but so that I had some evidence to offer colleagues at the appropriate time.

Knowing the staff and the school situation, I believe I made reasonable choices in that instance. The topic sheets were gratefully received by the staff and most made encouraging noises about how useful they were in planning science.

The "policy" document was duly filed, though the headteacher seemed quite pleased (he had something to offer any external agency should they wish to see how the school's curriculum was developing).

The resources base was used to varying degrees. Ideally I should have had the opportunity to put on workshop sessions so that the staff could become conversant with all the equipment and resources. If teachers are to take up the challenges of introducing science to children, they need to experience and have some understanding of the processes themselves, especially as many may well be at odds with their own education in science. With hindsight it would also have been better if I could have involved staff more in selecting resources – if they have chosen them and know what they're for, they are more likely to use them.

In terms of what was happening in my own classroom I found the children to be a most useful asset. They produced work which was shown to other classes through displays and demonstrations, and their obvious sense of enjoyment and achievement meant the word was spread.

Generally I remained receptive whenever a colleague wanted to know about any equipment, or needed a source book for background information, or wanted some advice about dealing with a particular aspect of a topic. And when the head of the infant department asked me to join them in a series of activity afternoons to give a science input, I arranged for the headteacher to take my class, and went along joyfully.

Evidence of investigative science was becoming more apparent but any progress made was on an individual level and was not consistent throughout the school. A classic example came earlier this year when two teachers (one with Y3\Y4 children and the other with Y5\Y6) found themselves planning the same topic. The debate that followed was all about the lack of communication.

Then, for this academic year, the classes were rearranged so that there are now parallel groups in Reception, Yl\Y2, Y3\Y4 and Y5\Y6. Staff gradually realised that they could no longer work in isolation but that there had to be planning in phase groups.

Also, in this year, my attending a Primary Science Co-ordinators' Course has focused the staff's attention as far as science is concerned. Colleagues have wanted to know what I was doing, and casual conversations about the course, and a sharing of ideas have become a very productive form of liaison and support. The headteacher finally decided that we must make good use of the opportunity to reorganise science throughout the school.

This term I have been able to work alongside a colleague through the use of the supply days which are part of my course. Having the opportunity to share ideas with another member of staff has helped the colleague to consider the sort of activities that can be developed and how to approach the work. For me it has been an opportunity to show how co-ordination can benefit the staff.

As the colleague's class is parallel one to my own we were already familiar with the idea of planning together, and I considered that, to begin with, it would be most valuable to work with someone whose attitude and approach suggested that they would develop the ideas that I hoped to see generally throughout the school.

The planning meetings were kept informal and friendly. I showed the colleague some of the methods I used in planning science activities. We talked about strategies that I had found useful in developing investigative work, and which skills and attitudes they could develop. We discussed her way of working at present, and the areas of concern that she was most aware of.

After she had produced her topic plan we talked it through, tried out some of the activities, rethought some of the questions and refined some of the activities to make the topic more focused. What I wanted, though, was for the colleague to feel that this was still principally her work.

When it came to implementing the plan I worked alongside the colleague at various stages, and helped with organising the equipment. Whenever we had worked together I found it important to make time at the end of the day (over a cup of coffee) to share our impressions of the activity – and to find lots of good things to say about it.

In between these sessions I "popped" into the classroom on a regular basis to ask groups of children how an investigation was going, for I feel that it was just as important for them to know that I was interested in the outcome of their work. When some groups of children wanted to use my classroom for one of their investigations, I made it readily available.

For the colleague the biggest benefit was the boost to her confidence through the obvious enjoyment of the children. Their enthusiasm made it difficult at times to bring work to an end or to stop it going off at all sorts of tangents. Importantly, the colleague feels motivated to carry on in a similar manner with succeeding topics.

For me, a number of useful strategies emerged:

- keeping the meetings informal and lively;
- the enquiry ("How's it going?"), and the resultant conversation at break time;
- praising the colleague on how effective I thought an activity was;
- praising the children's efforts;
- keep providing little bits of information, background material and resources – not everything at once ("I found this in [such-and-such] book; I thought it might be useful to you.");
- making sure the rest of the staff (including the headteacher) were aware of what was going on.

As well as using this experience to show the staff how how co-ordinated planning could work, another useful stratety has been to bring the advisory teacher for primary science into the school. Closely allied to the support I had been offering he gave ideas on how to plan and carry out science investigations, and the staff were able to see him working with children in the school. The rationale used was not that this is *the* way to work but, rather, this is *a* way of working.

Again, using hindsight, having the particular type of planning session that we did first was not so successful. The amount of detail, coming all at once, caught some of the staff "off-guard", and was counter-productive. However, the lessons themselves, and the follow-up were very successful. The staff were more able to appreciate the planning that had preceded the activities, and it got them thinking about their own planning.

Now that the staff have realised the need for a much more co-ordinated approach to the school's science I have been able to give them a more detailed framework from which to work. As if to give this approach further credibility, the staff have realised that it is a framework that could be applied to other curriculum areas, especially the consideration of particular topics for particular phases, and the issues of continuity and progression. Indeed, all staff are at present working (in small groups of two or three) with a clearer idea that a topic may be repeated but the activities will not be exactly the same because the children will be at different levels of development.

The policy document that I introduced some time ago has come out of its folders. We are dissecting it bit by bit. I am trying to involve all the staff (working in groups and reporting back), making sure that they accept ownership and responsibility for the ideas that they are asking me to redraft. We are moving towards a whole school science policy for the first time.

On reflection it has been difficult knowing when to intervene and when to stand back, but I believe an important part of any co-ordinator's role is remaining sensitive to colleagues' needs. I could have "jumped in with both feet" and imposed a science curriculum on my colleagues – but at what cost? Rather, I feel that by supplying gradual support and a step-by-step raising of awareness we are moving in the right direction.

The next stage, as I see it, is to build on the sessions where two or three teachers are working together. These sessions, whilst providing opportunities for sharing ideas and creating a supportive structure for all the staff, eliminate the more threatening situation of having to share ideas at a whole staff meeting. I have found that with only two or three at a meeting the atmosphere is much more informal and friendly, and everyone feels they are able to contribute something. Inevitably, it will be time-consuming for me to be involved in several of these sessions simultaneously but I feel that it will be a more beneficial use of time than that experienced in the past. Hopefully these sessions will also give colleagues the opportunity to identify their on-going needs.

As part of these sessions I would certainly like to give the staff the opportunity and encouragement to undertake more scientific investigations for themselves. Given that the view of children's learning in science incorporated in the National Curriculum is one of active development through processes of exploration, I believe it is important for teachers to have similar experiences especially as it may well be at odds with their own education in science.

Hopefully by the time they have had sufficient opportunities to explore the practical activities and to share ideas on planning, the staff will have a clear view of what science means to them – not only in terms of content, but also of its overall place within their perception of children's learning and the related aspects of classroom management. Then, also, they might all be able to make considered decisions on the resources to be purchased.

A start has been made and I remain positive about the possibilities for investigative science in the school. Within this year the staff have come a long way. They may not be born scientists but equally I do not get the feeling that they believe science has been "thrust" upon them.

References   ASE (1981), Science and Primary Education Paper No.3: *A Post of Responsibility in Science,* Hatfield, Hertfordshire: Association for Science Education.

Questions (November 1988}, *Enter the Co-ordinator: Lighting the flame!,* The Questions Publishing Co. Ltd

Questions (December 1988}, *Enter the Co-ordinator: Taking the pain out of training,* The Questions Publishing Co. Ltd

Questions (March 1989}, *Enter the Co-ordinator: In at the deep end,* The Questions Publishing Co. Ltd

Questions (June 1989), *Enter the Co-ordinator: Working it out together,* The Questions Publishing Co. Ltd

Anthony Cudworth has 22 years' teaching experience and is currently Science Co-ordinator in a Norfolk primary school. He has enjoyed the challenge of changing disciplines from Geography through Mathematics to Science, an experience familiar to many primary teachers.

Formulating a School Science Policy

Deirdre Medler

16

Early Days

It was not without many misgivings that I listened to the head-teacher`s decree that I should produce a complete science policy for the school over the next few months. For it had only been days since my appointment to the school and I was already thoroughly overwhelmed by many of the new responsibilities that were being so quickly thrust upon me. I was`t exactly oozing with credibility at the time either. Only four years previously I had been a student teacher at the school, and was now appointed to one of the senior posts, being very much junior in age as well as experience ! So as you can imagine this initial encounter with my employer did very little to inspire confidence.

Prior to this incident I had been feeling more confident and reassured by evidence such as that stated in the IPSE project.

"The greatest progress (in developing and teaching science) has been made in those schools which have evolved a written document slowly, basing it on established practice and through staff discussion. The time taken has been of the order of two years to arrive at a reasonably complete document." IPSE (1989)

It reinforced my own notion that such a policy can only really be a true reflection of a school's aims and objectives after a long and often tedious process of consultation , discussion and development of good teaching practice. The fact that the "greatest progress" is made when such principles are adherred to served to convince me that this would be a worthwhile approach. However, as I was already finding out, that is not to suggest that it is necessarily an easy one. In real school situations there are many pressures which can threaten and intimidate such an approach.

This case study recounts how, as a newly-appointed Science Co-ordinator, I worked towards formulating a school science policy based on these working principles whilst coping with the reality and day to day pressures of the school`s unique situation.

The Headteacher

The headteacher's priority at the time was clear. It was to produce a school development and management plan for the whole curriculum. He had to take into consideration the National Curriculum, the Education Reform Act, the school`s curriculum policy and the LEA's own education policy. That is why he was determined that I should make an early start on a science policy.

Plan of Action

I had my reservations. I instinctively knew that I had to be careful how I tackled to process of formulating a policy. Initially, it was important to develop more knowledge of the school. For first impressions can so often be deceptive ! I needed time to observe and absorb the way in which the school functioned. Furthermore, it was vital to develop positive relationships with staff and children and to establish a level of credibility.

It was therefore essential that I discussed my perceptions of the priorities with the headteacher in order to avoid a direct conflict that could be detrimental in many respects. This was duly done. I explained my position and emphasised that there were issues which needed to be addressed in my own mind before I could confidently lead worthwhile and fruitful discussions which would result in the production of a science policy reflecting the true aims, objectives and practices of the school. Whilst still overwhelmed by the enormity of the task ahead, I took encouragement from the observations of G. Hall and S. Louks (1978), that

"...change takes time and is achieved only in stages."

The school

With this in mind, I was able to focus my attention more clearly on the initial task of establishing the current state of affairs within the school. I focussed my observations on five main areas and then raised a variety of questions:

a) Organisation

What is the school structure like ?
Are topics "subject -based" or "cross-curricular" ?
Does any specialist teaching take place ?

b) Resources

What is currently available ?
What needs are there ?
How are resources organised ?
Are resources accessible to staff, and pupils where appropriate ?

c) Attitudes

What attitudes are prevalent both between and towards pupils, staff and curriculum ?

d) What science is already taking place ?

How is it organised ?
How are the issues of continuity and progression being addressed ?
How confident and effective are staff in teaching science?

e) Relationships with "cluster" schools

What meetings are there between staff from the various phases of education ?
What time has been spent addressing the issues of continuity and progression?
What records are in existence ?
Has any joint INSET been planned ?

Working with colleagues

Obviously it was necessary to implement a range of strategies for answering such questions. I spent time observing what was going on in school and discussing issues with colleagues. It was also necessary to arrange and attend meetings with science co-ordinators from other schools within the local "cluster". Furthermore, with the support of the headteacher and the availability of funds to make it possible, I was able to spend time working alongside colleagues in their classrooms. Support was given in a variety of ways, as it was required. Initially a majority of the staff wanted me to give some demonstration science lessons. This was particularly daunting, as in most cases I had little knowledge of the children I was teaching. However, it was important to undertake this challenge to help my own credibility and to make it clear that my role was a supportive and not critical one. So, I tried to use every opportunity in a positive way – planning each of the lessons alongside the classteacher, with particular emphasis given to investigative science. I was careful to emphasise that Sc1, Scientific Investigation, should be central to our approach to the teaching of science throughout the school. Thus, each activity was planned with painstaking attention to the processes and skills involved. In these early stages I had to be content with "teaching by example", hoping that my attempts at good primary practice would be recognised and valued.

Raper and Stringer (1987) advise:

> *"Avoid making too many demands especially in the early stages. The change process is often a slow one."*

Consequently, I was encouraged to persevere with working on the science policy, with, what I hoped, was a sensitive and methodical approach.

Developing the Policy

It was only in the following academic year, when I had answered most of the pertinent questions and was confident that the climate within the school was conducive, that I set about discussing the policy further. It was important to ensure that any developments should be the result of collaborative views and contributions from all members of staff. For, without a considerable degree of staff ownership, any document I might produce would be of very limited usefulness whatsoever ! It was therefore essential to persevere with the evolution of a document which reflected good primary practice being undertaken throughout the school. So, alongside the development of a written policy it was important to seek to develop the teaching effectiveness of every member of staff. For, as a co-ordinator it was not my role to remove the responsibility for planning and teaching science from any colleagues, but rather to support, encourage and enable them to teach their own science effectively.

Cox and Taylor (1989) asked teachers to rate the type of support they would prefer to help develop their teaching effectiveness.

Methods of support rated most highly were:

- Having advice and support of school science expert'
- Attending in-service training course
- Better scientific equipment in schools
- More books, workcards and information
- Spending time in another classroom
- Seeing another teacher in my classroom.

Of medium usefulness were:

- Being involved in whole-school project
- LEA Adviser coming into school

Of low usefulness were:

- Being involved in local schools' project
- Being involved in national project

These findings accord with the views of the staff in our school.

A Programme of Support

Once staff had expressed such needs it was imperative that a programme of support be continued both throughout and beyond the production of the policy document. So, as well as continuing to improve supplies of science equipment, books, workcards and information, I sought to support staff in developing their own knowledge and understanding of science. This involved staff looking at each of the Attainment Targets and Programmes of Study to identifying particular areas of concern. Inevitably, not everyone was willing to be open and honest about their lack of understanding but those who were certainly provided scope for planning relevant INSET.

Having developed some good relationships with other science co-ordinators in the cluster group, it seemed sensible to enquire as to whether there were any common areas of concern within the schools that could be addressed in jointly planned INSET. Finding that there were areas of physics that were causing wide-spread concern s, we sought support from the science ESG team in planning an INSET day and several evening sessions for teachers from all the cluster schools. Each session followed a similar format. Firstly the ESG teacher provided background information and explanations of relevant scientific theories on an adult level. This was followed by an opportunity for staff to ask questions. Practical activities then followed which had been planned to meet both the requirements of PoS and to demonstrate continuity and progression throughout KS1 and 2. Furthermore, all the activities were centred around Sc1 and included possible follow-up activities. Each one of these required staff to identify for themselves ways in which the processes and skills of science could be kept central to all classroom work undertaken. Finally, at each session there was a display of pupil and teacher books, together with a selection of other appropriate resources for the staff to look at.

The benefits of these sessions were enormous in both developing knowledge and understanding and in providing ideas for planning practical science. They were also important in developing the confidence and expertise of all the staff who were willing to attend. Furthermore, the informal atmosphere on each occasion proved conducive to worthwhile discussions, particularly relating to continuity and progression between the different phases of primary education.

Staff enthusiasm

However, despite these very positive aspects of the INSET provision, it must be said that there were less encouraging factors, which, at times, made it difficult to maintain enthusiasm and momentum for the sessions. For example, it was particularly noticeable that the demand on staff to relinquish their own time to attend the sessions, was a heavy one. It was also apparent that there were some who felt that an undue precedence was being given to science at a time when other curriculum areas also needed to be addressed. Thus, we had to be as accommodating and flexible as possible to the timing and content of each of the sessions, to maintain staff enthusiasm and support for the development of the teaching of science.

It was in such a climate that attention was focussed on the production of a written science policy for the school.

A Policy in Eight Parts

Initially a decision had to be made regarding the *content* of the policy. It was agreed that the format be in keeping with the other school curriculum documents. Consequently eight issues were identified which needed to be addressed. It was impossible that the actual writing of the document be done corporately, so, following discussions, I undertook the writing, which I hoped would reflect the feelings and practices of staff within the school. Once a draft document was produced it was then discussed and amended where necessary by the staff, before being finally adopted as the school's current policy.

Essentially, the policy was intended to be concise – stating clearly and briefly the rationale and framework for science. Each of the following eight headings was used. Under each of the headings specific issues were addressed with statements clarifying effective approaches and the organisation of science within the school.

Aims First, we stated our overall purposes and intentions for science throughout the school . Our aims refer specifically to the importance of seeking to develop in all children, both knowledge and understanding and skills in accordance with their age, interests and abilities.

Goals Our goals state more specifically how we intend to develop each child's knowledge and understanding of the scientific ideas, processes and skills central to science.

Attitudes We feel that it is important for children to acquire positive attitudes and values through scientific investigation. These are not specified for assessment in the National Curriculum. DES (1985) offers this list of " of desirable personal qualities":

a. interest/curiosity
b. creativeness and inventiveness
c. willingness to co-operate and collaborate
d. perseverance
e. open-mindedness
f. care and sensitivity to the living and non-living environment
g. self-appraisal

It is a challenge to our teaching that such qualities be developed by both encouragement and example.

Processes and Skills It was difficult to make a statement expressing that the essence of Sc1 is at the heart of the school's science teaching. For, it is only with constant encouragement and sensitive monitoring that the policy really does reflect the true practices of all members of staff.

Knowledge and Understanding Having identified the areas of knowledge broadly defined by the NC, this section states how the school's science syllabus would be incorporated and developed alongside AT1.

Special Needs A statement regarding equal access for all children has to take into account the need for differentiation. With mixed-ability classes there is a need to structure activities to ensure success for all children, allowing too, for very able children to undertake work of a more challenging nature, where appropriate. For those children with severe difficulties (whether they be learning, behavioural or physical) who are identified and protected by a Special Educational Needs 'statement' under the 1981 Education Act, there was a need to consider staffing provision and classroom support for science activities.

Syllabus The actual science syllabus needs to be a practical guide which indicates what is taught in the school. Before undertaking it's documentation it was necessary to consider whether science is to be taught as a separate subject or as part of a cross-curricular topic. It was decided to adopt the integrated approach because it would provide more coherence in the children's learning experiences.

A working party, with one member from each year group, planned a scheme of work for the school. This team was able to plan with the emphasis on continuity and progression. Learning experiences were sequenced and where appropriate it was planned that PoS be revisited in different contexts to allow for the re-inforcement and development of ideas, skills and strategies of investigation.

Record Keeping It was only after considerable time had been spent evaluating a range of different types of record that we came to a consensus of opinion, as to what we could realistically cope with. We addressed two fundamental questions;

> Why keep records ?
> What kinds of records should be kept ?

They should provide information on the context of science work undertaken, the coverage of PoS and Attainment Levels achieved by each child. We decided that that both Class and Individual records should be kept. The class record should be an aid to preparation and evaluation of specific schemes of work. The individual record of a child's progress should be both formative and summative and should provide the opportunity for self-assessment.

The issue of assessment remains to be addressed by the staff. Although we are constantly involved in the continuous assessment of children's learning, it is important that we develop a more objective range of assessment techniques for the gathering of information. Such techniques must obviously be matched to the nature of the learning which is taking place. Assessment in science must be seen in the context of the whole school policy on assessment, which is currently being developed.

Overview I would not be truthful if I did not admit that there have been occasions during the past two and a half years when I have doubted my effectiveness as Science Co-ordinator and my ability to formulate a science policy for the school. For, as I recall that initial, rather daunting encounter with the headteacher I sometimes wonder why I was unable to meet the request for a policy within the few months expected. It is only in my better, more confident moments, that I am re-assured that a completed school policy should be seen as a long term aim, and in it's written form should reflect true classroom practice. All that takes time to achieve!

My experience has made me aware that there are some basic principles and considerations for any Science Co-ordinator entrusted with the responsibility of writing a science policy to adhere to.

a) Communication   It is always important to seek, develop and maintain positive, professional relationships with all members of staff. It's worth spending time and effort to ensure that goals are agreed and that everyone is working towards the same end.

b) Priority   If staff are to concentrate fully on the development of a school science policy, it is important that science is identified as a priority within the school over a period of time. Otherwise, with many other competing demands, momentum becomes lost.

c) Time   Any major developments in a school science curriculum requires a whole school approach. All members of staff must be actively involved if any real progress is to be made. Time must therefore be found for staff meetings and to allow for INSET support.

d) Resources   In order for developments in the teaching of science to be successful it is essential that a range of resources is available for teachers and children alike. It is impossible to fulfil the practical aspects of science and adopt appropriate ways of working unless there is a range of general and specific science equipment. Good organisation and easy access to resources is essential if staff are to be encouraged to properly undertake the teaching of science.

e) Outside Support   Links with other schools in the area are vital in ensuring continuity and progression in the science curriculum. Joint INSET can be a valuable exercise and can provide the opportunity to maximise the use of outside support. Resources and expertise shared between schools can be a valuable asset.

f) Headteacher Support   Ostensibly, any real progress requires the active support of the headteacher. Heads must be responsible for nominating and supporting a science co-ordinator, and making his / her role clear to all members of staff. They must be a motivating force, ensuring that science is given a high profile, priority of time and of funding during the process of curriculum development.

Finally, a sobering thought for those who are comfortable in the knowledge that they have completed their science policy. Consider the recommendations of IPSE:

A science policy "...needs updating regularly."!

References ASE (1988) *Initiatives in Primary Science: An Evaluation.* The School in Focus. ASE (Herts)

Hall, G and Louks, S (1978) *Teacher's Concerns and Staff Development.* Teacher's College Record (Vol 80–1)

Harlen, W and Jelly, S (1989) *Developing Science in the Primary Classroom.* Oliver and Boyd

A Guide to Primary Science Development. (1992) Norfolk County Council Education

Raper, G and Stringer, S (1987) *Encouraging Primary Science.* Cassell Education

Deirdre Medler qualified as a teacher seven years ago. She has taught in three primary schools and is currently Year Leader with responsibility for science and IT in a Junior school.

17 | Home-School Relationships

Anne Watkinson

What are the benefits of developing home - school relationships?

...for parents?

A late entrant into the teaching profession, I came in because I found my own small children so interesting, so I have a personal conviction of the value of parental interest. I came into the educational world through the playgroup movement, whose philosophy was to involve parents at a time when nursery education was the province of professionals. Fairly early on, while running my own playgroup, I was asked to tutor parents for other community groups. These young mums had not been inside a classroom since leaving school (usually at the earliest opportunity). Their attitudes to their children, their families and the world changed with their participation in their children's education. They found their own children more interesting; positive intervention in discipline even worked on recalcitrant husbands; some went on to further and higher education as their children grew up. They began to understand the value of play activities, which do not only to occupy, but educate. Involving parents is not just informing them about their children, the school or the education system, but is also about increasing understanding of the potential that might otherwise remain hidden. I found myself wanting to know what my children were learning, and I wanted to be part of it.

...for the children ?

The development of home-school relationships benefits parents and children too. Christian Schiller, at the end of a long career as an Inspector, said:

> *"Young children learn through experience. They learn through exploring and experiencing the world around them..." no more so than in science! ..."And then at five we suddenly face them with two different worlds – the world of school and the world of home.......We must bring those two worlds together........Mum must be able to come into school and feel at home there. And when she comes to school it must be a place she understands. We shall not do that by PTAs or odd meetings on Friday afternoons.......she will understand, only as she experiences what happens in school. It is no good telling her or giving her lantern- slides......We need a school where Dad can go and feel at home......... And then there's Grandma.....there's the family and the neighbour next door......." (1975)*

Tizard's studies with young children show how the home provides a very powerful learning environment. She identified five significant factors. One was the wide range of activities that take place within the home; the second the common background shared by the members of the family, both in the past and for the future; the third is the beneficial adult child ratio, the fourth is the great meaning given to learning by the familiar context of the learning environment; and the fifth, the intense relationships particularly between mothers and their children. Although some of these can create adverse circumstances, particularly the last, generally they do not. She also argues that the de-contextualising of school learning creates in children the ability to generalise, and concludes that home and school learning should be complementary, not alternative or conflicting.

The *1986 Act* and the *Education Reform Act* have enshrined in law the need to inform parents about their children's progress. The *Parent's Charter* mentions documents: the child's report, Inspectors' reports, Annual Governors reports, a school Prospectus, and performance league tables. It mentions the right of choice and how to complain. It puts the emphasis on information transfer. It is not until the last paragraph that it mentions the value of parental involvement in education:

> *"As a parent, the biggest help you can give your child is to show that you are interested and to see the value of what he or she is doing at school. Such support can have a real effect on your child's performance – and on his or her future."*

...for the school? It is not only the children, but the whole school which can benefit. In School Matters, the writers define 12 key factors which increased the learning of children in the junior schools of London which were studied. One of the most significant is parental involvement.

They made it clear that positive involvement, not just meetings is the key:

> *'Parent-teacher associations ...... were found to be related negatively to progress, but (it) did apply to parents helping in school and in working with their children at home."*

And offer this advice:

> *"These two types of parental involvement need careful management but offer practical ways of increasing the effectiveness of the school."*

...for partnership with the school community? The value of partnership is, I believe, in the involvement and understanding, and not in just passing on reports, attending meetings or helping with the PTA, (although these must be part of the whole).

The school, in turn, must be responsive to the local community, not only to understand their children better and harness the ideas and resources, but to promote their community's understanding of education. All our futures depend on it. We can no longer justify an 'I know best' attitude. We must take note of the world outside the school.

Developing home-school relationships is no easy task. In these days of perceived overload, teachers are reluctant to take on yet another thing. Kath Beck (1989) says

> *"I am not arguing against it. It would be unwise though to pretend there are no difficulties. Teachers and parents need to acknowledge the difficulties openly and honestly in order that the communication lines can be kept open".*

Current Developments

There have been several long term projects to help schools and parents get closer, but only recently has science become a focus of attention. ASE has been very concerned to help in this area, and has been part of two recent initiatives. Concurrently, the BBC has launched a series of ten – minute programmes for parents at home. They have produced a free companion booklet and a book which can be purchased . The BBC theme was "to show parents how to help their children discover that science is fascinating and fun".

The number of 'Help your children with science' booklets on the supermarket bookstalls has risen , as have the 'Have fun with science" books in the general book shops. Most of the books take a similar theme, and have lots of splendid ideas, but they are rather like recipe books, which give 'set piece' experiments. They are fun, but do not often relate to what is going on in school, they do not promote the experiencing, exploring, or systematic investigative approach we pursue. Open ended questioning is rare, as is the feeling that children can be helped to pursue their own interests and questions.

The SHIPS Project

The ASE's second initiative is in the *School Home Investigations in Primary Science* – SHIPS – funded by ICI.Joan Solomon has directed a two and a half year research project, working with a number of schools developing activities to be done at home but which fit in with school topic work. The sheets of instructions go home twice a term, the parents and children do the investigation over the course of a week, then the teacher brings all the children together for a sharing time. The material, which is being published, records parent's, children's and teacher's comments on the activities. They also investigated how parents and children work together at home and are developing networks of schools to use the materials. The books contain activities for the children, with notes for teachers and parents, but, as Joan Solomon says,

> *"This is not a textbook for schools. Neither is it a set of science homework tasks. Neither is it a resource for home tutoring. It is a way of linking school and home, teacher and parent, in primary school children's learning of science."*

The home context for the work gives the child the familiar background , the teachers provide the unifying element. Some parents amplify the scientific background, some see it as a "homework" exercise. A problem is that parents, and maybe most adults, still see science as a collection of facts. They sometimes worry if children are still asking questions at the end of the investigation, whereas teachers would be delighted. Enjoyment and interest is frequently mentioned. Partnership and involvement are the spin-off and constitute a very real plus for the project.

The Primary Pack The Primary Committee of ASE took a slightly different focus and have produced a resource book for teachers to develop their own way of involving parents and the wider community of the school. Many people contributed to the pack, in various forms. The logo is a Venn diagram which embodies the idea of a tripartite partnership – the interaction of all the facets of a child's world.

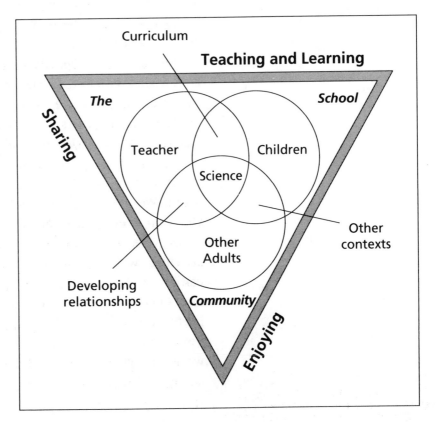

Figure 1 Venn diagram to show the interaction of all facets of a child's world

The pack contains reprints of articles of successful initiatives, involving parents, local industry, museums and others, which develop the excitement of science for young children. It has plastic pockets for inserts of information about places to visit. The pockets also contain a colour A2 poster for schools to complete, to attract parents to a meeting or exhibition or whatever your school might choose as their communication venture. It has a large section on involving parents in the school itself. If confidence in developing science with children is a problem for teachers, how much more is telling other adults what you think you are doing! The pack has a checklist for how to run open evenings, or workshops, with four workshops spelt out in some detail. There is a variety of material, some pictorial, some humorous, some based on DES material, so that teachers can select something to suit. There is an emphasis on reaching a common understanding of what science is, that it is fun, relevant, and not just confined to the pages of a DES 4-ring binder! Lastly, this section addresses ways in which helpers in school can be used with small groups of science investigators.

The second section has photocopiable material with activities to give parents to do at home with their children, a little along the SHIPS lines. Many of these are particularly suitable for children in their early years at school, say three to eight.

The third section develops the idea that science can go on in the home and in the classroom concurrently. We give details of how to run clubs in or out of school using material from various organisations such as *British Association, WATCH,* or the *Royal Society for the Protection of Birds,* or *The Tidy Britain Group.*

Parents are not the only people who can help develop children's science. The fourth section is about involving others. The school community heavily involves governors in these days of Local Management. If they are going to make decisions on resources, they must be informed ones. I recently joined a group of local headteachers to explore science for Governors. The meeting was prompted by a discussion with an LEA inspector who kept referring to 'Good primary practice'. "What is this 'good primary practice' you keep talking about?" the Governors asked. We did not go on talking about it, we made them do it. Our first evening session was based on Beverages – close to some governors hearts, we thought! We included some science activities, with teas as well as alcohol, and made them actually participate. Just like children, once involved, they did not want to stop. On our second evening, we concentrated on scientific activities to do with eggs. They complained that they had only had time to try one or two of our activities! In the ensuing discussion, we asked 'what do you think science is?' The first reply, from an insurance broker, was "Facts". Luckily, or unluckily for him, I suppose, I had just the thing – an OHT from Dickens' Hard Times: "facts, all I want are facts", contrasting this quotation with what we had done in the workshop. I don't think he was convinced, but he certainly was interested, and now will look at his primary school with new insight.

Local industries are not only a source of waste materials but partnerships can be developed and become really helpful to both sides. Local people with fascinating hobbies or enthusiasms can 'adopt' the school. We had a governor who sailed, he brought his dinghy into the school grounds and fired the children's interest. They made boats, exploring materials, winds etc.. The governor returned to judge the results, and ended up accompanying a school journey to the Norfolk coast. A local farmers used to have a regular visiting group though the year to see his work, and follow up their interests back in class. Our baker has regular visits from classes, and the ensuing scientific and edible experiments are shared by all. The children's interest in his 'cottage' industry will help keep alive the purchase of the product into the next generation. He also explained the changes he had had to make through Health and Safety legislation.

Pre-school Liaison

Having worked with the Pre-school Playgroups movement, I went on to train as an infant teacher and then I had a nursery class. I am quite sure that there is science before the NC. A young child's learning is scientific, only requiring encouragement, refinement and direction to blossom. Children explore because of inbuilt curiosity, which is frequently dulled if not killed off by our modern lifestyle, our ultra tidy homes, our ability to purchase ready-made, our unsafe roads and parks.

A full nursery programme, involving parents, as in the playgroups, but with teachers trained in using all the potential of learning-through-play, would counteract some of the restrictions we have to impose on young children, and enable them to experience some of the activities otherwise denied to them. Unfortunately, I have not yet been able to get such a group attached to my school, but I do talk in depth to all the parents before their children start, to start the 'record of achievement' programme, to appreciate the first five years of learning before they start. We cannot start with children as clean slates.

I give parents a simple questionnaire on their first visit, ask them to fill it in with their children, and come back to see me on their own. I ask the usual questions about health, writing their name and so on, but I also ask about interests, visits they make and questions their children ask. We talk together my reasons for asking these questions. I started this a couple of years ago, and followed up later to find out whether it was worthwhile. The overwhelming response from parents and teachers was 'please continue'.

The teachers get the parental questionnaire which becomes the first page in the child's record book. The teachers refer to it in subsequent interviews with parents. Who is to say what it will do for long term relationships, and understanding of the reporting process about children's achievements? A mother of a three year old in the village came in after the grapevine had worked for a few months. She said

"I understand you are interested in where the children are when they come into school. Would it be alright if I..."

Conclusion

Science is important and can be fun, its development in young children should be shared with parents and the community. This process will benefit all parties, and especially the children. It will help children's scientific education and increase that of any other adults involved. No-one pretends that it is an easy option, it involves time being spent by the teacher, but it will be time well spent on our children's future.

References

Schiller, C. (1979, 1984) *Christian Schiller in his own words.* NAPE

Tizard, B. and Hughes, M. Young (1984) *Children Learning Talking and thinking at home and at school.* Fontana

Mortimore, P. et al (1988) *School Matters – the junior years.* Open Books Publishing Ltd

Beck, K.(1989) '*Parental involvement in school: some dilemmas*', Education 3–13, 17: 3: 10

DES (1991) *The Parent's Charter*

Pollock, S. and Marshall, J. (1992) *Help your child with science.* BBC Books

Solomon, J. and Lee, J. (1991) *School Home Investigations in Primary Science*, The 'SHIPS' project ASE

Watkinson. A., (Ed.) (1992) *Primary Science – A shared Experience.* ASE.

Anne Watkinson has a pathology degree from Cambridge and worked in cancer research. She became involved in playgroup work and then in infant and nursery teaching. She is now a primary school head teacher and the Chair of the ASE Primary Services Group.